MIRACLES OF HEALING

Scottish Religious Cultures *Historical Perspectives*

Series Editors: Scott R. Spurlock and Crawford Gribben

Religion has played a key formational role in the development of Scottish society shaping cultural norms, defining individual and corporate identities, and underpinning legal and political institutions. This series presents the very best scholarship on the role of religion as a formative and yet divisive force in Scottish society and highlights its positive and negative functions in the development of the nation's culture. The impact of the Scots diaspora on the wider world means that the subject has major significance far outwith Scotland.

Available titles

George Mackay Brown and the Scottish Catholic Imagination
Linden Bicket

Poor Relief and the Church in Scotland, 1560–1650
John McCallum

Jewish Orthodoxy in Scotland: Rabbi Dr Salis Daiches and Religious Leadership
Hannah Holtschneider

Miracles of Healing: Psychotherapy and Religion in Twentieth-century Scotland
Gavin Miller

George Strachan of the Mearns: Seventeenth-century Orientalist
Tom McInally

Forthcoming titles

The Scot Afrikaners: Identity Politics and Intertwined Religious Cultures
Retief Muller

Dugald Semple and the Life Reform Movement
Steven Sutcliffe

Presbyterianism Re-established: The Presbyteries of Dunblane and Stirling after the Williamite Revolution
Andrew Muirhead

William Guild and Moderate Divinity in Early Modern Scotland
Russell Newton

The Dynamics of Dissent: Politics, Religion and the Law in Restoration Scotland
Neil McIntyre

The Catholic Church in Scotland: Financial Development 1772–1930
Darren Tierney

edinburghuniversitypress.com/series/src

MIRACLES OF HEALING

Psychotherapy and Religion in Twentieth-century Scotland

GAVIN MILLER

EDINBURGH
University Press

Edinburgh University Press is one of the leading university presses in the UK. We publish academic books and journals in our selected subject areas across the humanities and social sciences, combining cutting-edge scholarship with high editorial and production values to produce academic works of lasting importance. For more information visit our website: edinburghuniversitypress.com

© Gavin Miller, 2020, 2022

Edinburgh University Press Ltd
The Tun – Holyrood Road
12 (2f) Jackson's Entry
Edinburgh EH8 8PJ

First published in hardback by Edinburgh University Press 2020

Typeset in 10/12 ITC New Baskerville by
Servis Filmsetting Ltd, Stockport, Cheshire

A CIP record for this book is available from the British Library

ISBN 978 1 4744 4696 9 (hardback)
ISBN 978 1 4744 4697 6 (paperback)
ISBN 978 1 4744 4698 3 (webready PDF)
ISBN 978 1 4744 4699 0 (epub)

Contents

Acknowledgements

The research for this book has been supported in various ways by a variety of funders and organisations over the years. My thanks go to the Institute for Advanced Studies in the Humanities at the University of Edinburgh (Postdoctoral Fellowship), the Leverhulme Trust (Early Career Fellowship), Manchester Metropolitan University English Research Institute (Research Fellowship), and the Arts and Humanities Research Council (Research Assistantship on Religion and Society Large Grant: 'Theology and Therapy: Christianity, Psychotherapy & Spirituality in Scotland 1945–2000'). For their early encouragement in this area of study, I thank Daniel Burston, Cairns Craig, Colin Kirkwood (and the Sutherland Trust), Allan Beveridge and the late Ronald Turnbull. My gratitude also goes to the Theology and Therapy Project team: David Fergusson, Liz Bondi, Steve Sutcliffe and Alette Willis. For their encouragement and critical friendship, I thank also the Transcultural Histories of Psychotherapy Project group: Sonu Shamdasani, Sarah Marks, Rachael Rosner, Akihito Suzuki, Chris Harding and Cris Facchinetti. My ideas have also benefited from conversations with Cheryl McGeachan, Chris Philo, Sarah Phelan, Mark Gallagher and Adrian Chapman. The research for this book has depended upon many significant archival collections. I particularly thank: the National Library of Scotland; Special Collections, University of Glasgow Library (and the R. D. Laing Estate); Special Collections, University of Edinburgh Library; and the National Library of New Zealand. I am also grateful to Edinburgh University Press, and particularly Scott Spurlock in his role as Series Editor for Scottish Religious Cultures.

Some of the methodological discussion in the Introduction to this book is derived in part from Miller, G. (2018), 'Inferiority and bereavement: implicit psychological commitments in the cultural history of Scottish psychotherapy', *European Journal of Psychotherapy & Counselling*, 20, 1, 76–87. The discussion of Henry Drummond's influence on Fairbairn in Chapter One develops ideas previously published as Miller, G. (2014), 'Making Fairbairn's psychoanalysis thinkable: Henry Drummond's natural laws of the spiritual world', in G. S. Clarke and D. E. Scharff (eds) *Fairbairn and the Object Relations Tradition*. London: Karnac, 41–8. Chapter One draws in various ways upon Miller, G. (2008), 'Scottish psychoanalysis: a rational religion', *Journal of the History of the Behavioral Sciences*, 44, 1, 38–58. The discussion of John Macmurray's Adlerian influences in Chapter One develops ideas previously published as Miller, G. (2007), 'John Macmurray's psychotherapeutic Christianity: the influence of Alfred Adler and Fritz Künkel', *Journal of Scottish Thought*, 1, 1, 103–21. The discussion of Laing's theological inheritance in Chapter Two elaborates upon: Miller, G. (2009), 'R. D. Laing and theology: the influence of Christian existentialism on *The Divided Self*, *History of the Human Sciences*, 22, 2, 1–21; Miller, G. (2012), 'R. D. Laing's theological hinterland: the contrast between mysticism and communion', *History of Psychiatry*, 23, 2, 139–55. The latter informs also my account of Laing's New Age spirituality in Chapter Three. My account of Winifred Rushforth and the Davidson Clinic in Chapters Two and Three develops arguments published in Miller, G. (2015), 'Winifred Rushforth and the Davidson Clinic for Medical Psychotherapy: a case study in the overlap of psychotherapy, Christianity and New Age spirituality', *History of Psychiatry*, 26, 3, 303–17. The discussion of Marcus Lefébure and Hans Schauder in Chapter Three draws upon Miller, G. (2013), 'Resisting Self-spirituality: counselling as spirituality in the dialogues of Hans Schauder and Marcus Lefébure', *Journal of Contemporary Religion*, 28, 1, 125–40. Some of the argument in the Conclusion is anticipated by Miller, G. (2012), 'Crossing the border: pastoral theology and psychotherapy', *The Expository Times*, 124, 4, 157–65.

Introduction

In early March 1983, the United Kingdom's Prince Charles, and his then wife, Princess Diana, visited the Edinburgh home of Winifred Rushforth (1885–1983), a 97-year-old psychotherapist, New Age guru, and retired medical doctor (Rushforth 1984: 174). Prince Charles – or the 'Duke of Rothesay' as he is officially known while in Scotland – was prompted to visit Rushforth after receiving copies of her 1981 book, *Something is Happening* (Rushforth 1983, Rushforth 1984: 174), a collection of essays, as its subtitle announced, on *Spiritual Awareness and Depth Psychology in the New Age*. Notes made during the Prince's visit, and preserved in Rushforth's papers, indicate that he and Rushforth discussed a number of topics in their hourlong meeting, including: their shared admiration for the Jungian primitivist guru Sir Laurens van der Post (later exposed as an unsavoury criminal charlatan (Jones 2001)); the Prince's enjoyment of *Something is Happening*; his interest in holistic forms of healthcare; and his difficulties in meditating (Summary of conversation). Charles and Rushforth also corresponded after their meeting (Rushforth 1984: 174), although this was cut short by the latter's death a few months later, in August 1983 (Rushforth 1984: 176).

The encounter between Charles and Rushforth testifies to the latter's local prominence in the mingling of religion and psychotherapy. As later chapters in this monograph will show in detail, Rushforth exemplifies a Scottish interweaving of psychoanalytic psychotherapy, a seemingly clinical activity, with both Christianity and an emergent post-war New Age spirituality. Rushforth and the Davidson Clinic – the psychotherapeutic clinic which she founded, and which ran in Edinburgh from 1941 to 1973 – renewed the discourses of Christianity using the idioms and practices of psychoanalytic psychotherapy. In 1942, the Clinic's *Annual Report* declared unabashedly that 'psycho-therapeutic treatment can bring about miracles of healing which are the fulfilment of the Divine purpose' (*Annual Report* 1942: 2). Even as the medical prestige of psychoanalytic psychotherapy waned in the post-war years, Rushforth, as Edinburgh's resident matriarch and guru of the New Age, continued to promote a psychotherapeutically informed spirituality which was clearly attractive to those seeking spiritual enlightenment – including the future monarch. Her New Age 'Self-spirituality' (Heelas 1996: 18–20) promised to liberate the authentic, 'deep' self by renewing its connection to an inner wellspring of vitalist energy (see p. 110).

The religious meanings of psychotherapy were remarkably explicit within the discourse authorised by Rushforth and the Davidson Clinic. Yet while few Scottish psychotherapists were so frankly religious as to classify successful therapy as a 'miracle of healing' in an organisational report, there is considerable evidence of allied religious meanings within Rushforth's networks. Before moving to Edinburgh, Rushforth had received therapy at London's Tavistock Clinic, which was founded by the Scottish-descended psychiatrist Hugh Crichton-Miller (1877–1959) in 1920. In *The New Psychology and the Preacher* (1924), Crichton-Miller positions psychoanalytic theory and practice as an ally to Christian belief and practice: 'There is an Eastern saying: "No wind killeth the tree that Allah hath planted." Those who feel that their religion has this charter of inde-structibility will ... hasten to accept new scientific methods of investigation' (Crichton-Miller 1924: 21). The psychoanalytic psychiatrist Ian D. Suttie (1889–1935), who was educated in Glasgow and later practised in the Tavistock Clinic, argued that psychotherapy was the rational inheritor of Christian practice, and states in 1935 that the ideal therapeutic attitude 'is very like that of Christ': the therapist is 'serene without being aloof, sympathetic without being disturbed: exactly what the child desires in the parent' (Suttie 1935: 217). In Edinburgh, Rushforth's contemporary, the psychoanalyst W. R. D. Fairbairn (1889–1964), was a pioneer in 'object relations' theory, which, *contra* Freud, understands the infant as born with the capacity for social relationships. He states in a 1958 conference paper addressed to an audience of clergy that '[i]n my own personal opinion, it is something very like *salvation*, rather than medical cure, that the average patient is seeking when he embarks upon a course of psychotherapy'; what the patient requires is 'something very like the forgiveness of sins and the casting out of devils' (Fairbairn 1994f: 364). Perhaps the most celebrated Scottish exponent of religious and spiritual psychotherapy was the countercultural guru and 'anti-psychiatrist', R. D. Laing (1927–89). Laing's spiritual and religious borrowings are manifold. Rudolf Bultmann's existentialist hermeneutics, for instance, offer to Laing the possibility of understanding the seemingly incomprehensible disordered speech of psychosis (see p. 83), while Evelyn Underhill's account of Christian mysticism underwrites a phenomenology of psychotic experience, particularly of the supposed schizophrenic journey through madness (see p. 96). Laing also shows, like Rushforth, a movement between heterodox Christianity and New Age spirituality. Laing's 1983 lecture, 'Psychotherapy as celebration', was delivered to a large public audience in Edinburgh under the auspices of Wellspring, a spiritually inflected successor organisation to the Davidson Clinic. It illustrates some of his (not necessarily authentic) religious and spiritual proclamations, for Laing presents the psychotherapeutic relationship as essentially one of 'communion': 'nothing is more enjoyable than communing with other people' (Celebration: 10); in such enjoyment, 'I cease to be a psychiatrist and the patient ceases to be schizophrenic' (Celebration: 9). The renewed

Christianity in this account of therapeutic spiritual communion is explicit, for Laing claims that '[i]n Christian terminology the name that is given to this healing force is – Christ' (Celebration: 10).

These quotations illustrate briefly some of the religious meanings attached to psychotherapy by a few key Scottish practitioners, ranging from the internationally famous (Laing) to those who are obscure even with practitioner histories of psychotherapy (Rushforth). While this monograph focuses largely on developments within Scotland, or the work of Scottish pioneers, from the 1920s to the 1980s, it sees these developments and initiatives as crucially shaped by import from, and export to, a wider geographical context, including England, Continental Europe, North America, India and New Zealand. Various case studies and vignettes will illustrate the traffic between Scotland and other parts of the world. Moreover, this monograph is sensitive to the eclectic intellectual context of its field of study. There is no desire to excavate or validate some putatively authentic religious tradition of Scottish psychotherapy. Rather, the overlap of religion and psychotherapy in Scotland is understood as a nexus where a contingent series of psychotherapeutic practices emerged from cross-fertilisation with ideas and practices from Freudian, Jungian and Adlerian psychotherapy, as well as from religious traditions such as existentialism, personalism, Christian mysticism and contemporary vitalism.

Psychotherapy across time and place

The argument in this book addresses the period *c.*1920–*c.*1990, an interval extending from the early clinical applications of psychoanalysis in the pioneering work of W. R. D. Fairbairn in Edinburgh and Scots associated with the Tavistock Clinic in London, to the emergence of New Age forms of psychotherapeutic theory and practice pioneered by Rushforth and Laing, and sustained by lesser-known figures such as Hans Schauder (1911–2001) and Marcus Lefébure (1933–2012). As well as contributing to the history of religious cultures in Scotland, this book also enriches the history of psychotherapy in particular regional contexts. Liz Bondi points out that Freud's vision of psychoanalytic diffusion understood place as 'a more or less idiosyncratic local context from which universal and implicitly placeless ideas and practices need to be abstracted' (Bondi 2014: 60). Yet the historical and geographical development of psychoanalysis has belied the intentions of its founder:

> Since Freud's death, different 'schools' of psychoanalysis have developed, broadly aligned with national states or geographical regions ... These schools have not remained bound by national boundaries but have themselves travelled, shaped by and shaping cultural and political circumstances they encountered and in which they became embedded. (Bondi 2014: 63)

The importance of national difference as a factor in psychoanalytic history
has also been suggested by Paul Roazen, who contends 'that every country
has received Freud's teachings in accord with its own national needs and
traditions of thought' (Roazen 2001: 45). As John C. Burnham explains,
the history of psychoanalysis has come to recognise both 'the importance
of psychoanalytic theorists other than Freud' (Burnham 2006: 221) and
'the historical change that takes place when someone reads and learns a
new set of ideas and then integrates those ideas with others that the consumer already holds from the rest of the culture' (Burnham 2006: 227).

Although this monograph focuses on Scotland, it situates the nation
within a wider transnational approach to history of psychotherapy that
'focuses on movements, flows, circulation and intersection of people, ideas
and goods across political and cultural borders' (Damousi and Plotkin
2009: 4). In so doing, it recognises also, as Keir Martin points out, that
'the idea of bounded homogenous cultures linked to particular bounded
groups is made increasingly untenable by intensifying patterns of global
interconnection' (Martin 2018: 117). The cultural differences invoked in
this monograph are the praxis of agents and organisations who are nego-
tiating with particular cultural inheritances, complex contemporary circumstances, and the possibilities of imported discourses and practices.
Scotland emerges clearly as a place where psychotherapeutic ideas are
imported, reciprocally modified in interaction with local cultures, and
then re-exported. The first chapter, for instance, pursues the reciprocal
'dynamic interaction' of psychotherapy with local cultures (Pols 2018: 91)
by tracing the Scottish importation of Freudian and Adlerian psychoanalysis, its adaptation by Scots into object relations theory (of various kinds),
and the exportation of these ideas, with further adaptation, to post-war New
Zealand. While this investigation will frequently invoke Scottish culture to
explain how psychotherapy is locally adapted, there is no assumption that
Scottish cultural particularities represented by key agents and institutions
are held unanimously as the expression of some supposed Scottish national
character. Fairbairn, for instance, was socialised within an upper-middle-
class Presbyterian stratum of Edinburgh society which in many ways sought
to maintain late-Victorian values. But even Rushforth, a contemporary who
had in many ways a similar upbringing in terms of place, class and religion,
had a quite different worldview, in part because of her gender. Nor are
certain kinds of Scottishness, such as middle-class Protestant Christianity,
assumed to be more authentically Scottish than others, and thus to be
reawakened through a process of historiographic anamnesis. Scottish
culture is neither a static reified inheritance, nor *sui generis*, nor homogene-
ous, nor an 'essence' that could be obscured by some putatively misleading
'appearance'.

This investigation's focus on the circulation and adaptation of psychotherapy within a Scottish context challenges the 'continuist methodology'
which John Forrester and Laura Cameron argue is often unreflectively

adopted by historians of psychoanalysis, and which encourages 'judgements of importance' that are 'based on relevance (to today, looking backwards) or "influence" (on today, looking forwards)' (Forrester and Cameron 2017: 6). Laing is no doubt still an enormous influence on the present, particularly in the service-user movement and so-called 'critical psychiatry'; and contemporary psychoanalysis has also recovered and renewed the theories of Suttie and Fairbairn. But the 'continuist' or 'presentist' interest must yield to the 'historicist' interest in phenomena that – if not quite blind alleys and dead ends – nonetheless have a less distinct relationship to the present (cf. Stocking 1965). The Davidson Clinic closed, for instance, in 1973 and its psychotherapeutic successor organisation, Wellspring (1978–present), has shed the spiritual and religious meanings that were articulated in its founding (see p. 124): Rushforth's effect upon the present is now diffused amongst a variety of competing psychotherapeutic and spiritual traditions.

Moreover, the historiography of psychotherapy as a transnational movement routed through particular places invites greater diversity in historical causality. As Forrester and Cameron explain in their history of psychoanalytic diffusion in Cambridge from 1910 to 1930,

> Most histories of psychoanalysis have been overly influenced by two crude models: the 'Great Man' model, in which specific individuals have decisive influence in turning history their way; and the bureaucratic transplant model, in which the oversight of the International Psycho-Analytic Association (IPA) and its sub-committee the International Training Committee (ITC) determined the forms and procedures for establishing psychoanalysis throughout the world. (Forrester and Cameron 2017: 2)

While the present history involves some internationally significant actors, such as Laing, and to a lesser extent Fairbairn, it also tells the story of far more obscure agents who have had little or no effect upon the present. The organisations are also far more varied, with a number offering ideologically eclectic clinical services on a private basis, and in local organisational contexts that were largely independent of international or national oversight. The Davidson Clinic, for instance, was inspired by the Tavistock Clinic in London, but organisationally independent of it, even if conceived as a 'daughter colony' (see p. 59).

The burgeoning scholarly literature on the development of psychotherapy in a Scottish context, or by Scottish proponents, readily illustrates the preceding distinctions. In some of this research context, a presentist interest traces the work of acknowledged pioneers in order to inform the development of contemporary psychotherapy. This is particularly clear in work on Fairbairn by various proponents of object relations psychotherapy such as Grahame S. Clarke, and Jill and David E. Scharff (Clarke 2006, Clarke 2018, Clarke and Scharff 2014, Scharff and Scharff 2005). The same interest also motivates an extensive literature examining the contemporary significance of R. D. Laing for psychotherapy (e.g. Itten and Young 2012, Raschid 2005, Scott 2014). Another body of work combines both presentist and historicist interests, such as various psychoanalytic and cultural re-appraisals of Fairbairn (Beattie 2016, Beattie 2003) and the wider Scottish object relations tradition (Cullen et al. 2014), as well as Daniel Burston's pioneering work on R. D. Laing (Burston 1996, Burston 2000). Finally, the historicist interest dominates research re-situating Scottish psychotherapy in various biographical, cultural, spatial and societal contexts. This includes work on Laing by Allan Beveridge (Beveridge 2011), Cheryl McGeachan (McGeachan 2013a, McGeachan 2013b, McGeachan 2014a, McGeachan 2014b, McGeachan 2016, McGeachan 2017), Adrian Chapman (Chapman 2014a, Chapman 2014b, Chapman 2015) and Nick Crossley (Crossley 1998, Crossley 2006). It also includes research on the Scottish object relations tradition – particularly Ian Suttie – by Gal Gerson (Gerson 2004, Gerson 2009a, Gerson 2009b) and on the eclectic psychiatry of Laing's neglected mentor, the Glaswegian psychiatrist and academic T. Ferguson Rodger, by Sarah Phelan (Phelan 2017). My own work largely belongs to this final group, although I have sometimes written from a presentist perspective on the ongoing relevance of cultural and psychiatric critiques offered by Scottish psychoanalytic and psychotherapeutic ideas, particularly those of Ian Suttie and R. D. Laing (Miller 2004, Miller 2007, Miller 2010).

Symmetrical historiography

This monograph's historiographic analysis excludes, as far as possible, any privileged causal status for putative doctrinal truth – be this religious, spiritual or psychotherapeutic. The so-called 'symmetry postulate' (also 'symmetry principle') requires that social-scientific investigation of scientific knowledge should 'be symmetrical in its style of explanation' so that 'the same types of cause' are used to 'explain … true and false beliefs' (Bloor 1991: 7). David Bloor's important, but elliptical statement, contrasts with the asymmetrical style of explanation favoured in earlier histories of science:

> The general structure of these explanations stands out clearly. They all divide behaviours or belief into two types: right and wrong, true or false, rational or irrational. They then invoke sociological or psycho-logical causes to explain the negative side of the division. Such causes explain error, limitation and deviation. The positive side of the evalu-ative divide is quite different. Here logic, rationality and truth appear to be their own explanation. Here psycho-social causes do not need to be invoked. (Bloor 1991: 9)

The symmetrical style of explanation proper to the sociology of scientific knowledge, however, offers psycho-social causes for both 'right' and 'wrong' beliefs, rather than explaining the former's social currency by their truthfulness, and the latter's by extraneous historical factors.

To a largely secular age, it may seem uncontroversial that the history of Scottish religious cultures can be written without presuming that the currency and persistence of particular religious doctrines should be explained by reference, whether solely or in part, to divinely inspired truth – or, as Bloor puts it, to 'the historical unfolding of divine inspiration' (Bloor 1991: 184). However, it may seem improper, and indeed an invitation to relativism or irrationalism, to explain, as Bloor proposes, scientific belief without reference to the 'unfolding of rational enquiry, the "internal" history of science' (Bloor 1991: 184). One must acknowledge that the symmetry postulate contrasts with what might be called the everyday attitude of scientific agents, including psychotherapeutic researchers and practitioners. As a general rule, we may safely presume that psychotherapists – like other experts in the psychological disciplines, or in the life and natural sciences – typically hold their theory and practice to be valid and rationally justifiable. Obviously, there are caveats to such a rule: practitioners may believe that theory poorly understands practice, or requires refinement or elaboration – and perhaps there is even a minority who have no belief in their method, but practise psychotherapy in a spirit of conscious charlatanry. Nonetheless, the typical psychotherapist adheres to the doctrine of their particular approach, be what it may (cognitive-behaviourist, existential-humanist, psychoanalytic, etc.). And, no doubt, those of us who are potential consumers of psychotherapy are ethically reassured by practitioners who believe in what they do.

The reasons for adherence to a particular psychotherapeutic body of theory and practice are surely manifold. But, regardless of the exact reasons in any particular case, the practitioner's trust in the validity of their approach presents a potential obstacle to their historiographical competence. The practitioner's natural inclination is to explain the currency of their ideas by reference to their truth and rational validity. A follower of Fairbairn might argue, for instance, that the Scottish psychoanalyst's theory of the unconscious mind grasps more readily phenomena that evade the Freudian grasp. She or he might adduce the now widely recognised moral defence (Bliss 2010), in which the mistreated or neglected child internalises its own 'badness', rather than acknowledge the yet more terrible reality of its parents' abuse – to cite Fairbairn's celebrated apothegm, 'it is better to be a sinner in a world ruled by God than to live in a world ruled by the Devil' (Fairbairn 1994g: 66–7). Given the clinical applicability of such concepts as the 'moral defence', a Fairbairn-style therapist might therefore tend to offer asymmetric psycho-social explanations for the currency of rival, 'mistaken' approaches. If we ask her to explain the currency of, say, cognitive-behavioural therapy, our hypothetical practitioner may well make reference to the limited time available in professional practice, the restrictive and biomedically inflected evidentiary models that are promulgated in the health professions, and the bureaucratic fondness for therapeutic approaches that are readily translated into generalised protocols. In short, our hypothetical Fairbairn follower will (be inclined to): (a) explain the fact of her belief in Fairbairn's psychoanalytic psychotherapy by its rational validity; (b) explain the fact of belief by others in contradictory schools by reference to a host of economic, social, cultural and psychological motives and factors, such as economic expediency, cultural (including professional) prejudices, and organisational functionality.

This asymmetric style is entirely appropriate in the everyday attitude of the psychotherapeutic practitioner, for Bloor's symmetry postulate is a methodological principle rather than an assault upon scientific rationality (Bloor 1991: 175–9). However, with the aid of the symmetry principle, the historian or sociologist can deliberately neglect, suspend or bracket scientific validity and justification, in order to concentrate upon the kinds of explanation where socio-historical reasoning gains purchase. The symmetry postulate is a productive falsification, like such concepts as 'centre of gravity', 'economically rational actor', or 'square root of a negative number'. There is no absurdity in simplifying or falsifying an object to know it better. As Hans Vaihinger explains, 'many thought-processes and thought-constructs appear to be consciously false assumptions, which either contradict reality or are even contradictory in themselves' (Vaihinger 1924: xlvi–xlvii). The historian of psychotherapy may proceed as if disciplinary validity has no part to play in the explanation of why certain theories and practices are adopted. As a historian of Scottish psychotherapy, rather than a practitioner, I explain the fact of belief in psychotherapy by reference to non-rational factors, including economic, cultural, organisational, societal, and psychological causes. With regard to the distinctive schools of Scottish psychotherapy, I argue that these causes include: a context of Christianised evolutionary theory and sociology that operated as a philosophical customs-point for Freudian ideas; the ethical authority and social ambition of twentieth-century organisational Christianity; and the appeal of preserving Christian discursive patterns, including Christian life narratives, within an apparently secularising culture.

Psychological explanations

The symmetry principle precludes historical explanations that adduce the validity of a psychological theory as cause for its social currency amongst agents who regard it as truth. A separate question arises regarding the use of psychological (including psychoanalytic) ideas in my own historiographic discourse. To what extent are psychological (including psychoanalytic and psychotherapeutic) concepts invoked in my consideration of relevant 'psycho-social' causes (to echo Bloor)? Such psychologised explanations would seem to occur at two levels. First, one might adduce psychological and particularly depth-psychological explanations for the historically significant idiosyncrasies of particular agents. Secondly, one might offer psychological explanations that apply to individual agents but which have some wider cultural application.

The first approach is the realm of psychobiography, an approach which would favour depth-psychological accounts of key actors examined by this monograph. Admittedly, the religious sensibility of (amongst others) Fairbairn, Rushforth and Laing is certainly of explanatory significance, and there are also other individual traits that are relevant, such as Laing's ambition and grandiosity. However, there is no place in this investigation for extended psychobiographical explanation in the manner exemplified by Hilary J. Beattie's retrospective analysis of W. R. D. Fairbairn. Beattie argues that Fairbairn's life and work offer a rare 'opportunity to study directly the effects of internalized homophobia' on a major analyst of his generation (Beattie 2016: 891). Drawing upon a variety of evidence, including recently available archival sources, Beattie concludes that Fairbairn was a repressed homosexual whose 'blocked libido' contributes both to the failure of his first marriage and to his supposed theoretical deprecation of sexual pleasure for its own sake (Beattie 2016: 920).

My eschewal of psychobiography is motivated partly by its tendency to speculative and one-sided explanation. Even with the benefit of archival documents produced for psychoanalytic purposes, Beattie readily admits that her 'picture of Fairbairn as man and theorist is inevitably somewhat speculative' (Beattie 2016: 919). More importantly for the purposes of this monograph, however, Beattie's analysis of Fairbairn illustrates Thomas A. Kohut's contention that '[a]s clinicians, analysts are concerned with their patients; as historians, they are not much concerned with history. Even when they avow that their aim is historical, psychoanalysts approach the past for their own psychoanalytic purposes' (Kohut 1986: 343). Beattie's reading is, in all but name, an exercise in retrospective pathography directed towards a critique of contemporary object relations psychotherapy. As James William Anderson notes, 'Since a theory such as psychoanalysis was constructed through work with patients, the portions of the theory which deal with psychopathology are the portions which are most developed' (Anderson 1981: 456). Fairbairn's homophobic self-hatred is presented as an explanation for his psychoanalytic originality, and as a heuristic suggestive of his theory's inadequacies. On the one hand, his 'learned distrust of genital pleasure for its own sake echoes throughout his work, perhaps fostering his insights about attachment to early caregivers as the primary force in human development' (Beattie 2016: 920). On the other hand, his repressed sexuality provides him with rather a passionless model of heterosexuality, and a very negative view of homosexuality (Beattie 2016: 920). Even if Beattie's psychoanalytic explanation of Fairbairn's anti-hedonism it true, it is nonetheless a reductive account when taken in isolation. As later chapters in this monograph will show, Fairbairn's idea that sexuality was a 'signpost' to intimate personal relations was ripe for explicit statement within his cultural context.

My approach to psychological explanations that apply to individuals but which obtain at a wider cultural level is more sympathetic. This monograph will certainly avoid, however, the reductive stereotypes promoted by practitioner-led psychohistorical analyses of Scottish culture. The counsellor and trainer Carol Craig diagnoses the Scots in her manifesto *The Scots' Crisis of Confidence* (2003) by using Jungian typologies. In her view, the Scottish nation is psycho-culturally distinguished by a preference for 'thinking judgement' (Craig 2003: 58) and for dwelling in the 'extravert rather than the introvert world' (Craig 2003: 48). The consequence is that the Scots are practical fellows with lively inquiring minds, but are emotionally illiterate and hyper-critical of themselves and others – hence their typically low self-confidence (Craig 2003: 48–9, 59). The anthropologist A. P. Cohen dismisses Craig's account as 'misconceived theory' and a 'concoction of simplistic generalisations': 'She sees Scottish society as generalisable into a collective psyche to which she applies terms drawn from Jungian analysis, and from which she derives a deterministic culture which explains pretty well everything from economic failure to dreary conformity' (Cohen 2004: 160). I have therefore eschewed Craig's national diagnosis because of its tendency towards generalisations about Scottishness, as well as its rather outmoded vision of culture as a pattern that screens out non-conforming personalities (a kind of latent 'culture and personality' anthropology (Benedict 1935)).

However, I do not entirely dismiss psychoanalytic interpretation of Scottish culture. Such accounts, although they may continue some of the vices of Craig's approach, can have a heuristic value. In *The Eclipse of Scottish Culture*, Ronald Turnbull and Craig Beveridge use Franz Fanon's psychological critique of colonialism to argue that 'images of backwardness and inferiority ... govern the Scottish intelligentsia's discourse on Scotland', a rhetoric which can be explained in their view only by 'the loss of self-belief and acceptance of the superiority of metropolitan mores engendered by the sustained and ubiquitous institutional and ideological pressures which are exerted by "core" powers on their satellites' (Beveridge and Turnbull 1989: 112). The quasi-colonial status of Scotland is certainly debatable (although perhaps defensible in terms of 'internal colonialism' (Hechter 1975)), and a rigorous social-scientific investigation of Beveridge and Turnbull's thesis would indeed be daunting. Yet, I have found Beveridge and Turnbull's thesis a useful spur to historical investigation as part of what might loosely be called a sociological 'context of discovery', as opposed to a 'context of justification' (Swedberg 2012). Their ideas have offered a productive heuristic: what if Scottish intellectual life were systematically 'inferiorist' – what might have been overlooked?

Moreover, this monograph employs psychological theories and analyses not merely in the creation of fruitful lines of investigation, but in historical explanation itself. Steven Sutcliffe, following Callum Brown's historical analysis, refers to the 'striking response to the "discursive bereavement" (the grief at the cultural loss of religious certainties) experienced mid-century by Christians' (Sutcliffe 2010: 195) – including R. D. Laing. Brown's history of Christianity pursues Christian life narratives in which the believer (and often the secularised, former believer) understands him- or herself through 'a life-journey, using notions of progression, improvement and personal salvation, whether within religion or opposing it' (Brown 2009: 185). Following Sutcliffe and Brown, I will delineate in this monograph a cultural response whereby Scottish psychotherapy took on, and refurbished, such Christian narratives. Laing's autobiography *Wisdom, Madness and Folly* (Laing 1998), for instance, has an implicitly Christian biographical structure arranged around a series of turning points – this is why, for instance, he encodes his radical disenchantment with conventional psychiatry as a Pauline conversion (see p. 74). A similar pattern also appears when Rushforth and her collaborators self-consciously graft Christian life-narrative patterns such as rebirth and miraculous healing into psychoanalytic and psychotherapeutic discourse – even to the extent of seeing Providential forces at work in the founding of their organisation (see p. 63).

The work of Brown, and also Sutcliffe, has offered me a way of explaining the investment by some Scottish Christians in psychotherapy, even as post-war secularisation intensified: the scientific authority of psychotherapy legitimated their discursive and practical continuation of Christian life-narrative patterns to which they were deeply attached. However, Brown's concept of 'discursive bereavement' (Brown 2009: 184) clearly draws upon a variety of expert psychological positions. The Christian's life narrative selects and links together particular items of experience into a particular schematic pattern – such constructive activity is familiar from proto-cognitivist work such as Bartlett's famous study of memory (Bartlett 1995), and from self-consciously 'cognitivist' psychology in the research programme given an identity by Ulrich Neisser in the 1960s (Neisser 1967). Nor is this schematic pattern purely cognitivist in significance, for it is reflexively internalised in the way theorised by social psychologists in the constructionist school, such as Kenneth Gergen (Gergen 1973, Gergen 1985). Brown thus refers to the 'subjectification' of Christian discourses – not just 'a personal process of subscription to often very public discourses', but also 'very private (indeed sometimes intensely secret) protocols related to those discourses' (Brown 2009: 13). Perhaps most importantly, Brown's concept of 'discursive bereavement' manifestly identifies feelings of 'loss' experienced by Christian subjects who have witnessed, and undergone, the 'discourse change' of secularisation (Brown 2009: 184). The language of 'loss' and 'bereavement' implicitly deploys psychologised ideas of grief and mourning which have flourished over the past century or so, and it transposes them to the loss of a discourse rather than a person. As Leeat Granek explains, the work of psychological experts such as Freud and Helene Deutsch has made our common-sense about grief a highly theorised psychological construct

(Granek 2010: 50–4). Amongst our everyday psychologised assumptions are

> the idea that grief is an active process that involves an intense struggle to give up the emotional attachment to the person who has been lost, and that this struggle is a process that involves time and energy on the part of those mourning. (Granek 2010: 52)

Moreover, it is assumed that 'the death of a loved person must produce a reaction in the bereaved, and that the absence of such grief is as much pathology as is extensive mourning in time and intensity' (Granek 2010: 53).

Brown's complex syncretism of different concepts from quite varied psychological schools (some of which may be in tension with each other) has been important in my work at an explanatory as well as heuristic level. The concept of 'discursive bereavement' is more than simply a scaffolding that can be removed once the edifice of argument is complete. I see it evidenced in the life and work of Laing, Rushforth and others: the phenomenon seems to me real, and explicable in the ways implied by Brown's concept. This commitment to the reality of discursive bereavement prevents me from representing it merely as a productive methodological fiction. It is not *as if* R. D. Laing were adapting psychotherapeutic materials to Christian discursive patterns in order to deal with the potential loss of faith in an era of rationalisation and secularisation. That is what he was doing and why. There is, then, no magic chalk circle into which I can retreat: I am, in my historiography of Scottish psychotherapy, implicitly endorsing – via Brown's concept – social cognitivist and social constructionist psychologies, as well as psychoanalytic and post-psychoanalytic accounts of attachment, loss, and mourning.

Prospectus

This monograph is primarily a work of cultural history, but it necessarily expounds debates in psychotherapeutic and theological ideas. Although the symmetry principle discourages direct evaluation of such apologetics and polemics, the chapters described will from time to time reconstruct the internal logic of various developments. While I cannot claim expert knowledge of either psychotherapy or theology, I hope that these occasional expository reconstructions are good enough for the task at hand.

Chapter One, 'The Self in Communion', deals with the Scottish fusion in the inter-war period of psychoanalytic ideas with ongoing expert discourses from the Victorian period that understood human life as evolving, both biologically and socially, towards ever-greater altruism. The resulting intellectual hybridisation rejected Freud's hedonistic and solipsistic model of the personality. In Edinburgh, W. R. D. Fairbairn argued that mental illness was the result of a fall from an initial relationship of innate interpersonal communion. Similar developments were also promoted by Scots outside Scotland in the work of the Tavistock Clinic, where Crichton-Miller welcomed the psychoanalytic investigation of Christianity, arguing that psychoanalysis would purify Christianity to leave behind a progressive social impulse based on love. Suttie, his colleague, offered a withering critique of Freud's atomistic and hedonistic premises, and argued instead that the child was born with an innate associative attachment. Psychopathology was the outcome of infantile anxiety about the security of its first relationship, and psychotherapy was a means by which the therapist's Christ-like love healed the patient. The interpersonal Scottish psychoanalysis developed by Suttie was particularly influential in its impact upon the religious philosophy of the Scottish personalist philosopher John Macmurray (1891–1976), whose work was also extensively informed by – if not downright plagiarised from – the Adlerian theory of the German therapist, Fritz Künkel (1889–1956). The ideas of Suttie and Macmurray were exported to New Zealand from 1940 onwards by Macmurray's medical acolyte, Maurice Bevan-Brown (1886–1967), where they were endorsed by the New Zealand Association of Psychotherapists in the form of a preventative psychiatry which promoted a more loving and emotionally responsive mother–child relationship.

Chapter Two, 'Interpreting God's Psychotherapeutic Will', explores how Christianised psychotherapeutic ideas became ideologically and institutionally effective after the Baillie Commission had set out during the Second World War a new, socially active direction for the Church of Scotland. The activities and practices of Winifred Rushforth and the Edinburgh-based Davidson Clinic for Medical Psychotherapy offered a psychologically reinterpreted and scientifically authorised template for Christian life narratives, recovering and continuing diverse narrative elements such as rebirth or regeneration, 'miracles of healing', and providence. This discourse and practice of miraculous healing found temporary alliance with a broader interest in spiritual healing during the 1950s – an aspect of ministry which was to be carefully limited by the Church of Scotland's 1958 Special Report. In Glasgow, the psychiatrist R. D. Laing grappled with growing secularisation by assuming the previously feminised role of the 'angel in the house'. Laing acquired from George MacLeod (1885–1991), and the Iona Community, an incarnational, corporate theology which, when grafted into a psychiatric context, promoted social inclusion of the mentally ill. Moreover, Laing's first book, *The Divided Self* (1960), was extensively informed by Rudolf Bultmann's theology, which suggested to Laing that schizophrenic speech expresses the patient's existential truth in 'objectified' statements about the physical and organic world.

Chapter Three, 'Scottish Psychotherapy in the New Age', examines how Scottish Christian psychotherapy turned towards contemporary New Age spirituality. As Laing's career developed, he addressed a 1960s countercultural market by mixing mystical theology with psychoanalytic theory to form a New Age psychotherapeutic account of the recovery of authentic selfhood via *metanoia*, a transformative psychic journey. Laing's New Age affinities, however, brought him into conflict with the socially active Christianity that also informed his work – a tension that emerged with great clarity as he sought to renew his connection with the Iona Community in the 1980s. At around the same time, Rushforth's work promoted a psychoanalytically informed New Age spirituality that grew out of her earlier Christian orientation. According to Rushforth, psychotherapy brought the client into contact with an inner 'wellspring' of vitalist energy that engendered spiritual flourishing, mental wellbeing, and bodily health. When the Davidson Clinic closed in 1973, the name 'Wellspring' was bequeathed to the successor counselling and psychotherapy organisation, which found some early (albeit temporary) ideological co-ordinates in published dialogues on counselling between Hans Schauder, a medically trained counsellor, and Marcus Lefébure, a Roman Catholic monk. The dialogues, published between 1982 and 1990, present counselling as a form of contemporary spirituality, arguing that counselling facilitates spiritual experience and that psychoanalytic and psychotherapeutic concepts can be understood in spiritual terms. The dialogues also criticise the authorisation of subjectivity within both counselling and spirituality, indicating a politically critical attitude at odds with analyses of contemporary spirituality as capitalist ideology. However, the growing professionalisation of counselling from the 1980s onward meant that the Schauder–Lefébure model was only a temporary phase in a practice that was increasingly secularised, even where underwritten by religious organisations.

The Conclusion begins with an overview of the monograph's historical narrative. It then explores some of the 'trailing threads' that have been left unexamined, as well as potential and actual limitations that have emerged in the range of historical testimony employed, including with respect to place, gender and class. Finally, various practitioner-led accounts of the relationship between psychotherapy and Christianity are examined, and criticism is offered of the tendency to prescriptively model this relationship as a dialogue between science and religion.

CHAPTER ONE

The Self in Communion

On 12 March 1953, the widely read BBC magazine, *The Listener*, published a scathing but unsigned review ([Gorer] 1953) of W. R. D. Fairbairn's *Psychoanalytic Studies of the Personality* (Fairbairn 1994e). The book was issued in 1952 by Tavistock Publications, and contained a selection of the author's papers from 1927 to 1951. The review clearly displeased Fairbairn, who, as his personal papers reveal, launched a libel suit against the BBC supported by the Medical Defence Union (Letter, Hempsons Solicitors to Fairbairn, 22 June 1953; Letter, Fairbairn to Hempsons Solicitors [24 June 1953]). This action eventually issued in an out-of-court settlement from the BBC of £50 (waived by Fairbairn), his legal costs, and a letter of correction to be published in a later issue of *The Listener* (Letter, Hempsons Solicitors to Fairbairn, 30 September 1954; Letter, Hempsons Solicitors to Fairbairn, 14 October 1954). Fairbairn's legal case contended that the review attacked his fitness to sit on assessment boards for war pensions: this was plausible, since the review refers to 'a couple of rather uncharitable notes on war neurotics and the treatment and rehabilitation of sexual offenders', and states that Fairbairn regards the 'lapse from group standards' in such cases as 'wilful naughtiness' ([Gorer] 1953).

Fairbairn's irritation almost certainly ran deeper. The review, as he eventually discovered on the psychoanalytic grapevine (Letter, Jock [Sutherland] to Fairbairn, 22 September 1954), was authored by the psychoanalytically informed anthropologist Geoffrey Gorer (1905–85) – an intimation now corroborated by corresponding materials in Gorer's personal papers (Gorer Review). Gorer opened with the question: 'How many of Freud's concepts of the formation and development of the human psyche can be abandoned without abandoning the rightful use of the term psychoanalysis?' ([Gorer] 1953). According to Gorer,

> Fairbairn rejects nearly every one of Freud's central concepts: libido and the death instinct, the interpretation of dreams as wish-fulfilments, the Oedipus conflict, the theory of zones, the attempted link between psychology and physiology, the concept of guilt, [and] the super-ego as the surrogate of the Oedipus situation. ([Gorer] 1953)

He then summarises Fairbairn's theory as one in which libido is essentially 'object-seeking' – that is, a way to establish a personal relationship, originally with the suckling mother. As Gorer correctly perceives, Fairbairn contends that the infant is fundamentally born with a striving for social relationships, rather than, as Freud had argued, coerced by various mechanisms out of an initial state of hedonistic solipsism.

Gorer contends that Fairbairn's elaborate revision of the Freudian scheme is so thoroughgoing that 'it would seem more reasonable to coin another name for the ideas which are offered in its place' ([Gorer] 1953). Semantics aside, his review is suggestive for the argument of this chapter. Gorer argues that Fairbairn's work is based on 'analogies drawn from religion' that indicate a need to preserve a theological intellectual inheritance, but which are at odds with the empirical discoveries of his therapeutic practice: 'In the miscellaneous papers the Calvinist ecclesiastic seems to have taken the place of the psychotherapist; and, in the clinical papers, the psychotherapist seems not to have heard of the theorist' ([Gorer] 1953). Whatever the merits of Gorer's view on a split between the intellectual and the clinical Fairbairn, this public confrontation between different models of psychoanalysis illuminates the concerns of this chapter. It explores the development in Scotland, or by Scots, of a distinctly interpersonal theory of psychoanalysis that was informed by an aspiration to advance the Christian religion through a rational revision of its traditions. The chapter begins with the late-Victorian Scottish intellectual context that preceded the work of Fairbairn, the 'the lone, lorn member of the British Psychoanalytical Society practising in Edinburgh' in Gorer's disparaging description ([Gorer] 1953). After surveying a context of Christianised evolutionary theory elaborated by figures such as Patrick Geddes and Henry Drummond, the argument turns to the account of totemism developed by the theologian William Robertson Smith, in which communion between persons is seen as fundamental to 'primitive society'. The consequent modification of psychoanalytic ideas is clarified in a discussion of the theory promoted by Fairbairn in Edinburgh, and by the roughly contemporaneous work of psychotherapists Hugh Crichton-Miller and Ian Suttie, who were Scots active in the early days of London's Tavistock Clinic. There then follows a discussion of the importation and exportation that accompanied this programme of psychoanalytically re-imagined Christianity. There was comparatively greater interest in Afred Adler's 'individual psychology' in Scottish circles: a close textual analysis of the Scottish religious philosopher John Macmurray's work reveals the Adlerian tradition informing his redefinition of Christianity as a religion concerned primarily with a universal community of human fellowship. The ideas of Macmurray and Suttie were also exported in the post-war era. They were particularly effective in the founding of the New Zealand Association of Psychotherapists under the leadership of the Tavistock-trained New Zealander Maurice Bevan-Brown, where they informed a preventative psychiatry concerned with the salutogenic effects of loving communion between mother and child.

Christianised evolution and the ascent of love

As will be shown, Fairbairn's innovations (or deviations) indicate the challenge posed to Freudian ideas by a late-Victorian Christianised interpretation of Darwinian natural history that was prominent in Scottish cultural life. Although Freud's knowledge of Darwin is frequently forgotten by later psychological research (Young 2006: 179–87), it was an important resource for his ideas, and a way of securing their perceived legitimacy (Ritvo 1990, *passim*). As Allan Young explains, the 'evolutionary Freud' held to a Lamarckian model in which adaptive responses were transmitted directly via inheritance. The shocking contents of the unconscious mind revealed by the psychoanalytic method were thus a dissociated recapitulation of events that had actually occurred in the natural history of *Homo sapiens*, and which were imprinted on the species by collective racial memory (Young 2006: 175–9). Freud's evolutionary views led to the highly speculative psychoanalytic evolutionary anthropology presented in works such as *Totem and Taboo* (Freud 1955). However, when psychoanalysis entered a Scottish context, it encountered a quite different interpretation of Darwinian evolution which counterposed the evolution of love and sociability to the agonistic worldview of Social Darwinism. As Mike Hawkins explains, Darwin's theory had become for the Victorians the cornerstone of a larger Darwinist world view with the following tenets:

> (i) biological laws governed the whole of organic nature, including humans; (ii) the pressure of population growth on resources generated a struggle for existence among organisms; (iii) physical and mental traits conferring an advantage on their possessors in this struggle (or in sexual competition), could, through inheritance, spread through the population; (iv) the cumulative effects of selection and inheritance over time accounted for the emergence of new species and the elimination of others. (Hawkins 1997: 31)

Social Darwinism added a further element, namely that such processes extended 'to not just the physical properties of humans but also to their social existence and to those psychological attributes that play a fundamental role in social life, e.g. reason, religion and morality' (Hawkins 1997: 31). The leading originator of Social Darwinism was the philosopher and biologist Herbert Spencer (1820–1903) who offered what was in effect a natural law that justified laissez-faire capitalism as the most advanced form of evolutionary selection. In modern society, 'the struggle for existence took the form of industrial competition' (Hawkins 1997: 93), so that whenever the state 'attempted to regulate market transactions, promote individual welfare, or aid the sick, the poor and the unemployed, then they not only invaded personal liberty but posed a grave threat to future progress' (Hawkins 1997: 94).

From a contemporary perspective, this orthogenetic vision of evolution

would be generally regarded as mistaken. Mary Midgley for instance, identifies in such views what she calls 'the Escalator Fallacy', 'the idea that
evolution is a steady, linear upward movement, a single inexorable process
of improvement leading (as a disciple of Herbert Spencer's put it) "from
gas to genius" and beyond into some superhuman spiritual stratosphere'
(Midgley 2002: 7). Nonetheless, whatever its validity, the late-Victorian
Social Darwinist vision of evolutionary orthogenesis was a widely authorised discourse, which was also capable of further variation and adaptation.
A rival variant accepted the Social Darwinist presumption of an evolutionary 'escalator', but counterposed a narrative in which evolution brought
forth Christian virtues of altruism that sought their expression within late-
Victorian civilisation. This narrative, in which evolution progressed towards
a different end, was authorised in both academic and popular discourses
that circulated widely during Fairbairn's formative years. Such ripostes to
Social Darwinism were not confined to Scotland: as James R. Moore demonstrates, exponents of Christianised evolutionary theory were present not
only in Scotland, but also in the rest of Britain and particularly in North
America, as they sought a way to locate a progressive providential narrative
in the course of natural history (Moore 1979: 217–51). However, as David
N. Livingstone explains, the Scottish theological response to Darwinian
evolution involved an 'intellectual exchange across the borderlands of evolutionary science and evangelical theology' (Livingstone 2014: 201) that
was by no means universal across the Presbyterian church:

> While Belfast Calvinists winced over what they took to be the dark
> implications of human evolutionary prehistory, key spokesmen for
> their Scottish coreligionists found little that was objectionable in the
> idea of humanity's animal ancestry. Indeed, some ... extracted from
> the language of cooperative evolution ideas and idioms that could
> bolster their ethical and political ideologies and lend support to their
> version of Christianized socialism. (Livingstone 2014: 201)

Amongst such figures was, for instance, 'James Iverach (1839–1922), Free
Church Professor of Apologetics in Aberdeen from 1887' (Livingstone
2014: 35) who argued that 'the inclination of too many evolutionists to
naturalize struggle sprang from their eagerness to impute a capitalist mode
of production to the natural order itself' (Livingstone 2014: 37). Social
Darwinism was a 'kind of anthropomorphism', a 'reading of man's practices into the cosmos' based on assumptions from capitalist individualism,
claimed Iverach in *Christianity and Evolution* (Iverach 1894: 181).

A full exploration of the Scottish context of Christianised evolution
is beyond the scope of this monograph, so the following discussion is
necessarily selective. The Scottish polymath Patrick Geddes (1854–1932)
is perhaps best known for his contribution to the nascent disciplines of
sociology and urban planning. His civic and architectural regeneration
of Edinburgh's Old Town made him a highly visible presence in the city's

late-Victorian milieu. Two of his regeneration projects from the 1890s, the Outlook Tower (a sociological museum) and Ramsay Garden (a University Hall), are still prominent in Edinburgh's skyline, located as they are adjacent to the Castle Esplanade (Boardman 1978: 121–45). Geddes was also regarded as an expert biologist. Chris Renwick shows how Geddes used the ninth edition of *Encyclopaedia Britannica* (1889) to popularise his belief that evolution displays an inbuilt ethical orthogenesis in which co-operation and love within a species increasingly replace struggle between different species (Renwick 2010: 152). These views were stated at greater length in *The Evolution of Sex*, published in 1889, the year of Fairbairn's birth. Geddes and his co-author J. Arthur Thomson offer a striking vision in which the evolution of sexual reproduction, co-operative social structures, and mammalian nurture, demonstrate an ethical progression within evolution:

> that increase of reproductive sacrifice, which at once makes the mammal and marks its essential stages of further progress ...; that increase of parental care; that frequent appearance of sociality or co-operation, ... all these phenomena of survival of the truly fittest, through love, sacrifice, and co-operation, need far other prominence than they could possibly receive on the hypothesis of the essential progress of the species through internecine struggle of its individuals at the margin of subsistence. Each of the greater steps of progress is in fact associated with an increased measure of subordination of individual competition to reproductive or social ends, and of interspecific competition to co-operative association. (Geddes and Thomson 1889: 311)

This ethical progression extended into a narrative of human social evolution which explicitly refreshed longstanding Christian discourses:

> we see that it is possible to interpret the ideals of ethical progress, through love and sociality, cooperation and sacrifice, not as mere utopias contradicted by experience, but as the highest expressions of the central evolutionary process of the natural world. The ideal of evolution is indeed an Eden; and although competition can never be wholly eliminated, and progress must thus approach without ever completely reaching its ideal, it is much for our pure natural history to recognise that 'creation's final law' is not struggle but love. (Geddes and Thomson 1889: 312)

Geddes reiterated and elaborated these views with his co-author Thomson in *Evolution* (1911):

> We may therefore restate here the concluding thesis of our own 'Evolution of Sex' (1889), since elaborated in various ways by [Henry] Drummond, by [Peter] Kropotkin and others. It is that the general progress both of the plant and the animal world, and notably the great

up-lifts ..., must be viewed not simply as individual but very largely in terms of sex and parenthood, of family and association; and hence of gregarious flocks and herds, of co-operative packs, of evolving tribes, and thus ultimately of civilized societies – above all, therefore, of the city. (Geddes and Thomson [1911]: 175–6)

The city was the form of communal life at the top of the evolutionary ladder, and in it was found the fullest expression of the tendency to increasingly complex altruistic co-operation. As with Iverach, the authors' opposition to Social Darwinist ideology is explicit:

Huxley's tragic vision of 'nature as a gladiatorial show,' and consequently of ethical life and progress as merely superposed by man, as therefore an interference with the normal order of Nature, is still far too dominant among us. It threatens even to-day to confuse the nascent science, and still more to wreck the incipient art, of Eugenics, in fact to encourage and defend that massacre of the innocents which is expressed in the death-rate of every community; and to extend this to a corresponding view of legislation and government. (Geddes and Thomson [1911]: 176)

Fairbairn's personal copy of *Evolution* in the same edition (Fairbairn.S.108) was acquired in the year of publication (the flyleaf is annotated '13.10.11'). Marginalia and annotations show that Fairbairn was clearly engaging closely with the book's argument. Annotations on the inside back cover ('245–248 Evolution not individualistic'), and a corresponding marginal pencil line on these pages, demonstrate Fairbairn's close attention to the closing pages of the book's argument, which restate – almost word for word – conclusions from *The Evolution of Sex*. Geddes and Thomson repeat their account of the 'increase of the reproductive sacrifice' in mammals, which demonstrates the 'survivals of the truly fittest, through love and sacrifice, sociability and co-operation simple to complex' (Geddes and Thomson [1911]: 246), thus displacing 'the classic economic hypothesis of the progress of the species essentially through the internecine struggle among its individuals at the margin of subsistence' (Geddes and Thomson [1911]: 247). Accordingly,

The ideal of evolution is thus no gladiator's show, but an Eden; and though competition can never be wholly eliminated – the line of progress is thus no straight line but at most an asymptote – it is much for our pure natural history to see no longer struggle, but love as 'creation's final law'. (Geddes and Thomson [1911]: 247)

In a 1930s tribute to Geddes, his contemporary, the Scottish educationalist Stewart A. Robertson (1866–1933), testifies to the galvanising effect of Geddes's worldview upon a generation dismayed by Social Darwinism: 'Forty years ago, multitudes of young men in Scotland and in England owed their souls to the teaching of Patrick Geddes' (Robertson 1932: 395).

He continues,

> I recall the thrill which went through an audience, as Geddes traced
> the basal feature of all life to be the sacrifice of the mother for the
> offspring, and closed by saying with his usual fingering of the abun-
> dant locks and the phrase over the shoulder, 'So life is not really a
> gladiator's show, it is rather – a vast mothers' meeting.' Such biological
> teaching rallied young minds to faith in the rationality of the universe.
> (Robertson 1932: 395)

Fairbairn himself would appear to have been a young mind rallied in such
a way.

Geddes's reference to Henry Drummond in *Evolution* invokes a figure
who is today rather more obscure, yet who was also prominent within the
critique of Social Darwinism that circulated in Fairbairn's formative years.
The Scottish evangelist Henry Drummond (1851–97) developed and popularised a discourse in which natural history, when understood correctly,
demonstrated the Providential evolution of Christian virtues such as love,
tenderness and altruism. Drummond's *Natural Law in the Spiritual World*
(1883) and *The Ascent of Man* (1894) were hugely successful popular texts.
James R. Moore observes that Drummond's writings, including pamphlets
such as *The Greatest Thing in the World* (1890), were highly successful in the
late-Victorian book market. *Natural Law* was selling at over 1,000 copies
per month a year after its publication (Moore 1985: 385–6); *The Ascent
of Man* 'sold 10,000 copies within a year and 30,000 by 1902' (Moore
1985: 386); '*The Greatest Thing in the World* (1890), sold a third-of-a-million
copies in seven years and is still in print today' (Moore 1985: 386). As
Livingstone notes, Drummond's worldview permeated popular Christian
consciousness:

> Many preachers and evangelical workers found Drummond's writings
> to be a rich storehouse of sermonic analogy. To be sure, reviewers
> found flaws and quibbled about this or that, but by and large the
> thought that Drummond had creatively connected up God's world
> in a compelling saga of universal continuity gripped many readers.
> (Livingstone 2014: 41)

Drummond's literary success combined evangelical appeal with scientific
credibility built upon a modest track record: as well as holding an academic
post in natural science at Free Church College in Glasgow from 1877
onwards, Drummond also had experience as a field geologist, and was a
Fellow of the Royal Society of Edinburgh (Moore 1985: 392). Drummond
argued that nature was one continuous whole, and that the laws of biology,
in particular, were at one with the laws of the spiritual world that had been
revealed by Scripture (Moore 1985: 397). Because of this so-called 'Law of
Continuity',

Natural Laws ... do not stop with the visible and then give place to a new set of Laws bearing a strong similitude to them. The Laws of the invisible are the same Laws, projections of the natural not supernatural. Analogous Phenomena are not the fruit of parallel Laws, but of the same Laws – Laws which at one end, as it were, may be dealing with Matter, at the other end with Spirit. (Drummond 1884: 11)

Natural Law, to modern eyes, contains an extraordinary moralising of natural history, which Drummond views as an orthogenetic ascent from least to most complex, from less to more perfect. Drummond, for instance, upbraids the hermit crab for its evolutionary backsliding:

the Hermit tribe have neither discharged their responsibilities to Nature nor to themselves. If the end of life is merely to escape death, and serve themselves, possibly they have done well; but if it is to attain an ever increasing perfection, then are they backsliders indeed. (Drummond 1884: 324)

The hermit crab, in Drummond's view, has been providentially punished as a species for abandoning the difficult path to sturdy and self-reliant complexity in favour of (semi-)parasitism. This observation confirms, in his view, the general natural-spiritual law that '*[a]ny principle which secures the safety of the individual without personal effort or the vital exercise of faculty is disastrous to moral character*' (Drummond 1884: 326). Nor indeed was this some mere eccentricity on Drummond's part. Geddes and Thomson similarly use moralising language in *The Evolution of Sex* to condemn the parasitism of the cuckoo, employing vocabulary such as 'lazy', 'evil', 'selfish', 'cruel' and 'immoral' to characterise the bird (Geddes and Thomson 1889: 278).

Nonetheless, whatever the validity of Drummond's Christianised evolutionary narrative from a later perspective, 'To educated lay people *Natural Law* furnished proof that the latest science supported their faith' (Moore 1985: 399). Scripture was renewed via New Testament metaphors of organic life (vines and branches, grains of mustard seed, the body of Christ) that 'served as a point of contact with evangelical audiences for insinuating the claims of continuity and the authority of nature over a province that traditionally had been the most refractory to scientific explanation' (Moore 1985: 412). Although *Natural Law* was strongly criticised, Drummond, as Moore explains, maintained 'his grand unifying belief that natural laws are valid in the spiritual world. For ten years he illustrated this belief in essays and addresses, and in *The Ascent of Man* he made it the corner-stone of a thoroughgoing evolutionary cosmogony' (Moore 1985: 404). *The Ascent of Man* not only re-affirms Drummond's fundamental stance, it also clearly contributes to the Christianised evolutionary context which awaited the importation of Freudian ideas and practices. Moore explains:

Evolution, as we see in retrospect, wrote Drummond, has resulted from two factors: a Struggle for Life and a Struggle for the Life of

Others. The first, a struggle for nutrition, is competitive, individual-istic, and selfish. The second, a struggle to reproduce, is cooperative, corporate, and altruistic. But, although both factors are integral to the evolutionary process, they must be seen in due proportion. Since the dawn of man's ascent the Struggle for Life has been giving way to the Struggle for the Life of Others. As body and mind have evolved, self-sacrifice and co-operation, maternal and domestic virtues, have slowly but surely prevailed. Vestiges of animal nature remain, even in civilised man, but these will finally pass away in a further evolution of altruism (Moore 1985: 405).

Evolution, Drummond argues, gradually brings about an increase in Christian virtue: 'Evolution is Advolution [a rolling towards]; better, it is Revelation – the phenomenal expression of the Divine, the progressive realization of the Ideal, the Ascent of Love' (Drummond 1894: 435).

The revelation of a Providential design in evolution becomes apparent, Drummond argues, in the phylogenesis of mammalia. Drummond reas-sures his readers that '[i]n as real a sense as a factory is meant to turn out locomotives or clocks, the machinery of Nature is designed in the last resort to turn out Mothers' (Drummond 1894: 343):

Hitherto, the world belonged to the Food-seeker, the Self-seeker, the Struggler for Life, the Father. Now is the hour of the Mother. And, animal though she be, she rises to the task. And that hour, as she min-isters to her young, becomes to her, and to the world, the hour of its holiest birth. (Drummond 1894: 22)

Drummond specifically identifies suckling as a relationship between mother and child that provides both nutrition and love:

No young of any Mammal can nourish itself. There is that in it there-fore at this stage which compels it to seek its Mother; and there is that in the Mother which compels it even physically ... to seek her child. On the physiological side, the name of this impelling power is lacta-tion; on the ethical side, it is Love. And there is no escape henceforth from communion between Mother and child. (Drummond 1894: 358)

Suckling is the primal form of communion between persons, and meets biological, psychological and spiritual needs. The popular writings of Drummond, alongside that of more scholarly peers such as Geddes and Iverach, articulate a Christianised evolutionary narrative which was promi-nent in late-Victorian Scottish culture, and which saw evolution as the his-torical revelation of a providential plan for the creation of Christian virtues. Mammals, and pre-eminently humans, were at the top of this evolutionary escalator in which the sacrifices of motherhood were the prototype of loving communion, and in which late-Victorian urban life was (potentially) the most developed social context for its expression.

The anthropology of communion

The Christianised evolutionary biology of Geddes and Drummond was complemented by a further set of late-Victorian discourses propounded by Scots active in the emerging discipline of anthropology. If Christianised evolutionary biology illuminated the origins and prospects of all life on Earth, then anthropology complemented this knowledge with expert understanding of the fundamental nature and tendency of human social organisation, particularly as expressed in the discipline's reconstruction of supposed 'primitive society'. As Adam Kuper explains, this concept has been increasingly debunked in contemporary anthropology, since 'human societies cannot be traced back to a single point of origin. Nor is there any way of reconstituting prehistoric social forms, classifying them, and aligning them in a time series' (Kuper 2005: 5). Yet it has persisted because '[t]he theory generated a specialised tradition of puzzle-solving; it yielded a succession of transformations that could accommodate any special interests; and it referred to ultimate social concerns – the state, citizenship, the family and so on' (Kuper 2005: 222). The particular Victorian Scottish contribution centred on the phenomenon of 'totemism'. This was the supposed link between the religious life of 'primitive' peoples (whether prehistoric or contemporary) and their social organisation into 'clans', which were 'descent groups which were formed by the descendants of a man, in the male line, or of a woman, in the female line' (Kuper 2005: 5). 'Each clan', as Kuper explains, 'was thought to be descended from an animal or vegetable god, which it revered. This was "totemism"' (Kuper 2005: 5) – and, as he notes, it was a phenomenon reconstructed, or invented, by a small Edinburgh-based network of late-Victorian Scots, including the lawyer J. F. McLennan (1827–81) and the theologian William Robertson Smith (1846–94) (Kuper 2005: 86–90).

As a preliminary to discussion of the Scottish anthropological context, it is useful to turn briefly, by way of contrast, to Freud's account of religious communion in *Totem and Taboo* (1913). According to Freud, totemistic ritual meals are consumed in remembrance of the primal father who monopolised human females until he was slain by an alliance of his sons, who then instituted a system of clan organisation based on exogamous exchange and enforced by a taboo on incest (Freud 1955: 140–6). Guilt, passed down from generation to generation by innate mental inheritance, motivates religious observance: 'Totemic religion arose from the filial sense of guilt'; '[a]ll later religions are seen to be attempts at solving the same problem' (Freud 1955: 145). Freud's psychoanalytic account of human phylogeny, while citing Robertson Smith extensively, owes more to ideas from J. J. Atkinson's *Primal Law* (Atkinson 1903), which were in turn informed by Darwinian observations on social relationships in primates (Kuper 2005: 105–6) – Atkinson, perhaps predictably, was a Scot by descent and education (Morrison 1904: 246). This textual dependency helps to explain why

Freud's theory is so alien to the highly influential account of totemism and communion developed by Robertson Smith, for the Scottish theologian stresses neither the piacular (atoning), nor oblative (giving) dimensions of totemistic sacrifice. As Kuper explains, Robertson Smith regarded sacrifice as a ritual of communion between the totemic descent group and its god: 'The totemic gods were natural species, generally plants or animals. They were associated with shrines or sanctuaries, which followers had to visit. At certain times, a yet more intimate contact with the gods was required. This was achieved through sacrifice' (Kuper 2005: 89). Accordingly, in his *Lectures on the Religion of the Semites*, first published in 1889, Robertson Smith argues that the rituals of sacrifice are primarily social: 'The god and his worshippers are wont to eat and drink together, and by this token their fellowship is declared and sealed' (Robertson Smith 1894: 271). Sacrifice extends the everyday social relations that are sealed by rituals of food-sharing:

> The sacrificial meal was an appropriate expression of the antique ideal of religious life, not merely because it was a social act and an act in which the god and his worshippers were conceived as partaking together, but because, as has already been said, the very act of eating and drinking with a man was a symbol and a confirmation of fellowship and mutual social obligations. The one thing directly expressed in the sacrificial meal is that the god and his worshippers are *commensals* [i.e. table-sharers], but every other point in their mutual relations is included in what this involves. Those who do not eat together are aliens to one another, without fellowship in religion and without reciprocal social duties. (Robertson Smith 1894: 269)

The piacular interpretation of sacrifice, Robertson Smith insists, is a later development that is quite inappropriate to the earliest forms of religious life (Robertson Smith 1894: 401): the 'central act of primitive worship', as Marjorie Wheeler-Barclay explains, is 'a communion feast in which doctrine is subordinated to a corporate celebration and sanctification of divine and human fellowship' (Wheeler-Barclay 1993: 76).

In describing the earliest form of social relation between worshipper and God, Robertson Smith was therefore also outlining a theory of the earliest form of any social relation. The sharing of food between persons established the primitive relationship of *kinship*, a term which need not be understood genealogically since, as Robertson Smith indicates, it does not require or imply a blood relationship. The 'kindred', rather, is 'a group of persons whose lives were so bound up together ... that they could be treated as parts of one common life' (Robertson Smith 1894: 273–4). To the concept of the kindred as phylogenetically the most primitive social organisation, Robertson Smith added a matriarchal, ontogenetic dimension. Adult bonds of fellowship are sealed by commensal relations, but the original 'commensality' is between mother and child, whose kinship is established by suckling even when the two are not genetically related

(Robertson Smith 1894: 274). To establish kinship between biological father and child, a further commensal ritual is required, as described by Robertson Smith in *Kinship and Marriage in Early Arabia*, first published in 1885. The sharing between father and child of a customary 'morning draught' of wine 'acquires the same significance in constituting kinship as mother's milk had formerly done' (Robertson Smith 1907: 177–8). Robertson Smith's anthropology invokes the suckling relationship between mother and child as the earliest ontogenetic form of social relationship, and views later social relations as elaborations upon this primary bond.

Robertson Smith's inferences and speculations about the life of the 'nomadic Bedouins of pre-Islamic Arabia' (Bediako 1997: 320) were far from obscure, for they were the work of a thinker who was the focus of 'one of the most famous academic disputes in Victorian Britain' when his use of the Continental 'higher criticism' to historically interpret the Bible led to what was, in effect, a trial for heresy before the Free Church of Scotland's General Assembly that led to the loss of his professorship at Aberdeen Free Church Divinity College (Beidelman 1974: 13–22). Scottish Presbyterianism may have accommodated Darwinian evolution, but it was far more hostile to Robertson Smith's views on the evolution of religion: 'his radical reconstruction of the compositional history of the Hebrew Bible and his influential genealogy of sacrificial ritual seemed far more menacing than Darwin's theory of species change by means of natural selection' (Livingstone 2014: 201–2). Whatever Robertson Smith's own views on the implications of his analysis, the continuity between Christian communion and primitive sacrificial communion was perceived as implying that Christianity was a natural phenomenon, rather than divinely revealed (Wheeler-Barclay 1993: 77).

After dismissal from his academic position in 1881, Robertson Smith then garnered further fame and influence through his editing of the ninth edition of *Encyclopaedia Britannica* (to which Geddes was a contributor: see p. 19), where he contributed over two hundred articles, signed and unsigned, in his fields of expertise (Maier 2009: 184, 212–13). The so-called '"scholar's encyclopaedia"' covered nearly all of Victorian learning, and was distributed internationally and in affordable mass-market editions, so that 'Smith's achievement made a great impact upon the popularly educated thousands as well as upon scholars' (Beidelman 1974: 25). To understand Robertson Smith's life and work is therefore to appreciate further the peculiar cultural and intellectual resources upon which Scottish psychoanalysis drew. Opposing the Freudian lineage of ideas was a Scottish tradition with a quite different view of the relationship between religion and society. In Robertson Smith's account, the practice of communion was the central religious and social phenomenon, and it awaited rediscovery in industrial modernity by the expert methodologies of Biblical criticism and comparative anthropology. Communion existed *in nuce* in the primal religion and primitive society of the pre-Islamic Arabs, and promised fruition in modern Christianity. It is probably an overstatement to conclude that

Robertson Smith regarded Christianity as 'a religion of love, fellowship, joy, and communion with God, with little emphasis on sin, suffering, and guilt' (Beidelman 1974: 61); the spiritual ingredient of atonement was still a proper element of divinely inspired (i.e. Judaeo-Christian) religion (Segal 2008: 21–3). Nonetheless, his 'definition of religious faith centered on the relationship between the individual believer and God rather than intellectual acceptance of a creed' (Wheeler-Barclay 1993: 63), thereby giving the practice of communion a particular prominence alongside other elements of the Christian faith.

Religion and communion in Scottish psychoanalytic pioneers

Accounts of the importation of psychoanalytic ideas and practices into Britain have challenged the heroic narrative supplied by Ernest Jones (1879–1958), who 'claimed to have published, in 1909, the first favourable article on Freud's work in the English speaking world', and who later 'founded the London Society of Psycho-Analysis in 1913, which he disbanded because of its eclecticism in 1919, founding the British Society with more stringent membership rules in the same year' (Alexander 1998: 136). Philip Kuhn is particularly scathing of Jones's claims to priority, arguing that the Welsh psychiatrist provides 'a monolithic, often monomaniacal, history which he appears to have designed simply to aggrandize himself' (Kuhn 2014: 157). Research on the dissemination of psychoanalysis in Britain increasingly shows a longer history of diverse points of cultural entry and adaptation. R. D. Hinshelwood discovers 'seven points of access into British cultural life in the 25 years or so after 1893' (Hinshelwood 1995: 135): psychical research, sexual liberation, psychological and therapeutically optimistic psychiatry, empirical psychology, literary modernism, progressive education, and philosophy (Hinshelwood 1995: 147–8). Each different point of access 'tended to emphasise one element relevant to the cultural group and squeezed out other elements' (Hinshelwood 1995: 147) – for instance, psychical research regarded Freud 'as one who had contacted the "other world" through the unconscious life of hysterical patients' (Hinshelwood 1995: 138). Dean Rapp provides a broader picture of the non-specialist interest in Freud in his survey of British general interest magazines in the period 1912–19, where even large circulation magazines for the lay public are selectively favourable to Freud, ignoring his sexual theories, but introducing the concept of the unconscious mind and the techniques that access it (Rapp 1990: 242). General interest magazines were also sympathetic to Jungian psychology and the work of British eclectics (Rapp 1990: 232–4). Early clinics that specialised in psychotherapy, such as the Medico-Psychological Clinic (or Brunswick Square Clinic) which ran from 1913 to 1922, evidenced, as Suzanne Raitt has shown, 'an eclectic indigenous style which was gradually repressed and delimited as more and more early practitioners were converted to – or coerced into –

a strict Freudianism conceived along continental European lines' (Raitt
2004: 63).

As Freudian ideas and practices entered the United Kingdom through
these various channels, they came into a quite distinct dialogue with the
Scottish religious context, and were transformed accordingly, much as
Darwinian ideas had earlier been transformed in the nineteenth century.
The official Freudian line on religion had been set out in a variety of publications by Freud, and was antithetical to longer standing domestic discourses.
In *Totem and Taboo* (1913), as explained above, totemism, regarded as a
primitive form of religion, is depicted as a ritual of atonement preserved by
racial memory of the murder of the primal father. Freud's *The Future of an
Illusion* (1927) supplements this analysis of ritual with an account of later
patriarchal religion, and pre-eminently Judaeo-Christian belief, as a culturally institutionalised regression to a state of wishful childish dependency
upon an all-powerful protective father image:

> the terrifying impression of helplessness in childhood aroused the
> need for protection – for protection through love – which was pro-
> vided by the father; and the recognition that this helplessness lasts
> throughout life made it necessary to cling to the existence of a father,
> but this time a more powerful one. Thus the benevolent rule of a
> divine Providence allays our fear of the dangers of life; the establish-
> ment of a moral world-order ensures the fulfilment of the demands
> of justice, which have so often remained unfulfilled in human civiliza-
> tion; and the prolongation of earthly existence in a future life provides
> the local and temporal framework in which these wish-fulfilments shall
> take place. (Freud 1961: 30)

Although Freud carefully hedged his analysis with various emollient conces-
sions to religious adherence, his essential view was that religious phenomena were 'neurotic relics' from earlier stages of human civilisation which
modernity should, on an analogy with clinical psychoanalysis, replace with
the 'rational operations of the intellect' (Freud 1961: 44).

The incongruence between Freudian doctrine and the traditions of
inquiry in Scotland explicated above should be clear. The work of Geddes,
Drummond, Robertson Smith, and others, contradicted the Freudian view
that religion was a stubborn pre-rational residue that should be scoured
away by Enlightenment critique. They offered an alternative tradition of
inquiry into religion that scientifically modified and authorised Christian
discourses and practices. The natural history of evolution certainly dis-
proved naïve Creationism, but it also validated a Providential narrative
of evolutionary progression towards the emergence of Christian love in
mammalia, and, within the human species, towards the promotion of the
altruistic maternal ethic, rather than laissez-faire capitalism, in contemporary civilisation. Communion between mother and child in the act of
suckling was the paradigm of the social bond, rather than competitive

relationships of survival, sexual selection, and economic individualism. Anthropology offered complementary doctrines. The observation and reconstruction of supposedly 'primitive' human society showed that sacrifice was not originally atonement demanded by a wrathful deity (nor, by extension, was Christ's sacrifice simply an act of substitutionary atonement, although this penal element was present); sacrifice was ultimately a route to commensal fellowship between worshippers and their god.

There was not, of course, an explicit doctrine (of 'communion', for instance) that synthesised or even aggregated these various discourses, but they provided an important intellectual context against which Freudian and other psychoanalytic ideas were assessed, and (if necessary) rejected or amended. This worldview offers a likely provenance for the work of Fairbairn, who was reared in an intensely religious environment (Beattie 2003: 1175). As Marie Hoffman explains, Fairbairn's career path was at first clerical, before it became medical:

> Fairbairn did pursue an intermediate degree in divinity at the London University and then, at age 25, returned to Edinburgh, where he began his theological training in the Presbyterian church. These studies, however, were interrupted by World War I, Fairbairn serving in the army for three and one-half years. It was during this time that Fairbairn's vision shifted from curing souls through preaching to helping people through psychology. (Hoffman 2004: 772)

During his military service, Fairbairn was impressed by W. H. R. Rivers's employment of psychoanalytic techniques upon military personnel at Craiglockhart Hospital in Edinburgh, which seems to have confirmed his interest in the so-called 'new psychology' (Sutherland 1989: 8). After the war, he turned from ministry to medicine, and eventually to psychological medicine, as a way of helping others. His experience of psychotherapy had a strongly religious flavour imparted by the 'full-blooded' Christian convictions (Sutherland 1989: 7) of his analyst, friend, and (it seems) substitute father, Ernest H. Connell, 'a wealthy Australian who had trained in medicine and psychiatry in Edinburgh and had been analyzed by Ernest Jones' (Beattie 2016: 895). By 1925, Fairbairn was operating a private psychoanalytic practice in Edinburgh (Sutherland 1989: 9), and held various clinical and academic appointments in the city for the remainder of his career (Fairbairn 1994b: 463–4).

These biographical factors, and the wider cultural interest with communion inherited from the Victorians, resonate with Fairbairn's elaborately developed challenge to Freudian theory. Fairbairn proceeds from the principle that the supposed Freudian stage of oral infantile sexuality is really the earliest form of interpersonal relation between mother and child – a doctrine anticipated by Drummond and Robertson Smith. Fairbairn states: 'The first social relationship established by the individual is that between himself and his mother; and the focus of this relationship is the suckling situation' (Fairbairn 1994i: 10). The child's pleasure in suckling, in Fairbairn's view, is not an end in itself, but a 'sign-post to the object' (Fairbairn 1994h: 33) – an index of the mother's love. The infant wants above all to love and be loved by another person (the 'object'), but inevitably the mother (Fairbairn's theory is quite strictly gendered) must frustrate this narrow, possessive love. The child manages its insecurity and feelings of rejection through psychic mechanisms based on the principle 'divide et impera' (Fairbairn 1994c: 112). The actual mother is divided into separate mental (or 'internal') representations. The infant relates to a central good or 'accepting' object (a loving and loveable mother, 'desexualized and idealized' (Fairbairn 1994a: 135)), and two bad objects: the 'exciting object' (the mother as she provokes longing), and the 'rejecting object' (the mother as she fails to meet this longing) (Fairbairn 1994c: 109–11). The two internal bad objects, and the self's uncomfortable relations to them, become dissociated from the central ego, thereby creating two dissociated selves, mental 'pseudopodia' (Fairbairn 1994c: 112) inaccessible to the conscious mind: namely the 'libidinal ego' (compulsively lustful) and the 'internal saboteur' (obsessively guilty) (Fairbairn 1994a: 135), which are relational versions of the Freudian instinctual 'id' and self-persecuting 'superego' (Fairbairn 1994d: 147–8). Fairbairn's thesis that the fundamental defence is splitting of the ego (Fairbairn 1994c: 131) leads him to a distinctively relational paradigm of psychopathology, that of the 'schizoid' self who is so troubled by the demons of the libidinal ego and internal saboteur that he or she retreats from tangible, external relationships to a world of attempted intellectual self-sufficiency. The schizoid is cut off from human fellowship, and is consequently susceptible to 'intellectualization': 'Such individuals are often more inclined to construct intellectual systems of an elaborate kind than to develop emotional relationships with others on a human basis' (Fairbairn 1994i: 21). But neither intellectual nor emotional health can proceed from a life in which others are treated 'more or less as if they were lower animals' (Fairbairn 1994i: 12).

As Marie Hoffman observes, this theory resembles a Calvinist narrative of fall, estrangement, and (possible) return. The infant is born 'predestined ... to seek relationship' (2004: 785), but undergoes a 'fall from grace' which is a 'fall from relationship' (2004: 791). The child, unable to cope with its ambivalent feelings towards the mother, and unsure of whether to have faith in the goodness of her intentions, operates a protective process of dissociation. What remains in consciousness is a central ego with an idealised, rose-tinted attitude towards the mother that belies the emotions felt by the split-off portions of the self. Therapy, as Beattie indicates, is a casting out of these dissociated demons: 'It is the clinical task of analysis ... to permit the exorcism of the devils by which the patient is possessed and to open his closed inner world to the influence of outer reality' (2003: 1173). The exorcism metaphor used by Beattie is explicitly offered by Fairbairn when he states that psychotherapy is in part a psychological successor to

Christian ideas and practices. In a 1958 conference paper, 'Psychotherapy and the clergy', Fairbairn asserts an analogy between the casting out of devils and his brand of psychoanalytic psychotherapy:

> In my own personal opinion, it is something very like *salvation*, rather than medical cure, that the average patient is seeking when he embarks upon a course of psychotherapy. From a religious, or at any rate a Christian point of view, what man seeks salvation *from* is sin, estrangement from God, spiritual death, and that fear which is cast out by 'Perfect Love.'
>
> Correspondingly, from a psychotherapeutic point of view, what (in my opinion) the patient seeks salvation *from* is anxiety, guilt, his own aggression and the bad persecuting parental figures which haunt his inner world as the result of his experiences in childhood. What he seeks, accordingly, would appear to be something very like the forgiveness of sins and the casting out of devils. (Fairbairn 1994f: 364)

Fairbairn explicitly positions psychotherapy as a scientifically rationalised successor to some (though not all) elements of religious practice: 'Religion is the earliest and original form of psychotherapy. Psychotherapy as such may be said to have developed out of religion as an attempt to establish the cure of psychological troubles on a scientific basis' (Fairbairn 1994f: 363).

Fairbairn's religiosity, and its impact upon his psychoanalytic theory and practice, is already recognised. Less well-known, however, is the deeply Christian character of Hugh Crichton-Miller (1877–1959), the Edinburgh-trained medical doctor who in 1920 founded the Tavistock Clinic (originally, the Tavistock Clinic for Functional Nervous Disorders) in London, one of the earliest psychotherapeutic outpatient clinics in Britain (Lockhart 2010: 13). Like Fairbairn, Crichton-Miller had a religious upbringing: he was the son of the Scottish Protestant minister in Genoa, Donald Miller, who had risen up through the church from humble beginnings in a Scottish fishing community (*Hugh Crichton-Miller* 1961: 61–2). Crichton-Miller held strong Christian religious convictions as both 'an Elder of the Scottish Presbyterian Church of St Columba's, London', and as someone who saw 'Christian moral ideas as bearing upon human conduct' (Dicks 1970: 24). Crichton-Miller, with his colleague James Arthur Hadfield (1882–1967), who had also trained in medicine at Edinburgh (Lockhart 2010: 13), set about integrating Freudian psychoanalytic theory with Christianity via the general psychology of William McDougall (1871–1938), which 'emphasise[d] the purposive nature of the evolved and biological origins of the human individual' (Lockhart 2010: 16), and drew upon nineteenth-century British idealist philosophy (Lockhart 2010: 14–16).

In *The New Psychology and the Preacher*, Crichton-Miller welcomes the psychoanalytic investigation of religion, explicitly comparing it with Robertson Smith's earlier anthropological and textual criticism (Crichton-Miller 1924: 65). Crichton-Miller believes that psychoanalytic investigation will have a purifying effect upon the Christian community, preserving what is imperishable in religious sensibility: '"No wind killeth the tree that Allah hath planted." Those who feel that their religion has this charter of indestructibility will welcome all fair-minded criticism, and will hasten to accept new scientific methods of investigation' (Crichton-Miller 1924: 21). Rather than exposing religion *in toto* as a delusion or a symptom, psychoanalytic critique will, according to Crichton-Miller, remove those aspects of Christianity that are 'second-rate and extrinsic' such as wish-fulfilment, comforting regression, and compensation for inferiority (Crichton-Miller 1924: 39) – the phenomena identified by Freud, in other words. What will remain is an evolving 'progressive impulse' (Crichton-Miller 1924: 89) that is 'primarily affective' (Crichton-Miller 1924: 71), and to which history, doctrine and systematic theology are secondary. Crichton-Miller offers a socially progressive Gospel promoting personal relationships that are loving, rather than conceived of and practised on the model of subordination to the social organism: 'Christianity introduces a new principle – that of love. Society is therefore challenged to substitute for the power principle of biology, the love principle of the gospels' (Crichton-Miller 1924: 78–9).

Crichton-Miller's critical respect for religion is echoed in the work of Ian D. Suttie (1889–1935), a Scottish colleague at the Tavistock Clinic, who offers a trenchant critique of the atomism and hedonism of Freudian psychoanalysis, and whose ideas are now known to have informed Fairbairn's theorising in the 1940s, albeit without the Edinburgh psychoanalyst's explicit public acknowledgement (Clarke 2018: 3–21). Suttie spent his formative years in Glasgow, and it was at Glasgow University that he received both his Bachelor's degree in medicine and his MD; after a variety of posts in various mental health institutions in Scotland, Suttie took up in 1928 a clinical assistantship at the Tavistock Clinic (Heard 1988: xxxiii). Dorothy Heard remarks that 'there are few clues that indicate how and from where Suttie derived his ideas' (Heard 1988: xx), and this is partly because

> during her [his wife, Jane Isabel Suttie's] lifetime there was no one in the family who had a specialist interest in psychoanalytic psychotherapy. This lack and her known desires, to live as far as possible unburdened by possessions and to 'die tidy,' may explain why no papers relating to any aspect of Ian's or her own work or life survive. (Heard 1988: xl)

Like Fairbairn, Suttie repudiates Freud's egoistic hypothesis that 'the goal of life is self-assertion and self-seeking, limited only by fear of unpleasant consequences or retaliation' (Suttie 1935: 49) and argues that instinctual gratification is not an end in itself. Instead, whether in adult or infantile love, '[t]he emotions borrow, as it were, the *use* of organs ... and turn them temporarily to purposes that are definitely social' (Suttie 1935: 68). Thus, concludes, Suttie, 'it would be as absurd to regard the sex act as having a selfish "detensioning," evacuatory motive as to say that a woman desires maternity for the drainage of her mammary glands' (Suttie 1935: 72n).

Suttie's argument draws clearly upon the late-Victorian tradition that emphasises the evolution of motherly love. Evolution has dissolved the various instincts into a 'formless aimless attachment of the infant to the mother' (Suttie and Suttie 1932b: 209). This single instinct has numerous evolutionary advantages: it is adaptable and directable (and so can transmit culture); it is functional for self-preservation since it keeps the infant close to the mother; and finally it supplies what Suttie calls an 'associative need' that persists to maturity, and subsists under any merely selfish rationalisation of the individual's relation to society (Suttie and Suttie 1932b: 209). In the ideal case, says Suttie, the child comes to be with the mother by sharing her interest in the social and objective worlds in a process of 'endogenous repression'. This superior psychological maturation arises from the mother's rejection of the child's incestuous fantasies, as opposed to the father's patriarchal prohibition:

> I speak of endogenous repression, where the wishes of the loved person herself directly oppose those of the lover – the opposition in this kind of repression arises *within the love relationship and not from the interference of an outside party*, as in the exogenous, or Freudian repression proper (if indeed this ever effects true repression at all). (Suttie 1935: 106)

Suttie's critique of Freud, which seems to owe as much to Geddes and Drummond as to Darwin, was to later partly inform John Bowlby's empirically detailed work (Bowlby 1988: xvi–xvii) – indeed, Suttie anticipates Bowlby's central term, 'attachment', and also the metaphor of early loving relationships as a 'secure base' – or as Suttie has it, a '"base of supplies"' from which 'we can adventure into fellowship' (1935: 157–8). Suttie's challenge to Freudian theory is also explicitly informed by an aspiration to preserve and rationally revise Christianity in the manner suggested later by Fairbairn, and earlier by Crichton-Miller. Suttie argues that we are prejudiced against religion because of its dependence upon traditionary knowledge, and because of our suspicion of its socially powerful organised expression (Suttie 1935: 127–8). He therefore urges an unbiased attitude, and cautions that '[w]e must therefore study religion without making up our minds that it is either a disease or a cure, a psychopathy or a psychotherapy' (Suttie 1935: 138). Christianity in particular, argues Suttie, is essentially an ethic for the maintenance of loving social relationships, and is only accidentally superstitious or ideological: Christianity 'offers the conception of social life as based upon Love rather than upon authority' and it 'uphold[s] the notion of religious behaviour as concerned with good social relationships *between* men rather than with the individual duty of every man towards god' (Suttie 1935: 141–2). In a speculative historical anthropology of Christianity, Suttie argues that the religion was repeatedly retrogressed by its transmission through patriarchal cultures of the

Mediterranean, including Judaism and the Roman world. Gal Gerson ably summarises Suttie's view that

> [m]atriarchies provide the conditions for benevolent repression. Their beliefs and organization reflect the healthy approach that individuals take when their fundamental sociability is not warped by anxiety and aggression. Patriarchies, by contrast, foster submissive mothers, dominating fathers, weak and untidy forms of repression, and hence resentment and aggression – and the ideological tenets to justify them. The opposites of health and illness roughly correspond to the Nordic and Mediterranean regions. (Gerson 2009a: 32)

As Gerson rightly points out, this position means that Suttie 'grades regional cultures in a way that is hardly acceptable by later standards' (Gerson 2009a: 32). At the time, however, this was a common feature of evolutionist discourses, whether biological or anthropological, and evident in Geddes, Drummond, and Robertson Smith, amongst others.

Suttie concludes that psychotherapy (properly reconceived – that is in his own mould) is the rational inheritor of Christian practice, and that Freud's actual technique – as opposed to his theorisation of it – is in fact an offer of loving fellowship. The ideal therapeutic attitude, Suttie continues, is not the Freudian blank screen, but rather 'is very like that of Christ'; the therapist is 'serene without being aloof, sympathetic without being disturbed: exactly what the child desires in the parent' (Suttie 1935: 217). The task at hand, says Suttie in an unpublished lecture to the British Federation of Social Workers, is 'to exploit the resources of religious belief and feeling for the promotion of mental health and social harmony' (Emotional Development: 4). Religion already exists, for Suttie, as a repository of intuitive, symbolic and supernaturally conceived know-how; the goal is to rationally develop this already-existing expertise, rather than to dismiss it as mere neurosis or wish-fulfilment.

The selective adoption and adaptation of Freudian psychoanalysis pursued by Farbairn, Suttie and others was a consequence of their ideological formation by earlier rationalised investigations of Christian doctrine and practice. Although the preceding discussion has emphasised the efficacy of a distinctive cultural context, the suitability of object relations theory to contemporaneous British political discourses should also be noted. This factor has been extensively explored by Gal Gerson, who argues that object relations theory

> backs the welfare state by offering what amounts to a coherent political theory that starts from humanity's natural state, and then advances to define the entitlements that individuals hold in society and to outline the overall political order within which these entitlements may be enjoyed. (Gerson 2004: 770)

Since the supposed state of nature for human beings was not one of self-interested autonomy as presupposed by classical liberalism, but rather of infantile dependence, a different model of the social, political and economic order is implied (and becomes increasingly explicit in post-war developments such as attachment theory (Gerson 2004: 788) and its analogues, such as the 'new deal' for children promoted in post-war New Zealand (see p. 53)). The 'healthy, autonomous personality' of classical political theory was in fact a contingent product of complex familial interactions that begin in infancy, and which could derailed by '[b]reaks in the continuum of care, separation from parents, separation of parents, parental neglect, and external circumstances (such as poverty or war)' (Gerson 2004: 787). As a consequence, object relations theory focuses politically 'on maintaining the social unit where care is best given, a unit that the theory identifies with the family. Accordingly, the household is both supported by the broader society and exposed to its gaze through experts and officials' (Gerson 2004: 790). This psychoanalytic doctrine resonated with a broader progressive liberal worldview of the time which 'emphasized the constitutive nature of the sociable motivation', and which 'demanded that the family be protected from the market, and that government act to minimize pressures on mothers to leave their children for work' (Gerson 2009a: 34).

Scottish psychoanalytic ideas therefore have a quite peculiar character by the 1930s. The ideas of Fairbairn, Suttie, et al., are clearly informed by a context of Christianised evolutionary theory and anthropological speculation in which Scots were prominent. Moreover, the resulting adaptation of Freudian ideas to this context produced a psychoanalytic psychology that argued for innate sociability, and which was politically congenial to the emerging politics of the welfare state. Scottish Christianised psychoanalytic ideas emphasise the importance of the primordial communion between mother and child, which is an evolutionary analogue to the communion between God and worshipper. If the infant's familial environment is disrupted, whether by psychological or socio-political causes, then disturbances in early relationships lead to psychopathological consequences such as the dissociation of part-selves suffused with anger and longing, or the formation of an underlying morbid rage and anxiety that interferes with social relationships. The therapist, however, may, through a relationship that is primarily affective (loving, forgiving), restore to the adult patient his or her capacity for spontaneous and whole-hearted interpersonal life.

Selective importation: John Macmurray and Adlerian psychology

The adaptation of psychoanalysis to religious needs and interests went beyond the critical reassessment of Freud. By the inter-war years, a varied menu of psychoanalytic ideas and practices was circulating through Western countries, transmitted through various points of cultural entry. One important strand of psychoanalysis is the 'individual psychology' of Alfred Adler (1870–1937), which was formed in a schismatic split from the Freudian paradigm. Paul E. Stepanksy observes:

[i]t is a revealing oversight in the history of modern psychiatry that Alfred Adler has yet to be accorded his just due. Despite Adler's important role in the history of psychoanalysis and his obvious stature as the founder of Individual Psychology, the study of his thought and the explication of his system have remained the preserve of committed partisans. In the course of the continuing polemical exchanges between 'Freudians' and 'Adlerians,' Adler's thought has been deprived of the critical and contextual examination it warrants. (Stepansky 1983: 1)

Adler was a significant intellectual and personal presence in Scotland, partly because he was willing to venture beyond the metropolitan setting of London. While in Aberdeen on the northern leg of a British lecture tour in 1937, he visited the village of Corgarff, to meet the 'Rev. John Linton ... who was translating Adler's *Social Interest: A Challenge to Mankind*' (Bottome 1957: 256) – this translation was published in 1938 (Adler 1938). According to Phyllis Bottome, Adler gave a lecture in Aberdeen to the Child Guidance Society, with the result that '[t]he city decided to help the university to found a chair of psychiatry, each paying three hundred a year, so that they might have the right to send delinquent children from Aberdeen to the university for this special treatment' (Bottome 1957: 257). Adler died a few days after this lecture, struck down in Union Street by a heart attack on 28 May 1937 (Death Of Dr Adler 1937); his lecture tour was continued in June by his daughter Alexandra, who delivered in Edinburgh a series of ten lectures expounding her father's views (Adler's Beliefs 1937). In a curious, and long-delayed, epilogue, Adler's ashes were found in 2007 in Edinburgh (where his body had been transported for cremation). They had lain unclaimed until their rediscovery by the honorary consul for Austria, and were later formally returned to Vienna ('Adler's Ashes Found in Edinburgh').

Adlerian psychoanalysis has been quietly present in Scottish intellectual life since the 1930s, but its effects have gone unnoticed and unremarked until recent years, partly because of the relative obscurity of Adler within psychoanalytic historiography, and partly because his ideas were often used with only the scantest of attribution. One of Scotland's most significant twentieth-century philosophers and public intellectuals, John Macmurray (1891–1976), is, for instance, heavily indebted to the tradition of Adlerian psychotherapy. Macmurray was an academic philosopher who held a number of posts, including the position of Grote Professor of Mind and Logic at University College, London (1928–44), and then finally, until his retirement, the post of Professor of Moral Philosophy at the University of Edinburgh (1944–58) (McIntosh 2011: 2–4). Macmurray was nationally famous for a period in the 1930s, but, as Frank G. Kirkpatrick notes,

he never achieved the eminence of many of his peers, including, for example, his successor as Grote Professor at University College, London, A. J. Ayer. He seems always to have remained in the shadow of more prominent colleagues, associates and acquaintances such as

Leonard Woolf, R. H. Tawney, A. D. Lindsay, and Karl Polanyi. Much of his non-academic work was done with and for lay groups such as the listeners of the BBC, or the committed activists who made up the Christian Left in England [*sic*] in the 1930s, or with educational theorists. (Kirkpatrick 2005: 5)

Macmurray's work was particularly neglected during the post-war heyday of analytic philosophy in the United Kingdom, but, in recent years, has undergone a significant revival in fields such as psychoanalytic theory and practice (e.g. Clarke 2006, Dobbs 2008, LaMothe 2008, Sharpe 2016), theology (e.g. Fergusson 2012), political and religious philosophy (e.g. Kirkpatrick 2005, McIntosh 2011), and education (e.g. Fielding 2012, MacAllister 2014, McIntosh 2015). Although there has been substantial intellectual recuperation of Macmurray, and a lengthy biography (Costello 2002), the historiographic investigation of his activities and context is still at an early stage. It is clear though, as Philip Conford notes, that Macmurray 'achieved national notoriety in 1930 with a series of radio talks that sparked much controversy in the press', and which led to him being dubbed '"the Red Professor of Gower Street"' (where he was located, as an academic employee of University College, London) (Conford 2008: 320). Although Macmurray's radio talks and his accompanying pamphlet on the topic of freedom were immensely popular with the public, particularly in adult education 'Listening Groups' (Costello 2002: 179–81), they provoked a backlash in the columns of the national press, including *The Listener*, which 'bristled with letters to the editor that were virulently judgmental of Macmurray' (Costello 2002: 182). As Professor at University College, London, and a BBC radio personality with a gift for the medium, Macmurray was a significant presence in his local intellectual networks, which extended to the Tavistock Clinic, where both Suttie and Crichton-Miller were located:

> Throughout the 1930s, Macmurray was a central figure in what might be termed 'the other Bloomsbury Group', which centred on various venues in that area of north London. Just down Gower Street from University College, where Macmurray held his 'Red Professorship', the Serbian magus Dmitri Mitrinovic ran various groups at No. 55. From 1932, the Tavistock Clinic was even closer to University College than Mitrinovic was, having moved from Tavistock Square to the corner of Malet Street and Torrington Place to be in the heart of the University of London. The Tavistock Clinic developed a psychodynamically based approach to psychotherapy which influenced Macmurray and which he in turn would influence. (Conford 2008: 320)

By the 1930s, Macmurray had developed a political critique of Western society which posited relationships between persons as a way to prevent repetition of the horrors of the First World War. In a 1929 conference address (preserved in his papers), Macmurray argues that pre-War society was both in theory and in practice formed by an 'organic' social structure (Christian apologetic: 15) in which 'a process of "rationalization" on the grand scale welded the whole of society into one great functional organization' (Christian apologetic: 5). In this society, based on a constant struggle for survival, and legitimated by a philosophy of Social Darwinism, love became, to Macmurray's mind, 'sentimentalised' (Christian apologetic: 7): it was celebrated not as end in itself, but as an instrument, and a contingent one at that, to the functional goals of 'social prosperity and progress' (Christian apologetic: 8). Personal relationships within the family thus became 'a training-ground in discipline and self-sacrifice and subordination of the individual to a social end' (Christian apologetic: 8). Against this 'organic' or biological conceptualisation of human relations, in which individuals are bound together only in order to achieve some goal by co-operation in a functional unity, Macmurray posits a social unity in which personal relations are both freely chosen and intrinsically valuable – in a 1934 conference paper, Macmurray describes these relationships as connections of '"love", "friendship", "fellowship", [and] "communion"' (Personal and social: 3). Conford summarises Macmurray's political critique of the organic society, which the philosopher saw as dangerously renascent in the 1930s:

> To apply evolutionary ideas to society, he argued, was to reduce the significance of human life to its contribution to some future state rather than valuing it in its own right. In the social organism, people would be valued for their functions, as means to an end rather than as ends in themselves; this is why the 'organic' state was the totalitarian state. A biological interpretation of social life also tended towards a political philosophy based on kinship and rootedness (by implication, blood and soil), favouring hierarchy and emphasising the importance of breeding. (Conford 2008: 326)

The influences upon Macmurray's analysis of psychoanalytic or psychotherapeutic ideas are rarely explicit: Esther McIntosh, a perceptive commentator, suggests some links to Freud and Melanie Klein (McIntosh 2011: 92). Macmurray does, though, explicitly cite Ian Suttie's work in *Persons in Relation* (1961), based on his Gifford Lectures of 1954, where he describes the latter's *The Origins of Love and Hate* (1935), as an 'important contribution to psychotherapeutic theory' (Macmurray 1961: 45). In Macmurray's broader corpus of work, including articles and lectures, there is further evidence for the influence of heterodox strands of psychoanalysis, particularly the Adlerian school. In Macmurray's personal papers, the undated typescript 'Religion in the modern world' (which may be periodised to the 1930s or 1940s by its references to Hitler as a contemporary) sets out some of his seemingly idiosyncratic views on what psychoanalysis can teach theologians and philosophers. The elements of religion that interest

Freud, such as wish-fulfilment or irrational guilt, are to Macmurray merely 'the religious phenomena of our familiar world' (Modern world: 3). Such phenomena are indeed *prima facie* evidence for the illusoriness of religious belief, and for the propriety of its analysis as a symptom. Yet, while conceding that our religious life is typically irrational, Macmurray argues, in a parallel to Crichton-Miller, that such illusory religiosity arises from the repression and dissociation of a genuine religious impulse:

> the conscious life of Europe is inimical to religion and contains a powerful inhibition which forces its natural religious impulses into the unconscious. The form of our conscious life is determined by this inability to bring our religious nature into consciousness. So all our European religions have been 'unconscious' – phantasy fulfilments of suppressed wishes, childish and illusory; while our *conscious* efforts in the field of religion are efforts to prevent our religious nature finding a real expression. (Modern world: 2)

By using the logic of psychoanalytic explanation against its founding father, Macmurray can contend that just as there are 'people who adopt a mode of life which has no place for any natural expression of sexual impulses' (Modern world: 6), so too there is 'a religious impulse in us, which the form of our social life prevents from expressing itself in a real and actual form' (Modern world: 7). Macmurray, with his broader account of the unconscious mind, argues that the philosopher of religion therefore has to 'do what the psycho-analyst has to do in the interpretation of dreams. For all European religion is dream religion. It is a highly disguised expression of the real substance which lies behind it' (Modern world: 3). The nature of Europe's repressed Christianity may, Macmurray argues, be understood by interpreting psychoanalytically the Christian doctrine of salvation: the other-worldly community of the afterlife presented by organised Christianity displaces, and substitutes for, a universal Christian community in *this* world. As Macmurray has it in *Reason and Emotion* (1935), Jesus's task was not 'the creation of the Kingdom of Heaven in Heaven. ... It was the task of creating conscious community among all men everywhere' (Macmurray 1935b: 249). That we are not seeking more vigorously a real universal congregation can be explained by the dominance of institutional religion, which Macmurray characterises in 'Religion in the modern world' as 'the main social organization for side-tracking our religious impulses' (Modern world: 2) – a sceptical position which for Macmurray was confirmed by his experience of organised Christianity's propagandising subservience to the aims of the First World War (Costello 2002: 80–2).

Macmurray's 1938 article, 'A philosopher looks at psychotherapy' (Macmurray 1938b) further explains what he sees as the connections between religion and psychotherapy. He draws explicitly upon Suttie's *The Origins of Love and Hate*, arguing that the essence of love is to be found not in sexuality but in the inherent mutuality of the original relation of mother and child. The breaking of that relation in its original organic form sets the problem which is the general problem of human life. For it produces inevitably an anxiety reaction. (Macmurray 1938b: 21)

Thereafter, the ego is directed towards securing itself in a world perceived as inhospitable and dangerous: 'No situation and no person can be trusted. The available energy is all directed towards security and defence' (Macmurray 1938b: 19). But, although institutional religion may suppress our intersubjective life, Jesus himself was trying to overcome our anxiety, and to restore our original capacity for love. Christian faith is not adherence, rational or otherwise, to propositions set out in a creed; it is instead an emotional attitude – 'Jesus ... means by "faith" an attitude to life in which anxiety is overcome' (Macmurray 1938b: 17).

'A philosopher looks at psychotherapy' indicates the substantial influence upon Macmurray's thinking of Adlerian psychoanalysis, alongside that of Suttie. The article itself was published in pamphlet form by the Individual Psychology Association (IPA), a society dedicated to the furtherance of Adlerian therapy. Moreover, Macmurray met the New Zealand-born psychotherapist Maurice Bevan-Brown (see p. 49) in April 1939 when the former spoke at a conference in the village of Jordans, near London (Costello 2002: 281) – Bevan-Brown was closely associated with the IPA, and was for some time its chairman. Further evidence (and perhaps a reference to the same occasion) is provided by Phyllis Bottome in her biography of Adler, where she describes how 'Professor John Macmurray made an after-dinner speech at the Individual Psychological Medical Society in the early spring of 1939' (Bottome 1957: 238). According to Bottome's informant, a friend of Adler's who was present at the event, Macmurray '"was the only one who mentioned Adler. He said that we should think of Adler as one whose work is greater than that of any other psychologist"' (Bottome 1957: 239).

A more reliable index of Macmurray's debt to Adler is provided in the 1930 pamphlet, *Today and Tomorrow: A Philosophy of Freedom*, written to accompany Macmurray's radio broadcasts on 'Reality and Freedom' from the same year. Amongst the texts given as further reading to listeners is Adler's *Understanding Human Nature* (1928) (Macmurray 1930: 28). Adler's book, first published as *Menschenkenntnis* in 1927, clearly informs some of Macmurray's ideas. Adler refers to the inferiority complex – that 'mechanism of the striving for compensation with which the soul attempts to neutralize the tortured feeling of inferiority' (Adler 1928: 75). Just as Macmurray argues that those without faith strive anxiously for power in the midst of communal life, so Adler argues that a psyche beset by such a 'pathological power-drive' (Adler 1928: 76) participates only superficially in that inescapable 'logic of communal existence' that Adler terms 'social feeling' (Adler 1928: 167) (in Adler's original German, the term is *Gemeinschaftsgefühl* – a better translation would be 'community feeling'). Adler's likely influence upon Suttie, and so indirectly upon Macmurray, is also apparent in *Understanding Human Nature*. Suttie argues in *The Origins of Love and Hate* that the original social relation between mother and child is repressed and distorted into a power relation by a 'taboo on tenderness' (see Suttie 1935: 80–96) that prohibits harmless expressions of love and affection. Similarly, for Adler, at least one of the contexts that might provoke an inferiority response is that in which

> [t]he child's attitude becomes so fixed that he cannot recognize love nor make the proper use of it, because his instincts for tenderness have never been developed. It will be difficult to mobilize a child who has grown up in a family where there has never been a proper development of the feeling of tenderness, to the expression of any kind of tenderness. His whole attitude in life will be a gesture of escape, an evasion of all love and all tenderness. (Adler 1928: 38)

An appreciation of such connections with Adlerian thought is essential to an understanding of the way in which Macmurray's work incorporates psychotherapeutic ideas. Take, for instance, the concept of 'egocentrism' as it appears in Macmurray's pre-war publications such as *Reason and Emotion* (1935) and *Freedom in the Modern World* (1932; 2nd edn, 1935). The first chapter of *Reason and Emotion* argues that the central obstacle to emotional and intellectual development is egocentrism (and its various synonyms, such as 'subjectivity', 'immaturity', 'irrationality' and 'self-concern'). Although egocentrism does have a moral aspect (Macmurray implies that the morally egocentric act in terms of their 'subjective inclinations and private sympathies' (Macmurray 1935b: 23)), the phenomenon is clearly something more than the selfishness that might be traditionally opposed to the imperatives of duty. There is, for instance, an egocentrism in science, namely 'the desire to retain beliefs to which we are emotionally attached for some reason or other. It is the tendency to make the wish father to the thought' (Macmurray 1935b: 21). Egocentrism also has artistic and religious aspects, apparent when we 'try to distinguish good art from bad by the kind of pleasurable effect it has on the spectator or the listener' (Macmurray 1935b: 52), or when we 'think of religion as giving us something; as consoling us in trouble; helping us in difficulties, strengthening us in the face of death, and so on' (Macmurray 1935b: 53). There can also be egocentrism in emotions such as love:

> In feeling love for another person, I can either experience a pleasurable emotion which he stimulates in me, or I can love *him*. We have, therefore, to ask ourselves, is it really the other person that I love, or is it myself? Do I enjoy him or do I enjoy myself in being with him? Is he just an instrument for keeping me pleased with myself, or do I feel his

existence and his reality to be important in themselves? (Macmurray 1935b: 32–3)

The snares of egocentrism are legion: even those who feel keen guilt, and so seem to possess a properly altruistic morality, may be using duty to cloak their own unconscious egocentrism. Macmurray considers the example of a woman who has wronged her friends, and who revels in her guilt, rather than feeling concern for those she has injured:

> self-abasement is just as unreasonable, perhaps even more unreason-able, than her previous state of mind. It is a compensation which still enables her to be concerned with herself. It is still childish, immature and egocentric. Self-pity and self-disgust are just as irrational as self-assertion. (Macmurray 1935b: 30)

Even morally good actions can be corrupted by self-concern: Macmurray explains in *Freedom in the Modern World* that '[b]y being good and unselfish we can feel good and important and kind, and we can make other people feel how good and kind we are' (Macmurray 1935a: 160). In summary, ego-centric or 'unreal' people, as Macmurray calls them, are

> out of touch with the world outside them and turned in upon themselves ... What they demand of the outside world is that it should stimulate them and be agreeable to them and satisfy them ... They are not interested in other people; they want other people to minister to their self-esteem, to recognize them, think highly of them, respect them and love them. (Macmurray 1935a: 159)

To understand the centrality of egocentrism in Macmurray's thought requires further investigation of his relation to Adlerian psychotherapy, and in particular to the work of the German therapist, Fritz Künkel (1889–1956). Künkel trained as a medical doctor, before fighting in the First World War, and – like Macmurray – being wounded by shrapnel (Sanford 1984: 2). Künkel's injury was so serious (the loss of an arm) that he aban-doned work as a physician, and retrained as a psychotherapist. After close involvement with the Adlerian group in Berlin during the 1920s, Künkel began to establish himself as a theorist and populariser of psychotherapy, developing and disseminating a psychotherapy in which the practitioner's main goal was, in the words of Martha Deed, 'to help his patients to give up their egocentricity and to become more and more able to participate in the process of creation' (Deed 1969: 41). Whether by accident or design, Künkel was working in the United States when the Second World War broke out, and there he decided to stay, living and working in Los Angeles until his death (Sanford 1984: 4).

As ever with Macmurray, there is little in the way of explicit reference that might reveal Künkel's influence: Macmurray's only direct state-ment is apparent in the bibliography to *Today and Tomorrow*, where he refers to Künkel's *Let's be Normal!* (Künkel 1929) – albeit as '*Let's be Moral*' (Macmurray 1930: 28). Künkel, for his part, is far more explicit and generous in his recognition of Macmurray's elaboration of his ideas. In the foreword to *In Search of Maturity* (1943), Künkel names Macmurray in his acknowledgements:

> The conclusions of the following presentation are largely based on well-known facts as discussed in psychotherapeutic literature. Sigmund Freud, Alfred Adler, and C. G. Jung should be mentioned as the teachers to whom I owe most. In the religious field, Reinhold Niebuhr, John Macmurray, and Gerald Heard have contributed considerably to the clarification of my thinking. (Künkel 1949: ix)

Examination of Künkel's *Let's be Normal!*, the English translation of which precedes *Reason and Emotion* by six years, convincingly reveals at least one source for Macmurray's vocabulary of 'egocentrism'. (And, as set out in *Reason and Emotion*, its antonym, 'objectivity' (see Macmurray 1935b: 155–6).) In his book, Künkel gives several very similar examples of the egocentric attitude corrupting an apparently 'objective' interest. For instance, 'When a man takes a trip for egocentric reasons, to be able to say, for instance "I have been there and there," he has no pleasure in the trip itself. He wishes it were over before he starts' (Künkel 1929: 92). Or, if a student studies for an examination egocentrically, he 'uses the examination to quiet his need of recognition, or, what amounts to the same thing psychologically, he needs it to lessen his feeling of inferiority' (Künkel 1929: 91). In both these examples, the acquisition of knowledge is in the service of one's self-image. Something similar is proposed by Künkel for egocentrically motivated moral behaviour:

> Let us imagine that an old man has fallen on the street, and that a young man hurries to help him up. Such assistance can serve one of two purposes. Either the purpose is to help the person hurt, or the helper performs his good deed for a reward. If the first purpose outweighs the second, we call the man's behavior 'objective'; if the latter purpose is determinant, we call his behavior 'egocentric'. (Künkel 1929: 31)

Indeed, egocentrism is to Künkel the central psychopathology. In *What it Means to Grow Up* (first published in English in 1936) he asserts:

> The most important of the distinctions which occur in the more recent books analyzing character is that indicated by the two words Egocentricity and Objectivity. The words designate the two opposed attitudes, the two different kinds of behaviour, or we might even say, the two different sets of purposes that prevail generally, in ourselves and in others. A boy who makes an electric bell because he enjoys working with his hands, or because the bell is a necessity, is acting

objectively. But a boy who installs a bell with the one idea of earning the admiration of his parents, or his uncles and aunts, or his schoolfellows, is acting egocentrically. (Künkel 1936: 3)

For the egocentric personality, claims Künkel (and Macmurray clearly agrees), an objective relation to the world is a means to some other end – namely, the 'ego-ideal':

> the egocentric, whether he knows it or not, always acts according to self-evaluation. He has an ego-ideal which he strives to attain, a guiding image by which he measures his worth or worthlessness. He judges everything that happens on the basis of whether it brings him nearer this guiding image or not. (Künkel 1929: 32)

In Künkel's words, '[t]he purpose of every objective function is service to the world. The purpose of every egocentric function is service to the ego' (Künkel 1929: 31–2).

Künkel's vocabulary of the 'ego-ideal' and the 'guiding image' develops Adler's account of the way in which a fictional self-image may act as a goal for the personality. According to Adler, the child 'obtain[s] security by striving towards a fixed point where he sees himself greater and stronger, where he finds himself rid of the helplessness of infancy' (Adler 1918: 53). For the healthy personality, this fictional goal is merely a crutch, which may be given up when one actually reaches the powers and privileges of maturity, and no longer feels so acutely one's weakness and incapacity before the world. Rather as an architect might erase the guidelines on a drawing, so the healthy individual is 'able at all times to free himself from the bonds of his fiction, to eliminate his projections (Kant) from his calculations, and to make use only of the impetus which is given him by this guiding line' (Adler 1918: 54). To take a simple example (my own, not Adler's): the child who is told that eating spinach will make him as strong as Popeye uses this fantastic ego-ideal in order to force down an unfamiliar and unappetising food. But, as the child develops, the fictional goal of being like Popeye disappears, to be replaced – in the ideal case – by a realistic appreciation of a wholesome food, both as a pleasure in itself, and as a means to health. However, the neurotic personality (and for Adler this particularly means that created in the constitutionally inferior child),

> keeps before his eye his God, his idol, his ideal of personality and clings to his guiding principle, losing sight in the meanwhile of reality, whereas the normal personality is always ready to dispense with this crutch, this aid, and reckon unhampered with reality. (Adler 1918: 66)

The neurotic, in other words, clings to the ideal or fiction of future power and potency, hypostatising it into a reality, albeit an unconscious one. Somewhere at the back of his mind, the neurotic is still eating his spinach in the hope that he will (eventually, one day) turn into Popeye – or, as

Adler puts it, that he will 'escape from the feeling of inferiority in order to ascend to the full height of the ego-consciousness, to complete manliness, to attain the ideal of being "above"' (Adler 1918: 37).

The ego-ideal or guiding fiction, in Adler's system, provides a fictional end that eventually is dispensable to the mature, healthy personality; accomplishments once imagined as a means to the fictional goal of security and power come to be valued as ends-in-themselves. To be egocentric in the sense developed by Künkel's appropriation of Adler, and then adopted by Macmurray, is therefore not essentially to be self-interested, or whimsical, or merely subjective in one's attitudes: it is instead to treat any relation to the world as *in fact* a means to the (illusory) imago of security and power. Even the most moral and realistically minded of individuals may be egocentric if these attitudes are in the service of such a guiding image. As Stepansky points out,

> Adler did not contend that the neurotic character was incapable of altruistic behaviour, but he did argue that such behaviour only became manifest when it could be incorporated into the neurotic's 'search for significance' ... when it served to promote interpersonal superiority in contexts where the display of overt ambition would be a liability. (Stepansky 1983: 123)

But where Adler frequently uses constitutional inferiority to explain the hypostatisation of the ego-ideal, Künkel emphasises instead problems in the early relationship between mother and child in order to explain why the latter should feel so acutely its own weakness, and so cling, in neurotic compensation, to a guiding image. Künkel's account of the origins of egocentricity is provided in *Character, Growth, Education* (first published in English in 1938). The scenes described within are strikingly familiar to anyone acquainted with Macmurray's account of the mother–child relation in post-war publications such as *Persons in Relation* (1961). Egocentrism, says Künkel, is a sign of 'previous disturbance of the Primal-We' (Künkel 1938: 18) – this curious phrase indicates, says Künkel, that in early life, 'The acting subject is not the child himself, but the community of mother and child, the Primal-We in its entirety' (Künkel 1938: 21). For Macmurray, too, 'the mother-child relation is the original unit of personal existence' (Macmurray 1961: 62), 'a "You and I" with a common life' (Macmurray 1961: 60). In normal development, claims Künkel, the primal community is maintained by a relationship of faith between child and mother (who is stereotyped by Künkel, and also Macmurray, as the child's primary or sole caregiver). He gives the example of a mother who must leave the room in order to prepare some food for her infant, and so appears to abandon her child, and to break the norms of feeding that ruled their Primal-We:

> With her voice and her expression she affirmed unequivocally her loyalty to their community. Nevertheless her departure was felt to be

a denial of the We-subject, and hence a betrayal. Yet not a complete betrayal. Should one trust that reassuring look in her eye more than the evidence of one's own eyes which said 'she has gone'? Was it perhaps possible that she had gone away without breaking up the We? The child is unable to arrive at any clear understanding. His tension capacity is not yet sufficient. He cannot yet recognize in his mother's absence the contribution of service to the We. His tension capacity is, however, already sufficiently great for him not to forget the oath of fidelity that lay in her eyes.

Amidst all this uncertainty his mother returns. That decides every-thing. (Künkel 1938: 47)

The comparisons with Macmurray are again clear, for the Scottish philoso-pher refers to what he calls a 'rhythm of withdrawal and return' (Macmurray 1961: 87). If the child is to become a competent agent, he must endure the 'deliberate refusal on her [the mother's] part to continue to show the child those expressions of her care for him that he expects' (Macmurray 1961: 89). However, since 'the child's stock of knowledge is too exiguous, the span of his anticipation too short', he can only appreciate that '[t]his refusal is ... an expression of the mother's care for him' (Macmurray 1961: 89) if he maintains a 'positive attitude of confidence that the expected response will come in due time' (Macmurray 1961: 87–8). Indeed, Macmurray merely generalises Künkel's concrete example of withdrawal and return in which the mother 'goes into the kitchen and comes back again' (Künkel 1938: 46).

For the non-egocentric personality, claims Künkel, 'all kinds of unpleas-antness will be borne in the consciousness that, when all is said and done, the world-order merits confidence' (Künkel 1938: 47). However, there are also primal communities in which such restoration of the 'We' does not occur. For whatever reason – be it the child's anxious nature, the length of the withdrawal, the mother's inability to reassure, and so forth – the child is 'led astray by anxiety for the ego', and concludes, in effect, that '"[h]owever small one may be, one must look after oneself"' (Künkel 1938: 38). Macmurray, too, describes such egocentrism as what ensues when the child loses faith in the meaning of the mother's withdrawal: '[a]ctivity becomes egocentric, concerned with the defence of himself in a world which is indifferent to his needs' (Macmurray 1961: 89). Egocentrism, for Macmurray, is not strictly self-love, but is rather a 'fear of the Other' that involves 'a concentration of interest and activity upon the defence of the self' (Macmurray 1961: 94).

Künkel describes two modes of egocentric response: in the first, 'the child will try to master his surroundings, and external dialectical processes will play the chief part in the development of his character'; in the other, 'the child's behavior will be more passive' – he 'inclines toward dreami-ness or contemplativeness, and seeks to subdue the external world "from afar"' (Künkel 1938: 67). 'This contrast,' claims Künkel, 'corresponds ... exactly to the differentiation introduced by C. G. Jung ... under the names "Extrovert" and "Introvert"' (Künkel 1938: 67). As Künkel makes clear, these two responses, the assertive and the submissive, may mingle in one personality – one egocentric child, for instance, manifested a 'good deal of naughtiness and obstinacy, but also a certain amount of affectionate behaviour and cajolery ... for reasons of "policy"' (Künkel 1938: 50). This twofold taxonomy of the egocentric personality is echoed by Macmurray. If the child fails to 'overcome the negative motivation', then one of 'two courses will tend to become habitual',

> there will be produced an individual who is either characteristically submissive or characteristically aggressive in his active relation with the Other. This contrast of types of disposition corresponds to the distinction drawn by psychologists between the 'introvert' and the 'extravert' [*sic*]. (Macmurray 1961: 104)

Macmurray even repeats Künkel's characterisation of the submissive, introverted response as one of 'policy': the child 'remains egocentric and on the defensive; he conforms in behaviour to what is expected of him, but, as it were, as a matter of policy' (Macmurray 1961: 102).

Künkel's Adlerian theory therefore lies behind much of Macmurray's psychotherapeutic re-interpretation of the Gospels, a project which continues from the inter-war period to post-war work, such as the 1964 radio broadcasts for Lent given under the general title 'To Save from Fear', preserved in Macmurray's personal papers. In these talks, Macmurray explicitly casts Jesus as a psychotherapist who 'diagnosed the mortal sickness from which people suffer as fear' (Faith and love: 2). The fear in question is not rational fear towards some conscious object or possibility; rather 'the fears that matter are the deep fears, which we have suppressed so that we are unconscious of them' (Fear and faith: 3). The deep fear, of course, is that which may arise in the rhythm of withdrawal and return. An individual possessed by such unconscious fear of the other, 'will constantly act as if the world is a dangerous place, and live on the defensive' (Fear and faith: 3), and so will display two characteristic emotional attitudes – 'he hides himself from you behind a facade of pretence or formality, or else he tries to dominate you. He is either submissive or aggressive' (Fear and faith: 4). In either case, the genuinely intersubjective self is obscured by an ego-ideal built upon unconscious fear and anxiety. As Macmurray explains in *Persons in Relation*:

> Both dispositions are egocentric, and motivate action which is for the sake of oneself, and not for the sake of the Other ... Such action is implicitly a refusal of mutuality, and an effort to constrain the Other to do what we want. By conforming submissively to his wishes we put him under an obligation to care for us. By aggressive behaviour we seek to make him afraid not to care for us. (Macmurray 1961: 105)

The Adlerian lineage of Macmurray's psychotherapeutic Christianity should now be clear: indeed, these two egocentric responses of aggression and submission can be traced back, via Künkel, to Adler's account of '[d]efiance and obedience, *Trotz* and *Gehorsam*' as 'the two basic routes that the neurotic safeguarding tendencies could follow' (Stepansky 1983: 121).

For those who think of psychoanalysis and psychotherapy within Freudian or post-Freudian parameters, Macmurray's conclusions will seem to be merely *non sequiturs*. However, if Macmurray's work is related to Adlerian concepts, particularly those developed by Künkel, then the psychotherapeutic conceptual scheme in Macmurray's Christianity is clarified. The suppressed impulse that appears in disguised form in organised religion, and which Macmurray hopes to liberate, is the striving towards mature community rather than towards egocentric mastery. Where Freud's motto was '*Wo Es war, soll Ich werden*' (traditionally translated as 'Where Id was, Ego shall be'), Macmurray supposes that the real therapeutic aim is to replace the compulsive and deadening ego with the emotionally mature and genuinely other-centred self: 'Where Ego was, We shall be' would be a fair summary of Macmurray's position. Without such liberation of genuine mutuality, Macmurray believes, we shall remain egocentric in the specific psychotherapeutic sense developed by Adler and Künkel. Macmurray thus adopts only the barest essentials of the Freudian scheme (an unconscious mind formed by repression), and instead to turns to Suttie, Adler, and Künkel in order to find psychological and psychoanalytic thought patterns that articulate and support his attempt to scientifically rationalise the Christian religion.

Communion exported: Maurice Bevan-Brown and the New Zealand Association of Psychotherapists

By the 1930s, there was a clearly recognisable trend in Scottish psychoanalytic, psychotherapeutic and religious ideas which owed much to the nation's Darwinian and anthropological investigations of Christianity, as well as to an idiosyncratic importation and adaptation of psychoanalytic ideas and practices. The consequent emphasis on interpersonal communion by a small group of elite innovators exerted an influence in cultures and regions that are often overlooked in histories of psychoanalysis. Scotland itself was such a region, of course; later chapters will show how Scottish psychoanalytic ideas retained influence within domestic culture, even as newer ideas and practices were imported. However, a most striking illustration of Scottish psychoanalytic ideas at work occurs in their post-war exportation to New Zealand, a settler colony in which Scots were often highly influential.

As Warwick Brunton explains, the character of New Zealand psychiatry changed markedly with the establishment by central government of the Lunatic Asylums Department in 1876 (known from 1905 onwards as the

Mental Hospitals Department), which continued as a separate department until 1947, when it was merged with the Department of Health (Brunton 2011: 318, 331, Brunton 2003: 85). The Department became a vehicle for the dominance of Scottish approaches to psychiatric care: 'Scottish influence was marked throughout the life of the Department. Five of the six psychiatrist-administrators who ran the organisation for 66 out of the 71 years were Scottish-trained' (Brunton 2011: 318). Within New Zealand psychiatric care, which was modelled on Scottish principles, there was little room for psychological approaches, given the dominance of 'the somatic-pathological approaches that, together with an overlay of hereditary determinism and degeneracy theory, characterised British psychiatry in the late nineteenth and early twentieth centuries' (Brunton 2011: 321). Thus, the arrival in post-war New Zealand of Scottish psychoanalytic ideas on inter-personal communion was their transplantation into what was largely virgin territory (at least in terms of non-indigenous healing practice). This importation continued the tradition of looking to Britain, and particularly to Scotland, for intellectual and organisational leadership. As a result, the ideas of Suttie and Macmurray (although not apparently Fairbairn) were exceptionally influential, although not unmodified, within the early organisational forms of psychotherapy in New Zealand.

The New Zealand Association of Psychotherapists (NZAP) was formed in 1947 by C. Maurice Bevan-Brown (1886–1967), a New Zealander who studied medicine in his native country, before leaving for the United Kingdom on a travelling scholarship in 1921. Bevan-Brown settled in London, and became active in psychiatric and psychotherapeutic circles, undergoing personal analysis with, amongst others, Hugh Crichton-Miller. As the NZAP records show, he worked for the Tavistock Clinic from 1923 to 1939, first as a clinician, and then as a member of the lecturing staff (Bevan-Brown cv). Bevan-Brown knew Suttie well from the Tavistock Clinic, and refers in 1950 to the 'privilege' of having known and admired Suttie for several years before the latter's death (Bevan-Brown 1961: 101). As noted above (see p. 40), Bevan-Brown came into personal contact with John Macmurray in 1939 (Costello 2002: 281). Macmurray by that time had published with the Individual Psychology Association, an organisation that promoted Adlerian psychoanalysis, and of which Bevan-Brown was for some time the Chairman. These personal connections with Suttie and Macmurray are intellectually manifested in Bevan-Brown's first published book, *The Sources of Love and Fear* (1950) – the title itself is clearly indebted to Suttie's *The Origins of Love and Hate*, a book to which Bevan-Brown refers in his bibliography. The connection to Macmurray is also clear: in his acknowledgements, Bevan-Brown thanks, amongst others, 'Professor John Macmurray' (1950: v), and he refers to several of Macmurray's books in the course of his own, including *Freedom in the Modern World* (1932), *Creative Society* (1935), *Reason and Emotion* (1935) and *The Boundaries of Science* (1939).

When Bevan-Brown returned to New Zealand in 1940 (Manchester and Manchester 1996: 11), it was to proselytise for a psychoanalytic psycho-therapy that saw communion between mother and child as fundamental both to individual mental health and to the wellbeing of society as a whole. In *The Sources of Love and Fear*, Bevan-Brown proposes a 'preventive psychia-try' (Bevan-Brown 1950: xi) which recognises 'the importance of breast-feeding for subsequent mental ... health' (Bevan-Brown 1950: xv). Echoing Suttie, Bevan-Brown argues that the relation between mother and child is 'the first *personal* relationship, the first *social* relationship, the first *sensuous* relationship, the first *love* relationship ... this relationship, being the first, sets the pattern of all subsequent relationships' (Bevan-Brown 1950: 10). Only by appropriately protecting and cultivating this personal relation-ship, argues Bevan-Brown, can one avoid the 'illness and maladjustment of people in the Anglo-Saxon world' that 'is due to a failure of motherhood' (Bevan-Brown 1950: 34).

Bevan-Brown's concern for this perceived failure reveals the local context which further modifies the Scottish psychoanalytic ideas that he brings to New Zealand. Bevan-Brown alludes to 'a school of infant nurture which has held the view that it is good to let the baby cry and leave him alone, that, since there is no (adult) danger, he must learn that it is stupid to cry. They suggest that this is the way to teach him self-reliance' (Bevan-Brown 1950: 14). The school of child-rearing in question is that developed by the New Zealander Frederic Truby King (1858–1938), whose advocacy of breast-feeding, although radical in its day, was wholly concerned with the physiological benefits of the practice. King, who was Inspector-General of the Mental Hospitals Department from 1924 to 1927, was another Scottish-trained medical leader – he had been the top medical student in his year at Edinburgh University, and had also taken a degree in public health at the same institution (Brunton 2011: 320). Preceding his leadership in psychiatry, King began a crusade against child-mortality, forming in 1907 the Society for Promoting the Health of Women and Children – an institu-tion more commonly known as the Plunket Society, in honour of its first patron, Lady Plunket, the wife of the Governor-General of New Zealand. The Plunket Society was extremely successful. By 1947, 85 per cent of non-Maori children were under the Society's care (Olssen 1981: 11); and in the period from 1905 to 1946, infant mortality in the first year roughly halved (Olssen 1981: 12).

Yet the Society had aims far wider than merely the health of very young children. The Truby King method was also intended as a means by which to produce the character type demanded by a rapidly modernising society. King explicitly advocated 'perfect regularity of habits' as 'the ultimate foun-dation of all-round obedience' (King 1932: 98), and advised never respond-ing to a cry from the baby that was merely a cry for company or attention (King 1932: 149). The child had, as Erik Olssen puts it, 'to eat, excrete, sleep, and be washed according to the clock' (Olssen 1981: 14). Such regularity was supposed to promote self-discipline from an early age. What might be seen as ordinary expressions of parental affection were thus a danger to the child's moral development:

> mothers should not rock, tickle, or play with their babies ... If parents took the baby into their own bed, or kept the baby in their room at night, or gave a dummy to suck, they endangered the baby's physical health and its character. (Olssen 1981: 15)

Providing such dangerous indulgences could be avoided, the Plunket baby would grow up to be either a good mother, upon whose 'success and regular habits depended the health and happiness of the child, the stability and decency of the society, the future of the Empire and the white race' (Olssen 1981: 21), or an 'efficient, productive and self-contained' male, who 'could work easily in time-dominated organizations; and be capable of postponing present gratification for future rewards' (Olssen 1981: 19).

Such prescriptions were quite contrary to the psychotherapeutic ideas of those with whom Bevan-Brown had associated while at the Tavistock Clinic. As noted (see p. 41), Suttie had argued that because of a patriarchal disparagement of women in envy of their powers of child-bearing and greater opportunities for nurturing love, there had arisen a 'taboo on tenderness' – a repression of the touching, caressing and other behaviours that embodied non-sexual love, whether between adults, or between parent and child (Suttie 1935: 80–96). The result was a vicious circle in which parents starved their children of love, precisely because they themselves had experienced such deprivation:

> The mother who was herself love-starved and who, in consequence, is intolerant of tenderness, will be impatient of her own children's dependency, regressiveness and claims for love. Her suspicion and anxiety really amount to a feeling (rooted in self-distrust), that children are naturally bad (St Augustine!) and require to be 'made' good by disapprobation and the checking of all indulgence of 'babyishness'. (Suttie 1935: 89)

Suttie's account is echoed by Joyce Partridge, another contemporary at the Tavistock Clinic, whose 1937 guide to child-rearing, *Baby's Point of View*, is regarded by Bevan-Brown as 'the most valuable I know regarding infant welfare' (Bevan-Brown 1950: 13). Partridge states that 'never to be cuddled, or fondled, or nursed by Mother is leaving unsatisfied a need which is just as acute as the need felt by the adult for physical contact with his beloved' (Partridge 1937: 29–30).

As a child-rearing regime in which tenderness is tabooed, the Truby King method is an immediate object of Bevan-Brown's suspicion. If anything, his indictment is even more severe than that of Suttie and Partridge, who tend to focus on the consequences of the taboo on tenderness for individual psychology. Bevan-Brown goes further, and identifies the Truby King method and its analogues as causal factors in the World Wars through which he has lived. The Truby King method assumes 'that the baby is in some way a danger to the peace of the household, even a potential enemy', and so 'a war is set up between mother and child' in which 'the child feels that he must fight to survive in a hostile world' (Bevan-Brown 1950: 31). The child enters a world that he perceives as 'inhospitable, dangerous and lonely', and he learns to substitute power for love, so that '[m]uch of his subsequent conduct will be devoted to the object of making himself as secure as he can in an insecure world' (Bevan-Brown 1950: 14–15). Bevan-Brown eventually states baldly that 'if there is a large proportion of such individuals in a nation they will tend to assume that other nations have hostile intentions towards them, and will concentrate on national security as well as personal security' (Bevan-Brown 1950: 15).

The hostile, fearful personality, which substitutes power for love, is created by deprivation of what Bevan-Brown calls 'the first need of the infant', the '*security* which he derives from constant association with his mother' (Bevan-Brown 1950: 14). This emphasis on the fear which arises when the original communion is broken is derived from Macmurray, whose analysis is faithfully echoed by Bevan-Brown in *The Sources of Love and Fear* and in later addresses and publications. For example, 'Psychotherapy and religion', a 1951 conference address collected in Bevan-Brown's second book, *Mental Health and Personality Disorder*, urges 'all thoughtful people' to listen to John Macmurray, 'one of the leading philosophers of the day' (Bevan-Brown 1961: 128). From Macmurray, says Bevan-Brown, we learn that 'Love is the central theme of Christian doctrine', and that psychotherapy, which aims at the removal of 'fear and guilt, with the further aim of liberating the capacity to Love', is an expression of true Christianity (Bevan-Brown 1961: 130). Because of psychotherapy, hopes Bevan-Brown, we may come to live in a 'Love-determined' society, rather than a 'fear-determined' one in which persons seek power as a means to psychological security against their primitive anxieties (Bevan-Brown 1961: 133). Macmurray's use of the term 'communion' to describe loving rather than instrumental or functional relationships is also repeated in *The Sources of Love and Fear* not by Bevan-Brown (though it is everywhere implicit in his argument) but by R. S. Allan, a colleague who provides a 'Testimony to psychotherapy' originally published in pamphlet form in 1946. Psychotherapy is a religious enterprise because neurosis derives from damage to the 'first love-relationship between mother and child', which Allan refers to as the 'first communion' (Allan 1950: 78).

But although the NZAP under Bevan-Brown was clearly indebted to Christianised Scottish psychotherapy, it differed in certain respects. One of the 'surprising advantages' of the 'marginal position' (Bos et al. 2005: 216) is ease of self-definition: the NZAP benefited from the availability of a historic figure, Truby King, against whose methods it could clearly define itself. Furthermore, within a small country like New Zealand, where there was a lack of (non-indigenous) psychotherapeutic expertise, and a far smaller population, the NZAP could exert great influence. The kind of institutional and cultural reforms in childcare that were precipitated in the United Kingdom by attachment theory during the 1960s were demanded earlier by the NZAP, who had their own parallel (but genealogically related) preventative psychiatry. R. S. Allan makes the call to arms explicit in his 'Testimony to psychotherapy': 'What is needed most', he says, 'is a "new deal" for very young children. This "new deal" is primarily a task for parents, and the necessary reforms must be reforms in child nurture in the home and in institutions and societies which offer guidance to parents' (Allan 1950: 82). The reference to Roosevelt's programme is of course obvious; but to speak of a 'New Deal' is also to allude to the Biblical vocabulary of a 'New Covenant'. The raft of reforms that Allan demands is, in the conceptual scheme of the NZAP's founders, a religious transformation because these changes are intended to preserve and promote interpersonal communion, and '[t]his is a religious problem, if one believes that religion is ultimately concerned with personal relationships, with communion or fellowship' (Allan 1950: 86).

The group that formed around Bevan-Brown were therefore very active in the public sphere of post-war New Zealand. Peter Cook (himself the son of Enid Cook, one of the founders of the NZAP) records the pamphlets which preceded *The Origins of Love and Hate*: 'As a contribution to mental health education, the Lighthouse series of 11 pamphlets was published between 1945 and 1948 ... Topics included: war neurosis; mental health; nerves, nerviness and neurosis; sex education; psychology of, and preparation for, childbirth; and stammering' (Cook 1996: 406). As might be expected, the good news of Macmurray's psychoanalytic Christianity is readily found in these publications. The general editor of the series, Frank Cook, invokes Macmurray in his own contribution, *Ex-Servicemen Talk It Over: A Group Discussion on War Neurosis* (Cook 1945). The text is an imaginary dialogue that ends with 'Dr. Peter' describing to 'Sam' and 'Bill' the distinction between a religion of fear, and one of love; the session concludes with a prescription to the pair of Macmurray's *Freedom in the Modern World*. The word was also spread through radio addresses such as Bevan-Brown's 'The Foundations of Mental Health', a series of seven talks broadcast by the New Zealand Broadcasting Service prior to their publication in pamphlet form in 1956 (Bevan-Brown 1956). The ideology of the NZAP was even disseminated in North America. *The Sources of Love and Fear* was partly published as a response to the request of Gayle Aitken of New Orleans, who had read some of the NZAP pamphlets. When Aitken began the *Child-Family Digest* in 1949, she also brought to the advisory board Bevan-Brown and Enid Cook (Cook 1996: 406).

The publicising of Bevan-Brown's ideas soon encouraged an organised response to the methods of the Plunket Society. Cook records how the group centred in the NZAP directly influenced the formation of the first Parents' Centre in Wellington in 1951 through the initiative of Mrs Helen Brew, a speech therapist. The movement became nationwide, leading to the New Zealand Federation of Parents' Centres. After initial medical hostility the Federation was recognised by the New Zealand branch of the British Medical Association as an ethical medical auxiliary, acceptable in preparing parents for childbirth and parenthood. (Cook 1996: 406)

As a senior secondary school student, Brew had been highly impressed during her personal attendance at a lecture by Bevan-Brown, and found his views confirmed in her later professional dealings with children and families (Bell 2004: 3), and elaborated and buttressed by a broader context of progressive educational ideals expounded by international and domestic authorities (Bell 2004: 137–57). Under Brew's charismatic leadership, the Federation's efforts to 'counteract and modify the rigid teachings of the New Zealand Plunket Society in relation to infant care and training' (Cook 1996: 406) made it into an effective consumer organisation that spearheaded changes to childcare practices in New Zealand, including those formalised by the Plunket Society's guidance. As Marie Bell explains, the Federation was successful in changing such features of 1950s New Zealand healthcare as the medicalisation of childbirth, the bureaucratic regimentation of hospital care for neonates, the exclusion of fathers from ante- and post-natal education and care, and the separation of family members from children who required inpatient care (Bell 2004: 77–85).

Brunton notes the greatly reduced influence of Scotland on New Zealand psychiatry after 1947, with the merger of the Mental Hospitals Department into the Health Department, and the rise of a new generation of psychiatrists trained in England or New Zealand (Brunton 2011: 331). However, the character of the NZAP during the period of Bevan-Brown's formal and informal leadership, and successor movements such as the Parents' Centres, shows the post-war influence in New Zealand of Scottish Christian psychotherapy, as distinct from psychiatry. Suttie and Macmurray have a largely unmediated impact upon the early development of the NZAP as Bevan-Brown synthesises, disseminates, modifies and extrapolates their work, arguing that if the taboo on tenderness is not alleviated, then children will continue to fall into anxiety and mistrust, and to develop into power-hungry and warmongering adults. In this new national context, there occurs a further, significant transformation of Scottish psychoanalytic ideas: the NZAP extends their application from clinical work with adults to a preventative infant psychiatry opposed to the theories and practices of the Truby King school of child-rearing.

Conclusion

Scots were by no means alone in pursuing an 'an eclectic indigenous style' of psychotherapy (Raitt 2004: 63) during the early British importation of psychoanalysis, but they seem to have been more resistant to the marshalling of psychotherapy along Freudian lines enforced by the leadership of Ernest Jones in London. The importation and modification of psychoanalysis by key Scottish actors shows a complex process of selective appropriation whereby Freudian and other approaches were informed by an antecedent late-Victorian religious culture. Figures such as Geddes, Drummond and Robertson Smith had appropriated Christianity in light of contemporaneous expert discourses of the human: a Christian ethic of fellowship, rather than of competitive individualism, was legitimated by insights into 'primitive' society and religion, which showed the fundamental nature of both the human bond and Christian ritual, and by the providential movement of natural history towards the evolution of maternal virtues, epitomised by the 'communion' between mother and child. The resultant psychoanalytic theory developed by prominent Scots such as Fairbairn, Suttie and Macmurray understood the self as born into relations, and viewed psychopathology as a matter of disturbed personal relationships – whether this was Fairbairn's intellectually remote 'schizoid self', Suttie's culturally specific pathologies of Oedipal (rather than endogenous) repression, or the egocentric personality elaborated by Macmurray, which seeks security in a world understood to be fundamentally dangerous. This heterodox psychoanalysis not only selectively drew upon Freud, it also looked to other rival strands of psychoanalysis, particularly the Adlerian tradition with its far greater emphasis on interpersonal relations. The psycho-political project 'of creating conscious community among all men everywhere' (Macmurray 1935b: 249) was an implicit and sometimes explicit ideology of progressive welfare state capitalism, and was presented as the rational successor to the utopian aspirations preserved in, but also distorted by, organised Christianity. This ideology was adopted and adapted in its export by Bevan-Brown to the settler colony of New Zealand, where it found organisational expression in the early years of the New Zealand Association of Psychotherapists, and the New Zealand Federation of Parents' Centres, in their demand for a 'New Deal' for infants and children.

CHAPTER TWO

Interpreting God's Psychotherapeutic Will

In 'Religious Sensibility', a 1970 article for the BBC magazine *The Listener*, the radical psychiatrist and psychotherapist R. D. Laing (1927–89) describes his Scottish upbringing: 'I grew up theologically speaking in the 19th century: lower-middle-class Lowland Presbyterianism, corroded by 19th-century materialism, scientific rationalism and humanism' (Laing 1970: 536). Laing was brought up in the 1930s and 1940s in a culture that was still dominated by Scottish Presbyterianism. His experience was by no means exceptional, and was shared by many Scots until a wave of secularisation in the 1960s led to a decline in organised religious life in Scotland, particularly in the Protestant middle class. When Laing entered Glasgow University in the late 1940s, he was therefore surprised to 'meet for the first time ... people of my age who had never ever opened a Bible', and also to be

> regarded with incredulity by an 18-year-old French girl, a student from the Sorbonne, as some idealistic barbarian still occupied by issues of religious belief, disbelief or doubt, still living before the Enlightenment, exhibiting in frayed but still recognisable form the primitive thought forms of the savage mind. (Laing 1970: 536)

Nonetheless, Laing's article does not simply dismiss the religion of his upbringing. He concedes that psychoanalytic theory may reveal religion to be 'a comparatively harmless illusion, an opiate to which many people are addicted' that 'serves to shield them from reality or from their fantasy of reality' (Laing 1970: 537). But, he continues, 'every effective reductive attack from this position' should be welcomed by those who are religious, for 'it can only destroy what is perishable. What is imperishable can't be destroyed' (Laing 1970: 537).

This chapter explores a post-war Scottish context in which psychotherapy presented a way of continuing and preserving a supposed imperishable core to Christian belief, practice and inquiry. Although Laing's complex religious and theological hinterland will be considered at length, the investigation begins with the far more obscure Winifred Rushforth (1885–1983) and the Davidson Clinic for Medical Psychotherapy, which she directed. Conceived as a 'daughter colony' of the Tavistock Clinic, the Davidson Clinic's frankly Christian ethos was allied with the socially active direction of the post-war Church of Scotland. The Davidson offered its services in Edinburgh from 1941 to 1973, where it promoted 'Christian psychotherapy' as a mode of nigh-on miraculous spiritual healing.

Winifred Rushforth, the Davidson Clinic and 'Christian Psychotherapy'

Rushforth's gender makes her a particularly interesting figure in the historiography of Scottish psychotherapy. Motherhood was celebrated as the foundation of mental health by the emerging object relations paradigm, but this veneration of mothers and matriarchy could lead to a strictly gendered view of social roles. Gal Gerson contends, for instance, that 'object relations theory harbors the risk of idealizing power differentials and placing them beyond challenge. In Suttie, this danger stands out in his view of matriarchy as the rule of mothers within the home – and there alone' (Gerson 2009b: 390). Yet there are clearly significant female actors in the history of eclectic British psychotherapy, despite this apparent ideological limitation. Jane Isabel Suttie is one such agent. The public attribution of single authorship to *The Origins of Love and Hate* obscures the explicit collaboration between Jane Isabel Suttie (fl. 1926–35), and her husband Ian, on the earlier two-part article, 'The mother: agent or object?' (Suttie and Suttie 1932a, Suttie and Suttie 1932b), and ignores Jane Isabel's 1926 translation of Sándor Ferenczi's work (Ferenczi 1926). The Sutties' collaborative effort is also emphasised by H. V. Dicks, who refers to 'their joint work of revising psychopathology' (Dicks 1970: 40). Moreover, there were significant female-led eclectic clinics, such as the Medico-Psychological Clinic (or Brunswick Square Clinic) in London, which offered its services from 1913 to 1922, thereby pre-dating the Tavistock (Raitt 2004: 63). As Suzanne Raitt explains, the Clinic was 'founded and run, initially at least, by feminists and quite possibly by lesbians', and 'was dominated by women, who were drawn to the place by its open atmosphere, its eclecticism, and its willingness to accept trainees who had no medical qualifications' (Raitt 2004: 82).

Raitt concludes that the Clinic's female leadership and use of female lay therapists, as well as its eclecticism, led to its temporary exclusion from British psychoanalytic historiography (Raitt 2004: 82). A similar bias may explain the relative obscurity of both Edinburgh's Davidson Clinic (which also employed female lay therapists (Darroch 1973 *passim*)) and its founder Winifred Rushforth, despite their significant presence in wartime and post-war Edinburgh. Margaret Winifred Bartholomew (later Rushforth) was born on 21 August 1885 to an upper-class farming family resident near Edinburgh. After medical training at the Edinburgh Medical College for Women, she graduated MBChB from Edinburgh University in 1908. Domestic restrictions on medical practice for female doctors, and her marriage in 1915 to Frank Rushforth, a British officer in the Indian Regiments, meant that the first half of Rushforth's medical career was spent as a medical missionary and voluntary worker in India (Rushforth cv: 1). Her knowledge of psychology was initially acquired in this colonial context via her 'organisation of study circles for mothers of young children' (Rushforth 1984: 69); these were informed by the ideas of Alfred Adler and the general psychologist William McDougall, amongst others. (The fruits of this experience were later published in Britain in 1933 as *The Outstretched Finger* (Rushforth 1933), a child-rearing manual for mothers that had been prepared for 'Study Circles in Child Psychology' that Rushforth had organised in Calcutta, London and Edinburgh from 1930 to 1932 (Rushforth 1933: 69)). In 1929, Rushforth, having returned to the United Kingdom, began training as a psychoanalyst under Crichton-Miller at the Tavistock. As well as attending a course of lectures and seminars, she was required to undergo personal analysis, and to take on a psychoanalytic caseload. In 1931, she settled permanently in Edinburgh with her husband, and in 1933 began a private practice in psychoanalytic psychotherapy (Rushforth cv: 2). Rushforth seems to have continued her analytic therapy while in Edinburgh with Ernest Connell (Darroch 1973: 6), who had also analysed Fairbairn. Growing interest in adult and child psychotherapy in Edinburgh led Rushforth to a central role in founding and guiding the Davidson Clinic for Medical Psychotherapy, which ran in various locations in Edinburgh from 1941 to 1973 (see below). She also became a public spokesperson for psychotherapy, particularly in the regular bulletins published by the Davidson Clinic from 1946 to 1967, and also in the mass media, including BBC radio broadcasts in the late 1940s. After retiring from the Davidson Clinic in 1967, Rushforth continued to provide psychotherapy in various forms, including a regular dream analysis group (Rushforth 1984: 146). As detailed earlier (see p. 1), her 'guru' status was confirmed in 1983 when she received a visit from the Prince and Princess of Wales. She died on 29 August 1983 (Rushforth 1984: 176), and her memoir, *Ten Decades of Happenings: The Autobiography of Winifred Rushforth*, was published the following year (Rushforth 1984).

The Davidson Clinic opened on 24 January 1941 (*Annual Report* 1941: 3), but planning for a clinic began in 1938, as noted in the Clinic's first Minute Book, which covers the period 1938–45. On 18 November 1938, a group of ten people – the most important being Rushforth and an Edinburgh civic officer, John Falconer – met to discuss 'the formation of a psychological clinic in Edinburgh' (Minute Book: 1). Although some progress was made over a number of meetings, the eventual outbreak of war threw the provisional plan for a small clinic into disarray. The clinic project was revived, however, when Rushforth entered into a collaborative arrangement with the Reverend Roy Hogg, the minister of the Davidson Church in Edinburgh, from which the Clinic acquired its name (Rushforth 1984: 87–8). The first minuted meeting regarding the Davidson Clinic proper occurred on 20 November 1940, and was chaired by Hogg (Minute Book: 36–43). After formally opening on 24 January 1941, with first year attendances (albeit over 11 months) of 65 adult patients and 59 child patients (Darroch 1973: 7) (*Annual Report* 1941: 4), the Clinic grew rapidly, reaching the height of its activities relatively early in its existence. Adult patient numbers peaked in 1948 when 591 attended (*Annual Report* 1948: 4), and child patient numbers peaked in 1949 when 217 attended (*Annual Report* 1949: 6). Thereafter, patient attendance gradually declined: child attendance ceased altogether in 1966 after a recorded low of 59 in 1964 (*Annual Report* 1964: 11; the 1965 figure is not recorded in the *Annual Report*); adult attendance reached a recorded low of 128 in 1970 (*Annual Report* 1970: 5; 1970 is the last year this figure is given in the *Annual Report*). The decline in attendance, and a staffing crisis precipitated by the death of the Medical Director, Dr A. J. Bain, in early 1971 (Darroch 1973: 24), preceded the Davidson Clinic's closure on 29 June 1973 (Rushforth 1984: 143).

A full scholarly account of the Davidson Clinic's organisational rise and fall is beyond the scope of this monograph. A provisional narrative can be gleaned from the testimony of those associated with the Clinic. The most important factor, according to these sources, was the post-war creation of the National Health Service (NHS). Rushforth attributes the Clinic's closure to the rise of psychopharmacological treatments delivered by the NHS, and to the impossibility of competing with NHS salary scales (Rushforth 1984: 133–4). Jane Darroch, in her brief 1973 history of the Clinic, states that it could only find one-third of its requisite income from patient fees, and that it eventually lost its Child Guidance intake to the NHS and local authorities (Darroch 1973: 22–3). She argues that the Clinic could have continued as a modest enterprise (Darroch 1973: 23–4), except that it was unable to compete with the NHS for staff. A more extended explanation of the effect of the NHS is provided in Darroch's volume by J. D. Sutherland (1905–91), the Medical Director of the Tavistock Clinic in London from 1947 to 1968, who retired to Edinburgh, but remained active in various psychiatric and psychoanalytic organisations and endeavours. According to Sutherland, 'after the inception of the Health Service, it was virtually impossible for the Clinic to survive in an independent position' (Sutherland 1973: 27). There are various reasons for his conclusion (Sutherland 1973: 26–7): the NHS was culturally and economically unsympathetic to analytic psychotherapy, and so unlikely to refer patients; insofar as the NHS favoured analytic psychotherapy, it preferred in-house provision and its own standards of staff training; better NHS salaries meant that the Clinic could not compete to acquire new staff. Furthermore, in areas such as research and training, in which the NHS was not the main competitor, the Clinic was easily bettered by the universities.

From its inception, the Davidson Clinic was frank in its combination of religion and psychotherapy, a syncretism which was fully endorsed by Rushforth. H. V. Dicks explains that the Davidson Clinic was partly imitative – a 'daughter colony' (Dicks 1970: 3) – of the Tavistock Clinic, which had been founded, as noted earlier (see p. 31), by the deeply religious Hugh Crichton-Miller. His faith does not seem, however, to have led the Tavistock Clinic into a significant organisational relationship with the churches. In

Dicks's narrative, the clergy appear only marginally, as honorary support staff (Dicks 1970: 47), or attending extra-mural lectures (Dicks 1970: 30, 75). Alastair Lockhart's observations on the inter-war period corroborate Dicks's account: there were no more clergy on the Tavistock's governing body than, for instance, military men; the Clinic's lectures on religion were popular but outnumbered by other subjects; and less than three per cent of new patients were clergy or referred by clergy (Lockhart 2010: 14). The marginal organisational position of Christianity within the Tavistock Clinic, whatever its ruling ethos, may well explain Crichton-Miller's apparent sense, later in life, that the Davidson Clinic was truer to his ideals: Rushforth's 1959 tribute to Crichton-Miller in the *Davidson Clinic Bulletin* claims that he 'considered the work of the Davidson Clinic in the direct line of what he had sought to establish in the Tavistock Clinic, holding on to some ideals which, all too sadly, he thought had perished in the London work' (Rushforth 1959: 10).

As Crichton-Miller's sentiments imply, the Davidson Clinic was, at least for a time, in a closer collaborative relationship with the Christian Churches, particularly the Church of Scotland. J. A. Whyte claims that the Clinic 'began as an experiment in equal partnership between Church and psycho-therapeutic clinic' (Whyte 1967: 21). Although an offer of accommodation in Davidson Church property was refused by Rushforth, the Clinic opened in nearby rented rooms, and counted Margaret Allan, a Church of Scotland deaconess, amongst Rushforth's initial three colleagues (Rushforth 1984: 88). Allan, who, like Rushforth, had received analysis at the Tavistock Clinic, had her salary provided by the Christian Iona Community until 31 May 1941 (Minute Book: 73–4). Interest was also shown in the Davidson Clinic by the Roman Catholic Church, which had already supported the Notre Dame Child Guidance Clinic in Glasgow, which opened in 1931 (Stewart 2006: 61). This interest extended to the loan of a Notre Dame staff member, Dr Ruth Meier-Blaauw, who worked at the Davidson Clinic on Saturday mornings from May 1941 to September 1942 (*Annual Report* 1941: 4; *Annual Report* 1942: 3). The ecumenicism in the Davidson Clinic's Christian institutional connections is emphasised when, even after the closure of the Davidson Church in *c.*1943 (Darroch 1973: 8), 'a broader relationship with the Church' was enabled via approaches to the Church of Scotland's 'Women's Home Mission Committee and the Committee on Christian Life and Social Work' and to the 'Episcopal Diocese of Edinburgh' (*Annual Report* 1942: 4). There were also ad hoc collaborations with various Scottish churches, such as the programmed Sunday Service in a local church that featured in the Davidson Clinic's Easter and Summer Schools (as evidenced in Rushforth's papers: Summer School 1949, Easter School 1951, St Paul's search).

These relationships indicate a wider context of social and political activism by the Scottish Churches, and particularly the Church of Scotland. The latter's movement towards greater social criticism than had been apparent in the inter-war years was evident in the activities from 1940 to 1945 of the Commission for the Interpretation of God's Will in the Present Crisis, or 'the Baillie Commission' as it was more popularly known, after its convenor, the theologian Professor John Baillie (1886–1960). 'In its first report to the General Assembly of May 1942', notes Stewart J. Brown, the Baillie Commission 'decisively reversed the positions held by ... the older leadership that the Church should not speak out on economic and political issues' (Brown 1994: 27). The Davidson Clinic clearly located itself within the Commission's narrative of a turning point in the Church of Scotland's history towards 'working to inculcate a Christian morality in a pluralistic society and social welfare state' (Brown 1994: 28). Baillie, who was Professor of Divinity at New College, University of Edinburgh, appears in the Minute Book's account of the Davidson Clinic's second AGM on 5 February 1943: 'The adoption of the Report was moved by the Rev. Professor John Baillie, Moderator Designate of the Church of Scotland. Professor Baillie spoke of a recent visit to the Clinic, and expressed his admiration of the work being done' (Minute Book: 137).

Such connections were not merely a pragmatic alliance between the Davidson Clinic and socially active Scottish Christian organisations. The 'equal partnership between Church and psychotherapeutic clinic' described by Whyte extends to Clinic's account of its activities in the *Davidson Clinic Bulletin*. Dr William Kraemer (1911–82), the Medical Director from 1943 to 1958 (Minute Book: 118; Dr William Kraemer 1983), was a central figure during the Clinic's heyday. He was born in Germany in 1911 to Lutheran parents, but left his home country to escape the Nazi regime in 1933, before qualifying as a physician in Siena in 1936. He began training as a Jungian analytical psychologist in 1939, and relocated to the United Kingdom in the same year, where he was a schoolmaster at Lancing College prior to his appointment at the Davidson Clinic (Seligman 1983; personal communication, Sebastian Kraemer). In a 1951 article for the *Davidson Clinic Bulletin* entitled 'The Christian Label', Kraemer explains that

> we sometimes mention the name of God and Christ without apologising for it, and ... we sometimes refer to the teaching of Christ without seeing its possible social and political value as its only raison d'être, nor do we conceive this teaching to be merely the natural reactionary control to man's instincts. (Kraemer 1951: 2)

Kraemer's article promotes a subjective authorisation of Christianity whereby 'truth can reveal itself at all times and in all of us' rather than through 'the emphasis of the official Churches ... on the written word in the Bible or the inspired tradition' (Kraemer 1951: 4). Although Kraemer's avowal was for the limited circulation of the *Bulletin*, he does not seem to be merely tailoring his self-presentation to the Clinic's constituency. A 1954 letter to the *British Medical Journal* regarding the deliberations of the Wolfenden Committee is an equally frank Christian statement on the historically contentious topic of homosexuality: 'As Christians and physicians all our aim and interest is centred in love and healing, neither in condemnation nor punishment', declares Kraemer, as he expresses his hope for 'a new and more effective attitude towards homosexuality among the people of this nation and their leaders' (Kraemer 1954).

Kraemer's statement in the *Bulletin* that '[t]he Christian label ... turns out not to be a label but rather a mode of living and thinking' (Kraemer 1951: 6) is further elaborated in the Clinic's dual role as a provider of both 'medical psychotherapy' and 'Christian psychotherapy'. In publications such as the *Annual Report* and miscellaneous publicity materials, the Clinic is referred to as the 'Davidson Clinic for Medical Psychotherapy': in the 1951 *Annual Report*, for instance, Rushforth claims that '[o]urs is the only centre in Scotland which sets out to treat patients by medical psychotherapy on purely analytical principles' (*Annual Report* 1951: 13). But although the clinic may have provided medical psychotherapy to its patients (a term which at this time also included children attending the child guidance clinic), examination of the Davidson Clinic's public discourses, and particularly of the *Annual Report*, reveals a complementary discourse of 'Christian psycho-therapy' (*Annual Report* 1941: 7). The term 'Christian psychotherapy' was almost certainly contributed by the Reverend J. A. C. Murray (fl. 1938–47), who was a Church of Scotland minister in the Scottish town of Grangemouth, and then latterly in Edinburgh. Murray, who was amongst the Board of Governors of the Clinic, proposed on 22 January 1941 (two days before the Clinic's formal opening) 'that the words "principles of Christian psycho-therapy" be added to the objects of the clinic' (Minute Book: 45). Murray's 1938 book, *An Introduction to a Christian Psycho-Therapy*, expatiates on Christian psychotherapy, referring to 'a small band of ministers, of all denominations' who 'are convinced that Christ was the great Psychologist, and that the New Testament contains much which waits to be unfolded and fulfilled in the fresh light which psychology has shed' (Murray 1938: 15). By 'psychology', Murray means psychoanalytic psychology, which, he believes, 'has been stunted of its full growth by the swaddling bands in which the medical profession has enswathed it' (Murray 1938: 22). Psychoanalysis, Murray argues, must recognise not only the subconscious aspects of religion, but also 'make straight the way for the Faith by adventuring a geography of the super-conscious' (Murray 1938: 53), by which he means an account of states of 'expanded consciousness' (Murray 1938: 55) such as artistic inspiration, creative genius, prodigious skill, and – supremely – mystical experience (Murray 1938: 47–57).

Murray's Christian psychotherapy exposes the Christian discursive context in which Rushforth could locate her endeavours, even as post-war secularisation was about to transform Scottish culture and society. Those who affirm the reality of Western secularisation tend to see it as a gradual trend correlated with modernisation, and factors such as 'the fragmentation of the lifeworld, the decline of community, the rise of bureaucracy, [and] technological consciousness' (Bruce 2002: 36). There are, however, alternative accounts that are more productive for an understanding of 'Christian Psycho-Therapy', such as Callum Brown's claim that '[t]he social significance of religion ... can rise and fall in any social and economic context' (Brown 1992: 55). In Britain, Brown argues, secularisation was in fact a 'remarkably sudden and culturally violent event' dateable to the post-war period, particularly the 1960s (Brown 2009: 176). Brown concedes that quantifiable behaviours such as institutional membership (e.g. being a communicant member of a church), or a looser associational affiliation (e.g. use of a church for baptism, marriage and funerals), may seem to support the correlation of secularism with modernity. For Brown, however, Christian religious life is primarily discursive, and therefore less easily measurable. Faith in Christian life narratives is central, and upon it institutional and associational forms are dependent: the believer (and often the non-believer, in rejecting theism) understands him- or herself to be 'on a life-journey, using notions of progression, improvement and personal salvation' (Brown 2009: 185). Discursive Christianity, however, is a cultural and psychological phenomenon that translates less easily into statistical data, for it consists in a religious identity that shapes biographical narrative. Secularisation thus brings about a 'discursive bereavement' experienced in the declining currency of Christian life-narrative patterns: those reared in the Christian faith find their notions of a life journey increasingly out of kilter with the cultural dominant.

Murray's rhetoric offered to continue such Christian life-narrative patterns within psychological discourse. Murray refers to a 'life-curve' punctuated by 'several clearly definable danger-zones' in which the individual encounters a crisis precipitated – in Murray's characteristic movement between psychoanalytic and theological discourses – by 'some power from his own inner depths, or a command from God' (Murray 1938: 154). Puberty, for instance, 'biologically and psychologically, marks a crisis in the life-curve so radical as to deserve the description of a new birth' (Murray 1938: 154). The pubescent 'rebirth' described by Murray fuses somatic, psychological and theological discourses, so that puberty emerges as something like a synergistic opportunity for Christian regeneration: 'The nameless unrests and blind longings of puberty are in large measure due to the hunger on the part of the created for the Creator' (Murray 1938: 156); a 'deeper throb' (Murray 1938: 156) is felt as 'the religious instinct rises to consciousness as naturally as the sun' (Murray 1938: 155) in an analogue to the psychoanalytic account of the end of sexual latency.

Such psychoanalytic and psychotherapeutic repristination of Christian life-narrative patterns extends to the discourses produced by Rushforth and, under her leadership, by the Davidson Clinic. Providentialism is an aspect of the discursive Christianity re-produced by Rushforth. Her autobiography is filled with textual cues inviting the reader to perceive the providence at work in her life and in the institutional fortunes of the Davidson Clinic. Sometimes these cues are implicit, as when Rushforth reflects on the Davidson Clinic's hiring of Kraemer:

> Was it chance that brought to his notice an advertisement in which we offered the princely sum of £300 a year to an assistant medical direc- tor in the Davidson Clinic? Young and eager, he had been in touch with the Jungian fraternity in London; he was heaven sent. (Rushforth 1984: 93)

As the wider narrative context reveals, neither the rhetorical question, nor the idiom 'heaven sent', are innocent. The '"pennies from heaven" that maintained our work' (Rushforth 1984: 96) are a sign of Divine approval according to Rushforth, and to John Falconer, who 'shared my sense of assurance ... that we were being used in this service and should accept our role as part of the will of God' (Rushforth 1984: 116). Rushforth's dis- cursive Christian credo is that 'there is no such thing as chance', 'at each turning point there is *co-operation* with the Divine Purpose' (Rushforth 1984: 155).

Rushforth, like Murray, also exploits the idea of a rebirth. In a *Davidson Clinic Bulletin* article based on a lecture to the 1953 Summer School, Rushforth refers to the phenomenon (widespread, in her view) of analy- sands 'going through the curious birth experience' (Rushforth 1953: 6). She gives the example of a patient who 'took a new lease of life' which 'dates from that day on the couch in the consulting room when he was quite literally born again' (Rushforth 1953: 6). A more frequent motif in Rushforth's work, however, is that analytic psychotherapy works miracles of healing within the lives of patients. The 1942 *Annual Report* states explicitly that 'psycho-therapeutic treatment can bring about miracles of healing which are the fulfilment of the Divine purpose' (*Annual Report* 1942: 2), and a *Scotsman* article from 1943 also uses the phrase 'miracles of healing', though without reference to divine realities ('Davidson Clinic' 1943). The idea is still in circulation over a decade later in the 1953 *Annual Report*, where Rushforth in her later capacity as Honorary Medical Director testifies to 'constant miracles happening in the lives of our patients' (*Annual Report* 1953: 9). Rushforth's earliest experience of a putatively miraculous psycho- therapeutic cure seems to have been her first analytic case at the Tavistock Clinic, as she explains in the *Journal of the Indian Medical Profession*: 'my first case ... recovered miraculously. She was a woman in her thirties in the grip of a serious neurosis with conversion symptoms. This took the form of acute dysnoeic [i.e. dyspnoeic] attacks' (Rushforth 1962: 4098). The patient's attacks of breathlessness are, Rushforth infers, hysterical symptoms that arise from a 'conversion' of her psychological neurosis into a somatic form. For both doctor and patient, as Rushforth explains in the more personal discourse of her autobiography, the eventual psychoanalytic relief of these symptoms was a recovery of Christ's ministry of healing: '"The days of our

Lord have returned" was how Chrissie put it, and I was not averse to considering it as a marvellous happening' (Rushforth 1984: 75).

Rushforth's discourse of miraculous psychotherapeutic healing indicates the Clinic's alliance with a growth of interest in divine healing within the Church of Scotland during the 1950s, as evidenced by the Church's official monthly magazine, *Life and Work*. A 1952 article entitled 'The cure of souls: work of the Davidson Clinic' tells how

> [t]he Moderator of the General Assembly and Bishop Warner, along with a good representation of ministers, especially younger men, were present at a meeting organised by the Davidson Clinic a few weeks ago, which ought to be of considerable interest and significance for the Church. (Gunn 1952: 258)

The Clinic is depicted as a necessary auxiliary to pastoral work, but is associated also with 'the emergence and growth of prayer circles and services of intercession for the sick and suffering' (Gunn 1952: 258). Indeed, by 1957, J. A. C. Murray had moved from Christian psychotherapy to a fully developed spiritual healing: a round-up of healing activity in *Life and Work* records the opening of a centre for healing in Edinburgh's New Town 'under the auspices of the Fellowship of Christian Healing, and the direction of the Rev. J. A. C. Murray' (Anonymous 1957: 90).

The historical significance of spiritual healing should not be exaggerated. As the pages of *Life and Work* indicate, the Church of Scotland and its membership were far more concerned during this era with issues such as the Cold War, communism, decolonisation, evangelism, and youth culture. Nonetheless there is a definite interest in spiritual healing, which extends also to psychotherapy, particularly for psychosomatic disorders. A 1946 article entitled 'Does Christ still heal?' by the Reverend William Watson of Flowerhill Church, Airdrie, recounts three personal anecdotes of the author's healing ministry. A baptismal prayer for a dying baby 'restore[s] the sick child to health and vigour' by alleviating the mother's pathogenic anxiety (Watson 1946: 129). A nine-year-old girl suffering from St Vitus Dance (presumably Sydenham's chorea) is haunted by nightmares of a piebald man until Watson's suggestions cure her underlying anxiety: 'Deep down in the sub-conscious mind "something" began to drive out the fear. The St. Vitus dance disappeared, and soon she was quite well' (Watson 1946: 130). Finally, a young married man 'suffering from a divided self, mental disquiet, and spiritual starvation' is cured by unspecified spiritual means, leading the youth to declare 'that the day of miracles was not past, for he himself was a miracle, a new creation' (Watson 1946: 130). Moreover, interest in healing practice clearly grew in the immediate postwar years. A 1952 book review in *Life and Work* of Leslie Weatherhead's *Psychology, Religion and Healing* (Weatherhead 1951) discusses the state of healing ministry in Scotland, which is characterised as a revival of 'primitive Christian practice':

From Iona and from other sources influences have gone forth that have touched many parts of the Church. We hear of churches where from time to time Healing Services are held. We hear of others where after the morning service the elders and others meet round the Communion Table to pray for the sick by name. And we hear of inter-Church groups which meet for similar intercession. None of these activities has been without fruit. (McKenzie 1952)

This testimony is corroborated by a 1953 article which records an ecumenical (though largely Church of Scotland) healing group in Glasgow with around twenty clerical members; intercessory meetings for the sick are held as an adjunct to regular church services (Anonymous 1953). A pseudonymous 1955 article, 'Cured by faith? Experiences of a minister in healing', records the appointment by the General Assembly of a Commission to investigate spiritual healing (Clydesdale [pseud.] 1955). The author, perhaps rather bathetically, claims

I am convinced, from my knowledge of my own body, that some of us have certain powers, certain currents of power, within us which can be used to alleviate, if not cure, certain ailments, such as bronchial and catarrhal congestion and various forms of pain, by the application of both hands to the affected part. (Clydesdale [pseud.] 1955)

However, enthusiasm for the practice of spiritual healing within the Church of Scotland was limited by the eventual Report to the 1958 General Assembly of the Special Commission on Spiritual Healing, which had been appointed in 1954, and consisted of representatives from medicine, law, the Church and academia (Church of Scotland General Assembly 1958: 909) – including J. A. C Murray (Church of Scotland General Assembly 1958: 925). The Report includes a lengthy section on scriptural and historical precedent for healing ministry, including a firm statement that disease could and should not be attributed to individual sin (Church of Scotland General Assembly 1958: 910). The main business of the Report is, though, how to conceive and regulate the practice of spiritual healing within the Church given the diagnostic acuity and therapeutic efficacy of modern biomedicine. The Report sketches in the context that has prompted its work:

in about twenty Presbyteries some kind of healing activities are carried on, ranging from simple prayers for the sick to regular Services of Healing. There are some forty congregational groups in Edinburgh and a similar number in Glasgow; while here and there throughout the country individual ministers are working independently along similar lines. (Church of Scotland General Assembly 1958: 914)

As part of its work, the Commission surveys the available evidence from various informal healing ministries. While the Commission is theologically careful not to 'set any limit in our thinking to the power of God or his methods of operation' (Church of Scotland General Assembly 1958: 915), the Report is agnostic about the efficacy of spiritual healing for somatic disease, noting that the Commission has 'not found any case of physical disease, such as cancer, pneumonia, tuberculosis or leukaemia, in which it is possible to say that a cure has been brought about by spiritual healing alone' (Church of Scotland General Assembly 1958: 915). Indeed the Report indicates that assertions of somatic cure after intercession typically resort to the fallacy of *post hoc ergo propter hoc*: biomedical therapeutics have almost invariably been employed, and a very small number of cases will anyway result in spontaneous remission (Church of Scotland General Assembly 1958: 915). The Report is, though, more sanguine about psychological and psychosomatic efficacy: 'Among cases brought to our notice where prayer and the laying-on of hands brought relief of symptoms were persons suffering from bronchitis, asthma, skin diseases, paralysis, as well as many suffering from purely nervous disability' (Church of Scotland General Assembly 1958: 915). Nonetheless, despite this concession, the function of spiritual healing within the Church is very carefully circumscribed. Spiritual healing is complementary to expert treatment, not a substitute offered by clerical '"amateurs"' (Church of Scotland General Assembly 1958: 918) dabbling in psychology and medicine: 'Problems affecting physical and mental health require consideration *first* by a physician' (Church of Scotland General Assembly 1958: 918); ministers called to healing should always work 'in consultation with the patient's medical adviser' (Church of Scotland General Assembly 1958: 924). The minister may be able to assist directly in 'diseases of psychogenic origin arising through the inability of the persons concerned to adapt themselves satisfactorily to life' where he can address non-medical 'personal problems – doubts, fears, guilts, hopes, and aspirations' (Church of Scotland General Assembly 1958: 918). But beyond this therapeutic modality (which is perhaps that of a proto-counsellor), the main emphasis cannot and should not be on the directly curative possibilities of spiritual intercession. Rather, 'in all cases of healing the chief concern of the minister should be the reconciliation of the patient with God' (Church of Scotland General Assembly 1958: 915) – which is why the Report recommends that

[b]efore any person is given treatment by the methods of 'spiritual healing', he or she should be carefully prepared by pastoral instruction; it being made clear that the only proper attitude in receiving such treatment is a cheerful acceptance of God's will, whatever that may be. (Church of Scotland General Assembly 1958: 924–5)

The Report outlines a way forward for spiritual healing in the Church, and its recommendations include an enhanced role for hospital chaplains, who seem to epitomise the co-operation with biomedicine outlined by the Report (Church of Scotland General Assembly 1958: 925). Nonetheless, the Report disappointed a constituency who hoped for a more assertive statement on the reality of spiritual healing. The 'Extract Deliverance' following the Report records the formal deliberations of the General Assembly, which include a proposed but unsuccessful addendum stating that 'the healing ministry of Christ continues to-day' despite 'the impossibility of obtaining scientifically acceptable evidence of cure by spiritual healing alone' (Church of Scotland General Assembly 1958: 926). A subsequent editorial in *Life and Work* attempted to soothe the more enthusiastic proponents of spiritual healing, who clearly hoped for an authoritative statement on the practice's miraculous somatic efficacy:

> The Commission did not say, could not say, would not dare to say, that there is no evidence of healing coming immediately from the hand of God – as distinct from healing which comes through the recognisable therapeutic processes. What the Commission said was that it had no evidence of healing resulting directly from the special services and ministrations of 'spiritual healing', such as the laying-on of hands. (Stevenson 1958: 157)

The benefit of 'recognisable therapeutic processes' is glossed in the editorial as the miracle of God's non-intervention, which prevents us from 'living in a sort of cosmic circus, not knowing what a moment might bring forth, unable to predict with certainty the orderliness of the world around us' (Stevenson 1958: 158). The article argues for a rapprochement between the miracle of non-intervention that underlies biomedical science, and the ever-present (if seemingly very remote) possibility of a divine intervention:

> When we make our intercessions we ought to have in mind the 'miracle of consistency', the non-intervention which is often part of the divine purpose. But we cannot pray at all unless we ask, believing too in the other miracle of His intervention, whatever form it may take. (Stevenson 1958: 158)

Despite this accommodationist rhetoric, the Special Commission's Report marks a diminution in enthusiasm for spiritual healing, which was thereby officially conceived as more mundane than miraculous. In 1961, for instance, a small notice in the pages of *Life and Work* appears attempting to recruit for 'The Christian Fellowship of Healing (Scotland)' set up by Murray so that it can be established as a national centre for spiritual healing (Anonymous 1961). The Christian Fellowship of Healing, whatever its national significance, endured for several decades before closing in *c.*2011, but remained a sideline to the Church's activities: a 1973 article on the CFH (Scotland) in *Life and Work* admits that 'though it has been an active and live feature of the Church for all these years, there are many church members and even ministers who have little knowledge of its function and doings' (Weir 1973: 18). But although spiritual healing had a limited place within the Church of Scotland, the Davidson Clinic's narrower model of Christian psychotherapeutic healing continued to find favour with Church of Scotland clergy. As part of the Davidson Clinic Summer School of 1964, the Reverend John R. Wilson, minister of St Bride's Church in Dalry, Edinburgh from 1955 to 1968 (Young 1983: 1), preached a sermon (preserved in Rushforth's papers) on 2 August 1964 entitled 'St Paul's search for identity' – a topic intended to harmonise with the Summer School's theme that year, 'The Search for Our Identity' (St Paul's search: [1]). The essence of Christianity, according to Wilson, is a biographical progression that may be modelled in psychotherapeutic terms. To ground his thesis scripturally, Wilson offers a re-interpretation of Paul's conversion to Christianity in which familiar theological concepts are translated into psychotherapeutic discourse. Paul's famous conversion on the Road to Damascus 'was in fact a nervous breakdown, a mental collapse' (St Paul's search: [1]). This supposed nervous breakdown was ultimately the result, according to Wilson, of Paul's childhood, which was 'a strict one; he was made to be "Too good too soon"' (St Paul's search: [1]). However, in converting to Christianity, Paul found that '[h]e could be just as he was, and Christ would accept him like that' (St Paul's search: [1]), and so 'gradually a spontaneity came into his life; he was living by a spirit welling up from within, not according to a law superimposed upon him' (St Paul's search: [2]). The sermon's lessons for the present are that conversion to the Christian faith involves 'a deep depression', 'a collapse of the personality' quite unlike the 'wonderful elation' promoted by the evangelical tradition (St Paul's search [1]).

Wilson's investment in psychoanalytic psychotherapy is elaborated in a later, autobiographical article on 'The distinction between pastoral care, pastoral counselling and psychotherapy' (Wilson 1973), based on a 1969 conference paper. This additional testimony shows clearly that Wilson's sermon on St Paul alludes to his experience of psychoanalysis while a parish minister: 'Only as inappropriate defences were surrendered and the previously unacceptable "badness" accepted and made peace with, are we able to accept others and their negative aspects' (Wilson 1973: 198). This '"psychodynamic enlightenment"' (Wilson 1973: 200) was vital to Wilson's pastoral work in post-war Dalry, which he describes as 'a down-town parish in Edinburgh of teeming, overcrowded tenements where tuberculosis was and had been rampant' (Wilson 1973: 194). Conditions improve under the post-war consensus: antibiotics are introduced under the NHS to tackle tuberculosis, and overcrowded households find larger and more sanitary accommodation elsewhere. But the one-room 'single end' tenements are subsequently sold to what Wilson describes as 'the failures and misfits of society' (Wilson 1973: 195):

> For example, the middle-class woman who, having left her husband in a pleasant residential part of the city was living with her teen-age son in a 'single-end' which had only one bed, which tells its own story. Or perhaps it was the man who had left his wife and child in a new house, which he was still paying up, living by himself in a state of remorse and

regret. Or, the lonely homosexual whose hysterical advances made
one tensely defended. (Wilson 1973: 195)

The issues raised are less the traditional material concerns of inner-city
ministry, and more the difficulties of autonomous, individuated life. Wilson
laments the temptation to rely on 'prefabricated prescriptions' (Wilson
1973: 195) that enforce ascriptive roles:

> What use was it to say to the woman who had left her husband with
> her boy that the son needed his father, or that the marriage vows were
> sacred, and that she ought to go back and make a go of it! (Wilson
> 1973: 195)

Before psychotherapy, Wilson, when confronted with such cases, 'employed
the customary defences which one uses under stress, when threatened by
anxieties which one must hold at bay, so that the will to help is deflected
from its proper goal' (Wilson 1973: 195). But after therapy, his pastoral
work with such individuals is improved by his greater 'ability to come closer
to human need without undue anxiety' (Wilson 1973: 198) – a factor which
is 'much more important than the ability to see underlying patterns and to
make brilliant interpretations' (Wilson 1973: 198). He accordingly narrates
a variety of post-analytic pastoral successes, such as that of a middle-aged
single woman who has spent many years nursing first her parents and then
her older sister. This 'dutiful sister' feels bound to 'her duty to carry on
nursing her sister as a Christian should' but 'resents it and at times actually
hates her sister and this depresses her further' (Wilson 1973: 198). As her
minister, Wilson must 'be able to enter into her problem and to relieve her
of her harsh, punitive and masochistic feelings of hatred towards herself'
(Wilson 1973: 198). Moreover, the post-analytic Wilson has greater insight
into the organisational life of the parish. He recognises that the Church is
often 'regarded as an organisation to preserve "goodness" and to eliminate
badness, and because of this expectation, members prefer valiant calls by
the Minister to engage in energetic work for some laudable cause' (Wilson
1973: 202) – these members are exemplified by the case of a 'willing worker'
who 'needs the constant activity of Church life, working for a "good" cause,
to keep her depressive and guilty anxieties at bay' (Wilson 1973: 200).

   Although detailed testimony such as Wilson's article is uncommon,
Christian psychotherapy was clearly satisfying to other clerical consumers
of the Davidson Clinic's services. An anonymous 1951 contribution to the
Davidson Clinic Bulletin entitled 'An American looks at the Clinic' presents
the testimony of a US clergyman studying in Edinburgh. The author refers
to

> those hollow aspects of my personal life, those headaches every Sunday
> at two o'clock, those church promotional activities that left me so
> fatigued I was unable to drive home; and worst of all, those frantic feel-
> ings that my witness to Christ was being dulled. (Anonymous 1951: 11)

Yet, after twenty months of psychoanalysis, 'the Clinic has been working one of its standard miracles' – 'standard because I have met at least a score of other people who are finding the same thing happening in their lives as a result of analysis' (Anonymous 1951: 12). The sense of faith renewed by miraculous healing is shared by another clergyman, W. I. Ireland, whose 1965 contribution to the *Davidson Clinic Bulletin* describes his experience of an ecumenical Ministers' Group. Ireland argues for the purifying effects of psychotherapeutic critique, arguing that 'the enduring things of Christ will, in the end, only shine the more ... when attacked openly by our hidden and unacknowledged rejection of them' (Ireland 1965: 7).

The psychotherapeutic renewal of faith also seems to have satisfied Christian consumers who were not clergy. The anonymous patient 'D. A.' supplies a contribution to Darroch's history entitled 'To the Davidson Clinic: an appreciation' in which he or she presents the Clinic as a contemporary analogue to the early Christian Church. What the Davidson Clinic produces, at least in the personal experience of D. A., is not so much the relief of mental illness, as 'a new awareness of the real meaning of life and living' achieved through a 'labyrinthine journey of analysis and self-enlightenment' (D. A. 1973: 28). The 'integrated human beings' that result from the Clinic's psychotherapy are at work within society, transforming it from within, 'leavening the world' or propagating like a seed that has 'reproduced itself "an hundred fold"' (D. A. 1973: 29). The allusions to the Scriptural Parable of the Leaven (Matt. 13: 33, Luke 13: 20–1) and the Parable of the Sower (e.g. Matt. 13: 3–8) indicate that D. A. understands the Clinic as engaged in a modern missionary activity, transforming society from within by a process of contagious personal transformation – with Rushforth's gender perhaps being prophesied in the parabolic statement that 'a woman took and hid [the leaven] in three measures of meal, till the whole was leavened' (Luke 13: 21).

Such client testimony shows how the Davidson Clinic provided a psychoanalytic psychotherapy that was held to facilitate the narrative turning points of discursive Christianity. This, in turn, restored and renewed the faith of at least some of the Christians who felt themselves challenged by the apparent decline of Christendom. So-called 'Christian psychotherapy', and associated ideologies and practices, offered a new, psychologically reinterpreted and scientifically authorised template for Christian life narrative, thereby recovering and continuing diverse narrative elements such as conversion, rebirth or regeneration, miracles, providence, salvation and spiritual healing. Psychotherapy also provided a theoretical resource and psychological preparation for the everyday work of pastoral ministry. The Davidson Clinic, for its part, was especially active in this syncretism not only because of the personal inclinations of those associated with it, but also because of the Clinic's difficulties in achieving a secure medical status, and the consequent appeal of an alliance with a socially active Scottish Christianity in which spiritual healing had a definite if marginal niche.

R. D. Laing: the angel in the house

Tracing the history of Winifred Rushforth and the Davidson Clinic elaborates the neglected Christian context for psychotherapy in post-war
Scotland, helping to shed new light on R. D. Laing. Rushforth saw Laing as
sympathetic to the Davidson Clinic's aims: as correspondence in the Laing
archives demonstrates, she hoped in the mid-1960s to appoint him as successor to William Kraemer in the role of Medical Director (Correspondence
Rushforth–Laing). Laing declined Rushforth's offer, yet the remarks in
his 1970 *Listener* article (see p. 56) indicate the strength of his youthful
Christian belief, and his personal concern with what might be preserved in
the faith. In his 1985 quasi-autobiography *Wisdom, Madness and Folly*, Laing
describes further his religious socialisation. He was sent, for instance, to
Sunday School a year before starting primary school, where he won a prize
for his ability to recite the Books of the Bible in order faster than anyone
in his class (Laing 1998: 62–5). He also discusses the daily School assembly,
and his own habit of nightly prayers, maintained until his mid-teens (Laing
1998: 65–6). Laing refers to his temporary conversion at an evangelical
summer camp, an event described in greater detail in a 1968 manuscript
entitled 'Elements for an Autobiography' (Elements: 44–7). A year or two
after this experience, however, Laing 'gave up attendance at Bible Classes
and Sunday School' (Elements: 50), having been disappointed by what he
saw as the excessive sexual moralism and deficient scientific credentials of
evangelical Christianity.

Laing's mother, Amelia, parallels the wider societal fortunes of Scottish
Christianity, as she changes from a guardian of piety in the 1930s to an
atheist in the 1970s:

> My mother did not sing me lullabies but she taught me to say prayers.
> Almost fifty years later, after my father was dead, I asked her whether
> she believed in any of that sort of thing – 'It's all a lot of nonsense,
> Ronald.' (Laing 1998: 52)

Brown argues that discursive Christianity (and its secondary manifesta-
tions in church use and membership) were principally supported by the
conventional feminisation of piety in Britain from about 1800 to 1950.
During this period, the woman's task, as wife and mother, was to be
'the "angel in the house"', and 'to reign over the moral weakness and
innate temptations of masculinity' (Brown 2009: 9). Every household was
a domestic mission station led by a woman whose job was to discipline the
menfolk. According to Brown, Britain was only decisively secularised after
the Second World War when women challenged their traditional role
with the consequence that 'piety "lost" its discursive home within feminin-
ity' (Brown 2009: 179).

Brown's thesis has been criticised. Hugh McLeod, for instance, accepts
that '[t]he distancing from religion … of many women of the 1960s gen-

eration was a key factor in the weakening of the religious socialization of the next generation' (McLeod 2007: 186). But he cautions that 'many of the factors that were distancing women from the church were the same as the factors that were distancing men, and there is no evidence that women were leaving in greater numbers than men' (McLeod 2007: 186). Nonetheless, whatever the merits of Brown's argument as an explanation of a general cultural shift, it is informative for a reading of Laing's biography. The role of 'angel in the house' was normative during Laing's childhood: for instance, in the Scottish writer Willa Muir's modernist novel, *Imagined Corners* (published in 1935, when Laing was eight years old), one of the central female characters remarks that 'in Scotland man's chief end was to glorify God and woman's to see that he did it' (Muir 1987: 77). Yet although many women, including (it seems) Amelia Laing, shed the role of 'angel in the house', Laing's own words further substantiate Steven Sutcliffe's argument that the Scottish psychiatrist's life and work show a 'striking response to the "discursive bereavement" (the grief at the cultural loss of religious certainties) experienced mid-century by Christians' (Sutcliffe 2010: 195). Writing after British secularisation, Laing maintains the angelic, Christian discourse by retrospectively assigning it to the men of his household. *Wisdom, Madness and Folly* records a striking claim made by Laing's father, David:

> When my father was fourteen an angel had appeared to him while he was lying awake in bed at night and kissed him on the forehead ... He believed that this kiss had blessed his whole life. I never saw an angel. (Laing 1998: 65)

Curiously, Laing, who claims that he 'never saw an angel', then corrects himself – he has in fact seen an angel (of sorts): 'outside my bedroom window was the dome of a public library on the top of which was an angel, poised on one foot, as though to take off to the moon and the stars' (Laing 1998: 71). The public library in question is Govanhill Public Library, which Laing as a teenager read his way through voraciously (Laing 1998: 71). 'Elements', written in the late 1960s, shows that this displacement of the angel motif from David Laing to his son is based on the latter's inference about the view from his bedroom (a room which was his father's exclusively until 'I took it over "for my studies" when I was about 16' (Elements: 14)):

> At the age of 14, ... an angel came down and kissed his [David Laing's] forehead. He a number of times referred to this angel, and insisted it was not a dream. He probably selected the flat we lived in because 'his' room, overlooked the Govanhill Public Library, on the domed roof of which was an angel. (Elements: 7)

Laing's post-secularisation narratives transfer the previously feminised angel of Christian piety first to David Laing, and then to Laing himself, who emerges as the new custodian of the faith.

This symbolic displacement is matched by narrative structure, for 'Elements' and *Wisdom, Madness and Folly* both maintain a Christian biographical structure arranged around what Laing calls 'episodes that I regard as critical turning points, that determined a whole sector of my future for years, and may still be doing so' (Elements: 31). These conversion-like episodes are the 'single "convincing" moment[s]' (Laing 1998: 79) that Laing sees in *Wisdom* as the articulating points of his biography: they are 'things that "struck" me on the road to seeing and responding to the suffering with which psychiatry is involved in a different way from the usual' (Laing 1998: xvi). This allusion to Paul's (or Saul's) conversion on the road to Damascus – he is popularly spoken of as being 'struck' by a blinding light – echoes Laing's *The Politics of Experience* (1967), which celebrates the 'direct experience' whereby 'Paul of Tarsus was picked up by the scruff of the neck, thrown to the ground and blinded for three days' (Laing 1967: 118).

Laing's autobiographies present him as a successor to the 'angel in the house' whose piety is renewed by solitary engagement with the contents of Govanhill Public Library, and then by a spiritual development represented as a series of dramatic Damascene conversions. Sutcliffe's warning against 'our own predisposition to continue to render "life writing" in a "heroic" register' is salutary (Sutcliffe 2010: 183). As Allan Beveridge notes (Beveridge 2011: xv–xvi), Laing's heroic narrative obscures his mundane, gradual formation within an early professional environment in post-war Glasgow which facilitated theological engagement. Laing's grappling with problems of faith was part of a wider contemporaneous negotiation with religion in Scottish and British culture. Although the 1960s would bring increased secularism, '[f]rom 1945 to 1956, Britain experienced one of the most concerted periods of church growth since the middle of the nineteenth century' (Brown 2006: 188). This 'crusade decade' was marked in Scotland by a variety of missionary endeavours, such as the Tell Scotland Movement, the Radio Mission on BBC Scotland, and rallies led by the US evangelist Billy Graham (Brown 2006: 188). Glasgow was a hub of theological debate during this period, with a particular academic focus on German existential theology (Newlands 1993: 105). One already well-known locus for Laing was the Abenheimer-Schorstein group (as it has been retrospectively designated), which took a particular interest in theology (e.g. Rillie 1988, Collins 2008). Another, less well-known engagement occurred when Laing 'left Gartnavel Royal Mental Hospital in 1955 to take a National Health Service job as senior registrar at the Southern General Hospital, where the Department of Psychological Medicine of Glasgow University was located' (Laing 1998: 135). While Laing was in this post,

> The Department of Psychiatry was approached by a group of ministers who wanted to be given a course on human relations, interpersonal theory, counselling and so on. The professor took the group – seven

Protestant ministers of different denominations and a Rabbi – once a week, with me as his assistant. (Laing 1998: 135)

The 'professor' was T. Ferguson Rodger, Professor of Psychological Medicine at Glasgow University from 1948 to 1973, and 'perhaps the most influential psychiatrist practising in the West of Scotland in the 1950s' (Davidson 2009: 414). As Sarah Phelan explains, Rodger adopted an eclectic approach to psychiatry which 'was a critical response to the instability of contemporary psychiatric knowledge' (Phelan 2017: 92); he pragmatically mingled somatic and psychological explanations, classifications and therapeutics.

Rodger's facilitation of the Ministers' Group clearly shows that pastoral ministry was part of this eclectic approach. Although Laing's accounts of his Glasgow context can be selective and unreliable (Andrews 1998, Abrahamson 2007), his description of the group is broadly accurate. The archived minutes (Ministers' Group) confirm that there were seven attendees with the title 'Mister' (presumably ministers), and one with the title 'Rabbi'. Although Laing neglects to mention the other medical and/or academic participants (the various other 'Doctors' in the minutes), the records show that the group (usually called the 'Ministers' Group') met at roughly weekly intervals over ten weeks from 12 January 1956 to 15 March 1956. Although at least eighteen different people attended over this period, the average attendance was around twelve (with the caveat that two sets of minutes do not record attendance). Rodger set the structure for the course in the first session: each meeting would discuss case(s) from the ministers' pastoral work, and some set reading from Paul E. Johnson's *Pastoral Ministration* (Johnson 1955).

The Ministers' Group appears in *Wisdom* solely to furnish a 'turning point'. Although Laing is ostensibly present as an expert on human psychology, he is forced to concede that '[t]hese ministers ... had far more experience of actual human relations' (Laing 1998: 135). In particular, their discussion of bereavement compels Laing to discard certain psychoanalytic prejudices. The relevant meeting is likely the final one, on 15 March 1956, which, according to the minutes, contained 'an account of the chapter on Death in Johnson's book. Most of the ensuing discussion had to do with ... impressions and anecdotes derived from attendances at funerals'. In his chapter on death, Johnson argues that healthy grieving requires expression, rather than repression, of the inevitable painful emotions (Johnson 1955: 217). However, according to *Wisdom*, the ministers criticised Johnson's Freudian psychology, and his nomothetic account of bereavement: 'although some people were sad ... when someone close died, they [the ministers] were not sure that they should regard such grief and mourning as the rule' (Laing 1998: 136). Their doubts, based on far more worldly experience, challenged Laing's ostensible expertise, and his inclination to interpret the absence of grief as 'a manic defence' (Laing 1998: 136).

Although the Ministers' Group appears in *Wisdom* merely as a vignette, both the minutes and Johnson's *Pastoral Ministration* reveal that it was amongst the early sources for ideas later significant to Laing's work, such as empathy, the I–thou relation, object relations psychoanalysis, and community therapy. Johnson, despite his nomothetic model of bereavement, prescribes, as would Laing in *The Divided Self* (Laing 1965), the use of '*empathy*; the German equivalent is *einfühling*', defined as the 'social imagination to put yourself in another's position' (Johnson 1955: 72). In a further debt to Continental philosophy, Martin Buber's ideas on the I–thou relationship are discussed by one of the ministers (2 February 1956). Interpersonal relationships are a recurrent concern, particularly for Rodger, who relates Freudian ideas on the mother–child dyad to attachment theory in the second meeting (19 January 1956). On other occasions, Rodger valorises broader, adult forms of interpersonal life. He criticises the '"atomisation" of Western society' (23 February 1956), and argues that church community may itself be an appropriate therapy (2 February 1956). He also concedes that 'Ministers in fact play a more central role in the community than Psychiatrists who are peripherally situated' (2 February 1956).

The Ministers' Group not only shows a productive dialogue between psychiatry and religion in Laing's early context, it also anticipates his interest in communion as a healing practice. Johnson legitimates psychotherapeutic pastoral care by arguing that '[p]sychotherapy (mind healing) ... free[s] the soul from bondage to crippling fears and resentment' and 'release[s] the captive spiritual resources and redirect[s] them into channels of healthy social living' (Johnson 1955: 198). Psychotherapy, according to Johnson, is therefore 'holy' in an older (presumably more authentic) sense neglected by Anglophone culture: 'health means wholeness. This was the original meaning in the cognate European languages, in which "heal," "whole," and "holy" are derived from one linguistic root' (Johnson 1955: 198). The *Oxford English Dictionary*, one might add, is more cautious in tracing the etymology of 'holy': it acknowledges the sense of 'whole' as probable, with the sense of '*hail*- in the sense "health, good luck, well-being"' as merely a further possibility (*OED*, HOLY). Nonetheless, Laing echoes this idea in the archived typescript of a 1984 interview with *Laughing Man*, a periodical of New Age spirituality. He states that '[t]he first English translation of what is now called "the holy ghost" was by John Wycliffe, who translated it as "our healthy spirit"' (*Laughing Man*: 2–3). Laing then refers to the healthy spirit as a 'manifestation of Divinity', and describes 'companionability in the light of our healthy spirit' as something 'I have become less embarrassed about affirming in the course of the last thirty years or so' (*Laughing Man*: 3). Such references to a practical, socially active 'communion of spirit' expresses a Christian theology which Laing acquired in post-war Scotland, particularly from George MacLeod (1885–1991), the charismatic founder in 1938 of the politically progressive Iona Community, an organisation which was later formally associated with the Church of

Scotland in 1951. The Community still exists as a dispersed national and international network of members, with organisational headquarters in Glasgow, and a spiritual centre in the restored abbey on the small island of Iona, off the west coast of Scotland.

The evidence for Laing's connection with the Iona Community and MacLeod is fragmentary, but it indicates a relation that lasted from the late 1940s to the 1980s. Laing's first contact with the Iona Community was likely through the Community House in Glasgow, which was a hub of intellectual, political and cultural debate in the late-1940s and the 1950s (Ferguson 1988: 81–3, Ferguson 1990: 238–40). According to Laing's friend from this period, Walter Fyfe, Laing was a regular presence at the Community House, along with his intellectual mentor, Joseph Schorstein (Collins 2008), and the Community's industrial and political secretary, Penry Jones (Walter Fyfe, personal communication). It is presumably in this milieu that Laing first met MacLeod. A notebook from Laing's period of National Service gives an approximate date for the beginning of their relationship. In a page dated '16th Jan 1952' (possibly a later manuscript annotation made in 1981), Laing writes, 'I wish I could remember all the wise, silly, brilliant – but always arresting – remarks that George MacLeod made to me about myself and other people in the comparatively short time I've known him' (Notebook) – implying that Laing first met MacLeod *c*.1950. According to Laing's son and biographer, Adrian, his father also visited the Iona Community at the abbey on Iona 'in the early 1950s' (Laing 1997: 102). This relationship with MacLeod and/or the Iona Community continued into the next decade: Laing spoke, for instance, to the Community in 1960 on 'The Image of Man in Theology and Psychology' (Morton 1977: 53). The evidence for the later 1960s and the 1970s is less clear, but nonetheless indicates a continuing relationship. A newspaper article in *The Scotsman* of 12 August 1983, preserved in the Laing archive, interviews Laing on Iona, and refers to several visits. One visit apparently took place '21 years ago [i.e. *c*.1962]. "I warned George MacLeod I wouldn't take communion during the service, but he still came up to me and offered it"' (Glaswegian guru). The article also mentions a subsequent visit '[a]fter *The Divided Self* in which 'Laing was invited back to Iona to give a ten-day seminar'. The chronology is confusing since the supposed visit in 1962 would equally be 'after' *The Divided Self*, which was published in 1960. Nonetheless, it seems very likely that Laing was with the Community on more than one occasion in the 1960s. *The Scotsman* article also implies a visit during the 1970s, since Laing's current three-day visit in 1983 has occurred '[a]fter nearly a decade' of absence. Turning to the period post-1983, there is substantial documentary and audio-visual evidence for a 1984 visit (see p. 102), while Adrian Laing also records '1984 and 1985 visits to Iona' (Laing 1997: 234). The Reverend Donald N. Macdonald refers to a 1986 visit, claiming that '[o]n Iona, in the Summer of 1986', Laing 'made his own personal confession of faith' (Macdonald 1993a: 123). At any rate, Laing was either in

personal contact with MacLeod, or present at the Iona Community, at some
point in every decade from around 1950 onwards.

Laing's association with MacLeod and the Iona Community further
contextualises his psychotherapeutic practice. Three important characteristics of MacLeod's theology are set out in his manifesto *We Shall
Re-build* (1944), which argues that Christianity is essentially incarnational
and corporate, and that these two characteristics are united in the ritual
of communion. The 'meaning of the Incarnation – that God became
man', declares MacLeod, is that 'Holiness' is 'inseparable from "material" considerations' (MacLeod [1944]: 18). This could imply, MacLeod
concedes, 'new interest in the earth as a living organism, [and] the new
appreciation of the cosmos as a unity' (MacLeod [1944]: 19). But, by
using the 'holy-healthy' equivalence also set out by Johnson (above),
MacLeod emphasises that his incarnational theology focuses on human
living conditions:

> Political concern, economic obligation, social betterment and scien-
> tific search become not a derivative of our Faith, but the stuff in
> which our Faith is moulded ... healthiness becomes inherent again in
> Christian Holiness, as indeed (when our Bible was translated) the two
> thoughts were conjoined. (MacLeod [1944]: 13–14)

Since everyday embodied life is holy (in the putatively original sense), salvation enters history, where it is offered on a communal, corporate basis:

> no Church based on the Scriptures can ... deny that the offer is corpo-
> rate. Christ's challenge is ever to the individual soul; but ... [i]t is into
> a society that He calls a man, into an organism, the New Community,
> His Body. (MacLeod [1944]: 30)

MacLeod therefore concludes that

> the characteristic Act of Corporate Worship is ... Holy Communion
> ... there can be no better way of 'renewing our incorporation in Him'
> than by obeying His own command '*this do*', or of renewing our incor-
> poration with each other than by breaking bread and passing the cup
> from hand to hand. (MacLeod [1944]: 30)

A practical corollary to MacLeod's theology was therefore his expansion of
communion beyond its liturgical context. In the Iona Community during
the 1930s, there began, for instance, a practice in which

> [s]mall cakes (of bread) were offered to the congregation on leaving
> the main church after the Sunday Communion, with the request to
> break and share them with a stranger in the area designated as the
> place of the 'common life' – that is, the cloisters. (Power 2006: 44)

MacLeod also began the longstanding practice of a regular service of Divine
Healing, which variously involved intercessory prayers as well as laying-on

of hands (Monteith 2000: 106), and which (as noted at p. 66 above), was an inspiration to other healing services of the 1950s.

MacLeod elaborates his theology of incarnation, corporation and communion in *Only One Way Left: Church Prospect* (1956), based on his 1954 Cunningham Lectures to the University of Edinburgh's Divinity Faculty at New College (MacLeod 1958: vii). A copy of the 1958 second edition of *Only One Way Left* (Sp Coll Laing 646) can be found in Laing's personal library. Laing's autographed front flyleaf annotation records two years, '1958' and '1983', presumably indicating that he acquired his copy in 1958, and then consulted it again during the period in which he was later renewing his connection with the Iona Community and writing *Wisdom, Madness and Folly*. Indeed, Laing's autobiography clearly draws upon MacLeod's text. When MacLeod laments the individualism of Christianity that set in, as he sees it, in the late mediaeval period, and which culminated in nineteenth-century European capitalism and colonialism, he cites a particular etymology: 'Christian man ... forgot the word "companion" which means the sharer of the loaf' (MacLeod 1958: 6). This etymology is re-used by Laing in a passage which models the so-called Rumpus Room therapeutic community experiment at Gartnavel Royal Mental Hospital in 1953 (Cameron et al. 1955) as partly an experiment in non-liturgical communion:

> They [the patients] made tea and they made some buns. Ian Cameron, one of the psychiatrists, took some of the buns over to the doctors' sitting room and offered them around. There were seven or eight of us psychiatrists sitting around. Only two or three were brave, or reckless, enough to eat a bun baked by a chronic schizophrenic. This incident convinced me of something. Who was crazier? Staff or patients? Excommunication runs deep. A companion means, literally, one with whom one shares bread. Companionship between staff and patients had broken down. (Laing 1998: 127)

The complex reality of the Rumpus Room is no doubt belied by this anecdote, and by Laing's many other retellings of the experiment, which exaggerate in various ways the therapeutic efficacy of the setting (Abrahamson 2007, Beveridge 2011: 199–223). Nonetheless, the narrative clearly shows Laing glossing psychotherapeutic practice with Christian vocabulary.

MacLeod's corporate incarnational theology also draws upon John Macmurray's philosophy, indicating a further continuity between Laing and the inter-war tradition of psychotherapeutically reformed Christianity. In *Only One Way Left*, MacLeod implies that the Wycliffe translation of the Bible is superior to other English translations because it is closer to the original Hebrew senses: 'in the Song of Zaccharius ..., "knowledge of salvation" is translated "science of health". Salvation, for the Hebrew, is science of health' (MacLeod 1958: 63). This claim (regardless of its philological merits) indicates that MacLeod regards himself as purifying Christianity of its Greek philosophical accretions: 'The Greek element has brought us

to our present decrepitude. The Hebrew element should have its chance'
(MacLeod 1958: 74). In particular, MacLeod approves 'the startling
phrase of John MacMurray [*sic*], "The great contribution of the Hebrew
to religion was that he did away with it"' (MacLeod 1958: 67) – by which
Macmurray meant that Judaism (in his view) refused to separate sacred
and secular realms. There is further evidence of MacLeod's intellectual
debts in his personal connection to Macmurray. John E. Costello records
that 'Macmurray was a friend of George MacLeod', and that MacLeod's
vision of the Iona Community was partly shaped 'in conversations with
John Macmurray' (Costello 2002: 316). T. Ralph Morton further emphasises Macmurray's influence, by identifying his significance for the entire
Iona Community, particularly through his book '*The Clue to History*, published in the year of the Community's birth [i.e. 1938]' (Morton 1977: 54).
In this book, Macmurray argues that institutional forms of Christianity
have repressed, in both political and psychoanalytic senses, the original
Jewish teaching of Jesus that history must progress towards the creation
of a universal community, or, as Macmurray has it, 'the socialist common-
wealth of the world' that will – he believes – arise in the defeat of fascism
(Macmurray 1938a: 237).

Laing's connection to the Iona Community, including an extended visit
in the 1980s, will be examined further in a discussion of the New Age
elements of his psychotherapeutic theory and practice (see p. 102). His
longstanding connection to the Community, as with his participation in
the Ministers' Group, indicates his involvement with organised religious
life in Scotland, particularly the Church of Scotland in which he had been
raised. Laing models himself as a successor to the previously feminised
'angel in the house': he is a male agent who can, through his innovative
psychotherapy, preserve the 'imperishable' elements of the Christian faith
during an era of secularisation in Scotland and the wider United Kingdom.

Laing and hermeneutics

Laing's theological hinterland was broader than merely the social and
pastoral activities and ideologies of the Church of Scotland. He was clearly
fascinated by philosophical theology, including the ideas of the German
theologian Rudolf Bultmann (1884–1976), whose writings were being
translated, expounded and criticised by Scottish theologians in the 1950s
– a context in which Laing was an active participant. Laing's interest in
specifically scriptural interpretation has been neglected because analysis
of his ideas tends to focus upon their application to psychiatry of the
philosophical distinction between *Verstehen* (understanding) and *Erklären*
(explanation) – a distinction which, though it began with biblical hermeneutics, eventually came to be seen as constitutive for the human sciences
as a whole. Central to Laing's argument in *The Divided Self* (1960) and later
studies such as *Sanity, Madness and the Family* (1964) is the thesis that psy-

chiatry has been unable to understand schizophrenic patients, and so has been able only to classify and account for their words and actions using natural-scientific categories. It is possible, argues Laing, to have a 'thorough knowledge' of schizophrenia as a genetic, psychopathological or disease phenomenon, 'without being able to understand one single schizophrenic' (Laing 1965: 33). Laing seems therefore in *The Divided Self* to be developing and extending to schizophrenic patients the kind of psychiatric arguments presented by Karl Jaspers, who drew a methodological distinction in psychiatry between the causal, nomological claims of the natural sciences and the interpretative methods of the human sciences. He thus insisted on 'the unbridgeable gulf between genuine connections of external causality and psychic connections which can only be called causal by analogy' (Jaspers 1963: 301); the latter are understood '*genetically by empathy*' rather than through an inductive logic (Jaspers 1963: 301). Laing accepted this distinction, but repudiated Jaspers's claim that 'with schizophrenic psychic life we reach limits at a point where normally we can still understand and we find ununderstandable what strikes the patients as not at all so' (Jaspers 1963: 581). Much of Laing's psychiatric research was indeed informed by the hypothesis (or perhaps a dogma) that one could, with sufficient work and imagination, understand both the speech and actions of patients with schizophrenia (Miller 2008). With sufficiently developed empathic understanding, the therapist, Laing notes, can acquire 'the plasticity to transpose himself into another strange and even alien view of the world' (Laing 1965: 34).

Laing's relationship to Jaspers is elaborated by his critique of the latter's psychiatric formalism. Jaspers argues that the

> [f]orm [of a symptom] must be kept distinct from content which may change from time to time, e.g. the fact of a hallucination is to be distinguished from its content, whether this is a man or a tree, threatening figures or peaceful landscapes. (Jaspers 1963: 58)

Laing criticises the thesis that 'from the phenomenological point of view it is only the form that interests us' (Jaspers 1963: 59) by indicating what he sees as the corresponding position in textual criticism:

> Ancient documents can be subjected to a formal analysis in terms of structure and style, linguistic traits, and characteristic idiosyncrasies of syntax, etc. Clinical psychiatry attempts an analogous formal analysis of the patient's speech and behaviour. This formalism, historical or clinical, is clearly very limited in scope. (Laing 1965: 32)

Laing specifies that the textual objects he has in mind are 'ancient', 'documentary' and 'historical' – this means that the formal analysis in question is likely to be the tradition of form criticism established by the biblical scholar Herman Gunkel (1862–1932). In this approach, scripture is studied according to the hypothesis that 'each genre plays a certain role in life and that each may thus be used only or primarily in certain kinds of contexts' (Buss 1999: 234). Form criticism first determines the genre of the textual object under investigation. It then seeks, through this knowledge, to locate the textual object in the particular lived context from which it emerged, and from which it is now to some extent dislocated by its written transmission:

> By examining the institutions and situations in which a certain social group would have used a text (the so-called '*Sitz im Leben*' of a text), the real-life function of a text becomes an aid in our understanding of the interaction between linguistic shape and social meaning. *Form history* is thus concerned with the contextualisation of texts within specific social settings. (Oeming 2006: 37)

So, for instance, '[d]uring the early part of the [twentieth] century, a number of scholars were convinced that the poems of the Song of Songs were sung at wedding festivals' (Buss 1999: 400). Prophetic speech, too, might also be given a particular life situation: it was hypothesised that 'prophets played an expected role within, or in close connection with, established proceedings; associations with rituals were suggested especially by texts patterned as a liturgy with an interplay between several types of speech, such as prayer and oracle' (Buss 1999: 397).

The hypothesis that Laing intends an analogy between Jaspers's thesis and Biblical form criticism is confirmed by the argument against clinical and historical formalism advanced in *The Divided Self*. The problem with both formalisms, Laing believes, is that they tend towards 'dynamic-genetic hypotheses' (Laing 1965: 32). On one hand, we produce a historical causality for the text, since our knowledge of its form furnishes 'a knowledge of the nexus of socio-historical conditions from which it arose' (Laing 1965: 32) – a knowledge, broadly speaking, of the *Sitz im Leben*. On the other hand, 'our formal and static analysis of isolated clinical "signs"' can be supplemented with 'an understanding of their place in the person's life history' (Laing 1965: 32). But in neither case, Laing thinks, does this 'historical information, *per se*' help us better understand what is being said unless 'we can bring to bear what is often called sympathy, or more intensively, *em*pathy' (Laing 1965: 32). Formalism identifies a textual or clinical object, and places it in a historical sequence: this does not in itself lead (so Laing believes, rightly or wrongly) to an improved understanding of the object. Thus, when Laing dismissively remarks that 'Ezekiel, in Jaspers's opinion, was a schizophrenic' (Laing 1965: 27), the intersection between psychiatric and scriptural interpretation is far from accidental. Laing's reference is to Jaspers's 1947 article, '*Der Prophet Ezechiel. Eine pathographische Studie*' ('The prophet Ezekiel: a pathographic study'), in which the German psychiatrist 'comes to the conclusion that he is dealing with a hysterical schizophrenic' (Oeming 2006: 46). This diagnosis is based upon symptoms such as visions (especially of Jerusalem), abnormal states of mind such as long periods of staring into space, sudden influence by outside voices, moments of awakening, cataleptic seizures followed by states of paralysis and lack of speech, abrupt and direct comments on sexuality, strange and ever-changing symbolic rituals, as well as frequent alternation between cold, pedantic and abstract rationalism and coarse displays of unashamed emotion. (Oeming 2006: 46)

As Oeming's summary makes clear, the content of Ezekiel's words and actions is largely left to one side. What interests Jaspers is the form of these symptomatic behaviours, rather than whatever message the prophet might have been trying to communicate. From Laing's point of view, the provision of 'schizophrenia' as the cause of Ezekiel's symptoms bypasses a genuine encounter with his words as surely (Laing would argue) as does the hypothesis of a particular *Sitz im Leben* in which these words might be uttered.

Although Laing insists that empathy must be employed to understand the content of psychotic speech, it is not simply Laing's empathetic gifts (formidable though they might have been) that inform his clinical accounts in *The Divided Self*, which was first published in 1960. His exegeses are again guided by an analogy from Biblical interpretation – specifically, from Bultmann's project of scriptural demythologisation. The connection between Bultmann and Laing is easily neglected, however, because Laing's explicit use of Bultmann's work is as a conduit to earlier developments in the philosophy of hermeneutics. Laing does not quote Wilhelm Dilthey (1833–1911) directly; instead, he cites the account of Dilthey given in the 1955 English translation of Bultmann's essay, 'The problem of hermeneutics' (Bultmann 1955). Yet Bultmann is to Laing far more than simply a pipeline to earlier German philosophy, for Laing's exegesis of psychotic speech employs the methodology used in Bultmann's project of scriptural 'demythologisation'. Bultmann's ideas are implicit in two Laingian claims: first, that the schizophrenic's apparently nonsensical speech can, in effect, be 'demythologised' by an existentialist hermeneutic; second, that the spiritual position of the so-called 'schizoid' personality is analogous to, perhaps even identical with, the disembodiment promoted (in Bultmann's view) by Stoic philosophy. The analogy which eventually emerges from Laing's psychiatric application of Bultmann's ideas is striking: the psychotic is, in effect, something like a biblical literalist, who expresses existential truths in a naïvely objectifying language to which the modern scientific mind can react only with incredulity. To substantiate this claim about Laing's work, it is necessary to have some knowledge of Bultmann's thought, and of its significance in Laing's formative intellectual milieu.

Laing's knowledge of Bultmann's work is far from exceptional within the intellectual culture of post-war Scotland. Bultmann was, for instance, one of the thinkers studied by the Abenheimer-Schorstein group of which Laing was a member: 'existentialist theology' was one of its 'cohesive forces', and the German theologian was specifically amongst those discussed (Beveridge and Turnbull 1989: 110). Bultmann was also the subject of a popularising introduction written by Ian Henderson, who took the Glasgow University Chair of Systematic Theology in 1948, and published in 1952 'a slim but seminal volume entitled *Myth in the New Testament*. This at once became *the* authoritative introduction to Rudolf Bultmann's famous programme of demythologizing the New Testament, proposed in 1942 but delayed by the war' (Newlands 1993: 103). Henderson was just one amongst many of the Scottish exponents of German philosophical theology:

> There was something of a school of existentialist theology here [in Glasgow] with [Ronald] Gregor Smith and Ian Henderson, and then the advent of lecturers in the Faculty like John Macquarrie, soon to proceed to Union Theological Seminary, New York, and then to the Regius Chair in Oxford, and Iain Nicol, now Director of the Toronto School of Theology. (Newlands 1993: 105)

Macquarrie, who was known personally to Laing (Mullan 1995: 367), was also an expositor and critic of Bultmann in books such as *An Existentialist Theology: A Comparison of Heidegger and Bultmann* (Macquarrie 1955) and *The Scope of Demythologizing: Bultmann and his Critics* (Macquarrie 1960). This Scottish activity was supplemented by Bultmann himself, who '[i]n 1955, ... journeyed to Britain to deliver the Gifford Lectures at Edinburgh University' (Fergusson 1992: 2) – these were published as *History and Eschatology* in 1957 (Bultmann 1957).

This expository work was far from merely subservient to Continental theology. Macmurray's rejection of the explanatory modes inadequate to persons was, for example, seen as a domestic equivalent to existential theology. Macquarrie explains:

> Macmurray ... points out that the self or personal being of man was ... first understood on the model of a material thing or substance, and then, with the rise of biology, on the model of a living organism. But Macmurray, rather like Heidegger, claims that both of these models are inadequate for understanding a person and that we must work the other way around, understanding organism and even substance out of our own personal experience, which subsumes both the organic and substantial modes of being. (Macquarrie 1972: 74)

Even though *The Divided Self* is billed in its subtitle as 'an existential study in sanity and madness' (Laing 1965: iii), its introductory chapter openly locates Laing's project in Macmurray's schema: 'the theory of man as person', claims the author, 'loses its way if it falls into an account of man as machine or man as an organismic system of it-processes' (Laing 1965: 23). Laing cites Macmurray, contending that we should be able to *think* of the individual man as well as to experience him neither as a thing nor an organism but as a person and that we should have a way of expressing that form of unity which is specifically personal. The task in the following pages is, therefore, the formidable one of trying to give an account of a quite specifically personal form of depersonalization and disintegration at a time when the discovery of the 'logical form through which the unity of the personal can be coherently conceived' ... is still a task for the future. (Laing 1965: 23)

For Laing, hermeneutics was clearly vital to the project of thinking of the individual as a person, and this extended to a deployment of Bultmann's demythologising interpretation of scripture. Bultmann's hermeneutic project tackles a central problem of the Bible for contemporary Western culture: namely, the supernatural cosmology of Christian scripture. Bultmann argues that the Christian proclamation occurred in a world-view quite unlike our own, a 'mythical world picture': 'The world is a three-storey structure, with earth in the middle, heaven above it, and hell below it'; 'supernatural powers intervene in natural occurrences and in the thinking, willing, and acting of human beings; wonders are nothing unusual'; the world itself 'is hastening toward its imminent end, which will take place in cosmic catastrophe' (Bultmann 1984a: 1). We simply cannot accept this world picture in our own time, believes Bultmann; or, at least, we could only do so with an effort in self-division and self-deception that would 'affirm for our faith or religion a world picture that our life other-wise denied' (Bultmann 1984a: 4). This is why we must 'face the question whether the New Testament proclamation has a truth that is independent of the mythical world picture, in which case it would be the task of theology to demythologize the Christian proclamation' (Bultmann 1984a: 3).

To find such a truth, Bultmann argues, one must understand that mythol-ogy is not about the world, but about man: 'myth does not want to be inter-preted in cosmological terms but in anthropological terms – or, better, in existentialist terms' (Bultmann 1984a: 9). Myth is composed of 'objectifying representations' (Bultmann 1984a: 14) that transpose existential concepts into a naïvely reifying discourse (or, in Henderson's words, myth 'treat[s] of spiritual factors as if they were natural entities' (Henderson 1952: 46)). Bultmann argues, for instance, that the Christian antipathy to the 'flesh' – apparent in Paul's description of 'another law in my members, warring against the law of my mind' (Rom. 8: 23) – is not a 'complaint that we, our souls or selves, are imprisoned in material bodies or that sense has power over spirit' (Bultmann 1984a: 15). This material-cum-causal inter-pretation takes the objectifying language of myth at face value. Instead, says Bultmann, we must understand that the Christian opposition to the 'flesh' criticises a certain way of trying to find security in the world, one in which

the whole sphere of what is visible, available, disposable, and measur-able ... becomes a power over us insofar as we make it the foundation of our lives by living 'according to it,' that is, by succumbing to the temptation to live out of what is visible and disposable instead of out of what is invisible and nondisposable. (Bultmann 1984a: 16)

The kernel of Bultmann's concept of mythic objectification is almost certainly, as Henderson indicates, Martin Heidegger's critique of modern philosophy, and of its 'confusion of the categories of *Vorhandenheit* with those of *Dasein*' (Henderson 1952: 29). Heidegger criticised the Cartesian tradition for attempting to think about human existence (*Dasein*, 'being there') using categories appropriate to the contemplation of thing-like beings that were *Vorhandenheit* ('present-to-hand'). The result is an enormous conceptual confusion that develops because Descartes 'takes the Being of "Dasein" ... in the very same way as he takes the Being of the *res extensa* – namely, as substance' (Heidegger 1962: 131). Because of Descartes's error, there arises a picture of the self as an entity composed of two substances, *res cogitans* and *res extensa*, which are in some mysterious causal inter-relation. What was true for Heidegger of modern Cartesian philosophy and science is also true for Bultmann of Christian mythological thinking. Bultmann's demythologising programme calls for 'an understanding of scripture that is free of every world picture projected by objectifying thinking, whether it is that of myth or that of science' (Bultmann 1984b: 102). Heidegger's philosophy will clear away the scientific-philosophical misunderstanding of man; Bultmann's 'demythologising' will purge theology of the propensity to misunderstand the scriptural expression of existential phenomena as statements about the world of things.

The relevance of Bultmann's demythologising programme to Laing's work becomes apparent when one notices just how many of the case studies in *The Divided Self* claim to interpret the content (rather than the form) of a psychotic utterance as a statement about the patient's existential position. For instance, 'a schizophrenic may say that he is made of glass' (Laing 1965: 37): this Laing takes to mean that the patient experiences himself as having 'such transparency and fragility that a look directed at him splinters him to bits and penetrates straight through him' (Laing 1965: 37). Or, to take another example, 'Fire may be the uncertain flickering of the individual's own inner aliveness ... Some psychotics say in the acute phase that they are on fire' (Laing 1965: 45). Patients in Laing's studies also transpose existential concepts into biological as well as thing-like categories. Both modes of objectification are apparent when 'depersonalized patients ... speak of having murdered their selves and also of having lost or been robbed of their selves' (Laing 1965: 149): in the first instance, selfhood is thought of as biological life; in the second, it is conceived of as a possession that may be misplaced or stolen.

Laing's reflections upon such examples frequently invoke a hermeneutic identical with that developed by Bultmann. Such delusional statements, Laing remarks, are 'literally true within the terms of reference of the individual who makes them', but despite their literal falsity (to us, at any rate), they may nonetheless contain 'existential truth' (Laing 1965: 149). In one case study (that of a man who claimed, with literal falsity, never to have had sex with his wife), Laing refers to

> a loss of the sense of the realness of the Kinsey Report reality so total that the individual expresses the 'existential' truth about himself with the same matter-of-factness that we employ about facts that can be consensually validated in a shared world. (Laing 1965: 87)

'Julie', the subject of the lengthy concluding chapter of *The Divided Self*, also ends up in a similar relation to seemingly objective statements:

> [i]f she began by accusing her mother of never having let her live, in an existential sense, she ended by talking and acting more than half as though her mother had, in a legal sense, actually murdered an actual child. (Laing 1965: 193)

The presence of Bultmann's concept of objectification in this case study is unmistakable. Laing claims, for instance, that '[t]he existential truth in Julie's delusions was that her own true possibilities were being smothered, strangled, murdered' (Laing 1965: 193). Similarly, when Julie feels her sense of separateness is dissolved because she and Laing have the same thoughts, then '[t]he completely psychotic expression of this was to accuse me of having her brains in my head' (Laing 1965: 199). For the adjective 'psychotic' in this quotation, one could quite fairly substitute the word 'mythological' or 'objectified'. A schizophrenic patient such as Julie, who 'convert[s] existential truth into physical facts' (Laing 1965: 193), is, to Laing, a living scripture: to understand her, we must look through her naïvely objectifying, mythological utterances, to find their existential meaning and validity.

Allan Beveridge has carefully examined many of Laing's original clinical notes and draft material from the 1950s for the studies and vignettes that were eventually published in *The Divided Self* and in later works such as *Wisdom, Madness and Folly*. Julie was an in-patient at Gartnavel Hospital with whom Laing spent about 250 hours over 180 interviews, endeavouring to interpret her apparently incomprehensible speech (Beveridge 2011: 238). Amongst other approaches (such as psychoanalysis), 'Laing tried to decode Julie's mad utterances as statements about her existential predicament' (Beveridge 2011: 245). But, as Beveridge argues, both the validity of Laing's interpretations and their therapeutic benefits are unclear. Laing had acquired an enormous quantity of notes from his interviews, leading Beveridge to ask: did Laing 'highlight passages that fitted with his theory and ignore those that did not fit or were simply incomprehensible?' (Beveridge 2011: 246). Furthermore, alongside retrospective selection, Laing may also have co-constructed Julie's narrative in their interactions: 'Julie's comments were not made in a vacuum but in response to his interjections, which were informed by his concept of schizophrenia' (Beveridge 2011: 246). Moreover, there is 'no evidence that Julie improved or left hospital' (Beveridge 2011: 246) – which leaves unclear what the benefit was to Julie of her supposed existential self-clarification. There are no doubt multiple explanations, including personal ambition, for Laing's self-portrayal as 'the hero-therapist who alone possessed an understanding of the patient' (Beveridge 2011: 247). But the psychiatrist's dedication to hermeneusis, and in good part to a latently demythologising approach, displays clearly the extent of his investment in a theological tradition of inquiry into recondite meaning.

Alongside the demythologisation of the content of schizophrenic speech, there exists another unspoken genealogical line from Bultmann's theology to Laing's conceptualisation of mental illness. Many of Laing's case studies in *The Divided Self* discuss patients who experience themselves as divided between a true, inner, mental self, and a false, outer, bodily self. There is no single provenance for Laing's exploration of such 'schizoid' self-division: there are already various well-established relations between Laing's ideas and the philosophical and psychoanalytic context from which he emerged. One clearly attested source for Laing's account of the schizoid false-self system is, for instance, the object relations psychoanalytic theory developed by D. W. Winnicott (1896–1971). From the 1940s onward, Winnicott had argued that the mother's empathetic identification with her infant was necessary in order for the latter to develop a secure sense of self. In his 1960 paper, 'Ego distortion in terms of True and False Self', Winnicott summarises his views:

> It is because of this [empathetic] identification with her infant that she knows how to hold her infant, so that the infant starts by existing and not by reacting. Here is the origin of the True Self which cannot become a reality without the mother's specialized relationship, one which might be described by a common word: devotion. (Winnicott 1965: 148)

Laing certainly knew of Winnicott's work, even though he later tried to downplay its influence upon him. In biographical interviews with Bob Mullan, Laing claims that

> before I went down to London, when I was writing *The Divided Self*, Winnicott was not a major figure in my intellectual horizon, with *his* notion of false self and true self. Maybe I *should* have given him more credit, but I didn't think so. Mine was more a translation of the Heideggerian notions of authentic and unauthentic. (Mullan 1995: 152)

Laing's statement is misleading, and an example of his tendency to deny all but his favoured Continental antecedents. Heidegger, unlike Winnicott, had nothing to say on the importance of a facilitating environment to the infant's development of an authentic self. Winnicott has a great deal to say, and Laing certainly borrows some of it. A footnote in Chapter Six of *The Divided Self*, 'The false-self system', explicitly refers to Winnicott, as well as to the earlier object relations theory of W. R. D. Fairbairn (Laing 1965: 94n). Winnicott's thinking (and perhaps that of Macmurray as well) provides much of the psychoanalytic conceptualisation that Laing brings to his extended relationship with Julie. Laing gives a lengthy account of Julie's infancy as described by her parents, grafting his ensuing Winnicottian analysis onto a philosophical discourse in which she is described as 'an existentially dead child' (Laing 1965: 183). As Beveridge remarks, Laing approached Julie's narrative 'with a preconceived theory ... that links early infant experience to the later development of schizophrenia' (Beveridge 2011: 243).

While acknowledging these sources, one should not entirely discount Laing's stated dependence upon existential ideas. He enters in the bibliography of *The Divided Self* (Laing 1965: 207), but for some reason does not directly cite, the 1956 English-language edition of Bultmann's *Primitive Christianity in its Contemporary Setting* (Bultmann 1956). Despite this rather glancing acknowledgement, the peculiar condition of the schizoid in Laing's work often parallels the spiritual path analysed by Bultmann in his chapter from *Primitive Christianity* on 'The Stoic ideal of the wise man'. The modern spiritual plague, Bultmann thought, was to try to achieve security through instrumental mastery of the world. But there is also another mistaken path to security: this is the path pursued by the Stoics – or by Epictetus, at least, who provides most of Bultmann's quotations. Rather than advising us to live in the 'flesh' of the disposable, Stoicism counsels, in Bultmann's opinion, that we should flee from the body and the world – it tells us that 'freedom ... means independence of all reality, external to the subject' (Bultmann 1956: 143). Instead of trying to master the world, and to achieve security through (for instance) technological power, the Stoic accepts his helplessness before fate, and recognises that the greater part of his existence is subject to forces beyond his control. For the Stoic, security and freedom can be found only in 'our inner life – our imagination, our desire and will. Everything else is beyond our control, all that confronts us from outside, even our own bodies, every external situation in life, every blow of fate that strikes us' (Bultmann 1956: 138). He who is of the body, on the other hand, is bound (so the Stoic believes, in Bultmann's exegesis) to the contingencies of the physical and social world, of other things and other persons:

> Those who become slaves to their own bodies and to the powers and persons to which bodies are subject, are vulnerable to misfortune and suffering. If, however, they are inwardly free, nothing can assail them. All external evils are reduced to the level of indifference, like all external goods. (Bultmann 1956: 138)

Although Bultmann's account of Stoicism is now rather outdated, his idea of the Stoic (or, in psychiatric parlance, 'schizoid') separation of mind from body as an understandable choice (as opposed to an incomprehensible process) seems to have inspired Laing. The similarities between Bultmann and Laing are apparent when the latter discusses the false-self system as a rational decision, rather than as the psychopathological result of early personal relations. The Scottish psychiatrist believes that a particular decision has been made by some of the patients that he encounters. Rather than risk the self in the world of commitment, the schizoid personality has chosen to withdraw from every action, even though this only further imperils his own selfhood: '"All that you can see is not me", he says to himself. But only in and through all that we do see can he be anyone (in reality)' (Laing 1965: 37). The Stoic pattern emerges most clearly in *Wisdom, Madness, and Folly*, where Laing discusses the plight of 'David', a young patient who was in his care during the 1950s:

> His body: this place of rage, terror, desire and despair. This place of life, which is too harrowing and too fraught with too many conflicts and contradictions that entangle him, that he cannot resolve or transcend. What does he do? He withdraws from his body. He dissociates himself from it. He refuses to *be* it, live it, inhabit it, permeate it with himself. (Laing 1998: 147–8)

Laing emphasises that this withdrawal is not an involuntary mental mechanism but rather a course of action in which 'a process in which he originally felt himself to be the passive victim is *now* the outcome of his own action on his own experience' (Laing 1998: 148).

It may seem unlikely that Laing should draw upon Bultmann's rendering of Stoic philosophy in order to provide a paradigm of mental illness. After all, '[t]he Stoics … treated Socrates' life as a virtual paradigm of Stoic wisdom's practical realization, and … were especially impressed by accounts of Socrates' fortitude, self-control, and imperviousness to physical and emotional stress' (Long 2002: 68). How can the patients who interest Laing be compared to Socrates, the master of rational dialogue and founder of the Western philosophical tradition? Leaving aside any evidence for Socrates' actual mental health, there are two responses that may be made. The first is that Laing was not above diagnosing Western philosophy as psychopathological: in an interview with Mullan, he claims, 'I developed an idea that I never fully developed in writing that, with the Descartian [i.e. Cartesian] split, the mainstream western thinking had developed a psychopathological streak' (Mullan 1995: 112). The second is that Laing seems only to be drawing upon Stoicism as a model for the schizoid personality, rather than for the full-blown schizophrenic. The Socratic paradigm does not threaten this analogy: Fairbairn, for instance, argues that schizoid persons 'are often more inclined to construct intellectual systems of an elaborate kind than to develop emotional relationships with others on a human basis' (Fairbairn

1994i: 21). It is almost definitive of the schizoid that such introversion should lead to a corresponding intensification of the intellect.

Laing has been accused of mythologising schizophrenia by romanticising it as a journey or quest of masculine discovery and psychic exploration (Showalter 1987: 230). However, it is more accurate to say that Laing's original intention was to demythologise schizophrenia by employing upon psychotic speech essentially the same existential interpretation as that proposed by Bultmann for the understanding of scripture. The schizoid patient, at least as represented in *The Divided Self*, is stuck in the same spiritual impasse as the Stoic 'wise man'. A schizoid who reaches an existential crisis may express his withdrawal from embodied existence in objectifying language (for example, by claiming he is a ghost, or has killed himself), and may thereby be diagnosed as schizophrenic:

> A man says he is dead but he *is* alive. But his 'truth' is that he is dead. He expresses it perhaps in the only way common (i.e. the communal) sense allows him. He means that he is 'really' and quite 'literally' dead, not merely symbolically or 'in a sense' or 'as it were', and is seriously bent on communicating his truth. The price, however, to be paid for transvaluating the communal truth in this manner is to 'be' mad, for the only *real* death *we* recognize is biological death. (Laing 1965: 37–8)

Laing's depiction in *The Divided Self* of such a clinical situation is therefore bleak: psychotic patient and clinician simply talk past each other. Each objectifies existential issues and crises: the patient employs a mythological mode of discourse that he himself takes for literal truth; to this attempted self-disclosure, the psychiatrist applies various neurological, physiological and (in Laing's day) psychoanalytic discourses, and so further reifies what the patient is trying to communicate. The situation is analogous to that of a conversation between a Biblical literalist and a modern scientist: the former cannot express the Biblical proclamation except as literal, mythologised statements; the latter can only listen with bafflement to these irrational, superstitious and unscientific outpourings, and wonder what causality is at work in the mind of the literalist.

Conclusion

Brown's use of the phrase 'discursive bereavement' (Brown 2009: 183) in his account of the 'sudden and culturally violent event' (Brown 2009: 176) that, in his view, constituted post-war British secularisation, seems to imply that traditional discursive Christianity simply disappeared. The Davidson Clinic, however, belies this apparent assumption: the varied ideologies and practices of Christian psychotherapy were quite clearly a way of continuing the life-narrative patterns of discursive Christianity (and were no doubt on a par with Christian psychologies and psychotherapies elsewhere in Britain (see Richards 2011: 71–88)). However,

while the Davidson Clinic's brand of psychotherapy could ally itself with
the social activism of the post-war Church of Scotland, it did not find a
secure organisational and ideological niche. The Clinic's initial organisational alliance with the Davidson Church in Edinburgh ended within
two years of its opening because of the Church's closure and the consequent departure of the minister Roy Hogg, 'who was largely instrumental for the initiation of the Clinic by the association of himself and
the kirk session with the Board of Governors' ('Davidson Clinic' 1943).
The Church of Scotland's concern with spiritual healing in the 1950s
allowed a brief period of ideological and organisational alignment, but
healing was never sufficiently mainstream as to provide safe harbour
for the Clinic, which was forced to find its own way financially, and to
build ad hoc alliances with sympathetic clergy. Indeed, there was explicit
opposition to the project of Christianised psychotherapy from conserva-
tive clergy, who disputed the cultural authority of psychotherapy, particularly over issues of sexual morality. In a 1963 article for *Life and Work*
entitled 'Freud – or the New Testament', Donald Robertson repudiates
the psychotherapeutic re-interpretation of Christianity. Robertson, who
speaks as 'one who did accept far too much of the Freudian way of life'
(Robertson 1963), diagnoses psychoanalysis as a fad born of Modernist
crisis, and as a condonement of sin (verging, moreover, on casuistry and
antinomianism):

> When days of confusion followed the First World War, out of the smoke
> appeared a new figure with ideas of promise. I mean Freud. He fitted
> the time. He dealt with sin and guilt in a new way. Analysis and explain-
> ing away was the road to release. Guilt on account of moral defeat was
> false, and defeat in any case was not our fault; it stemmed from our
> childhood and from 'trauma' due to self-conscious ignorance. A little
> frankness at the right moment would prevent subsequent conflict and
> release the inner personality for a life of fullness and freedom.
>
> If in that life came adultery or sodomy or lesbianism we were not to
> be too much upset. It was not mortal sin but a cathartic experience,
> perhaps in our very special case almost right. (Robertson 1963)

In his polemic against 'Freud and his disciples, Jung and Adler' (Robertson
1963), Robertson also dismisses the scriptural re-interpretation that had
accompanied the emphasis on a supposedly authentic Christianity of love,
tolerance and healing: 'We were told that Jesus really believed almost this,
and it was Paul who had led the Church astray' (Robertson 1963).

Moreover, the Davidson Clinic, as noted above, was marginal to medical
psychotherapy, and indeed was the object of scepticism from the Edinburgh
academic establishment. In a 1948 letter to *The Scotsman*, James Drever, the
head of the Psychology department at Edinburgh University, rebuts what
he sees as the implication of an earlier fundraising letter that the Davidson
Clinic is the sole provider of psychotherapy in the city:

Anyone reading the letter which appeared this morning might well suppose that we have in Edinburgh only one group of psychothera- pists. This is not by any means the case. Sir David Henderson's Unit at Jordanburn and the Child Guidance Clinic at Merchiston Park, as well as a number of private practitioners, all deal, as does the Davidson Clinic, with the less serious types of mental ill-health. (Drever 1948)

Drever also takes issue with a possible suggestion of somatic healing in the Davidson's claim that anxiety is a 'complicating' factor in tuberculosis and cancer: 'Does this mean that anxiety causes tuberculosis and cancer, or that sufferers from tuberculosis and cancer are anxious? The latter is probably true, but I doubt if analysis would help' (Drever 1948).

The eventual closure of the Clinic did not mean that the psychothera- peutic rebirth of discursive Christianity was entirely lost. The Clinic also facilitated the formation of the Scottish Pastoral Association (SPA), an ini- tiative partly informed by the involvement of Margaret Allan (1893–1965), the deaconess of the Church of Scotland who was, from 1941 to 1962 (*Annual Report* 1962: 8), seconded to the Davidson Clinic as a lay analyst (P. S. 1965: 2), and who had earlier received analysis at the Tavistock (Darroch 1973: 6–7). Although the SPA had ceased to exist as a distinct organisa- tion by 1975 (Lyall 2010: 154), its journal *Contact*, which began in 1960, still exists, although it is now known as *Practical Theology* (Lyall 2010: 151). The formation of the Scottish Pastoral Association, and successors such as *Contact/Practical Theology* and the Scottish Association for Pastoral Care and Counselling, indicates a degree of enduring success for the Davidson Clinic's mission, although – as will be shown (see p. 139) – pastoral counsel- ling tends to a rather more cautious, dialogic approach to the relationship between psychotherapy and Christianity. In a more integrative mode, the 'Clinical Theology' devised by Frank Lake (Peters 1989, Lake 1966), which is roughly contemporary with these developments, offers a much stronger sense of identity between Christianity and psychotherapy. Elements of Laing's therapies and theories find correspondences in Lake's activities as the Director of the Clinical Theology Centre in Nottingham, and founder, in 1962, of the Clinical Theology Association (Peters 1989: 10). Lake, like Laing, experimented with the use of LSD in therapy – albeit far earlier, in 1954 (Lake 1966: xix). He also similarly argued that mental illness could be a transformative spiritual experience that required therapeutic guidance: confronted by 'the birth pangs of the spirit', the clinical theologian was called upon 'to give wise pilotage to souls in danger of foundering' (Lake 1966: xxvii). Lake also came to argue, much like Laing (Burston 1996: 126–8), that one could remember traumatic experiences from one's foetal existence – a belief for which Lake was severely taken to task by his critics (Lyall 1991: xiv, Peters 1989: 67–71).

The degree of interaction between Lake and Laing is as yet uncertain. There are certainly commonalities, but it may be that these indicate a shared genealogy rather than a significant interaction between the two. Lake had many of the same theological and psychoanalytic influences as Laing: the former's *Clinical Theology* (Lake 1966) contains references to Martin Buber, Macmurray, Fairbairn, Winnicott and others who were also known to the Scottish psychiatrist. However, it can be established that Laing encountered Lake in the early 1960s, and used the opportunity to expound what he saw as the theological roots of his own psychiatry. In a letter dated 28 June 1963, Lake thanks Laing for his contribution to a recent conference:

> so many of us being familiar with your books, there was a groundwork of familiarity with your line of approach. But none of us had any idea of its spiritual dimensions, if I can use that word. You made us think very deeply about the Biblical roots of so many of the realities to which you alluded so challengingly. (Letter, Lake to Laing, 28 June 1963: 1)

Lake clearly hoped the dialogue between his Christian theology and Laing's psychiatry would continue. On 19 September of the following year, he tries (perhaps unsuccessfully) to entice Laing with the promise of an upcoming conference on the connection between 'hystero-schizoid "breakdown"' and the 'twin aspects of "the negative way" – as they are manifest in the apophatic theology of orthodox Christian mysticism and in St John of the Cross's Dark Night' (Letter, Lake to Laing, 19 September 1964: 1). Laing's psychotherapy, however, was soon to find a more eclectic, New Age context in which its Christian genealogy would be strategically obscured.

CHAPTER THREE

Scottish Psychotherapy in the New Age

The Australian actor, Diane Cilento (1933–2011), records in her auto-biography how in 1960s London she met 'R. D. Laing, an iconoclastic Scottish psychiatrist and author of an astonishingly astute book called *The Politics of Experience*' (Cilento 2006: 234). Cilento was at the time married to another Scotsman who had relocated to London, namely the actor Sean Connery (b. 1930), whose fame in the role of James Bond far outshone even Laing's celebrity. Cilento, who came to believe 'fervently' in the ideas of *Politics* (Cilento 2006: 244), was inspired by Laing's therapeutic use of LSD (including allegedly with Connery (Cilento 2006: 235)) to later attempt her 'first guided LSD trip, which had a profound effect upon me' (Cilento 2006: 306). This spiritual technology for mystical experience not only effected a deep, personal transformation, it was also to Cilento a 'sacred matter' which revealed 'something beyond this material world' (Cilento 2006: 306).

This chapter explores the development of a psychotherapeutic 'New Age' spirituality from the earlier discourses and practices of Scottish Christian psychotherapy. (The term 'New Age', denoting an eclectic, mobile and subjectively authorised contemporary religiosity, is admittedly problematic (e.g. Chryssides 2012: 247–8), and a number of difficulties with it will be explored.) Laing's trajectory illustrates well the popularisation of a nar-rative of breakdown and breakthrough (or *metanoia*) as a means to the discovery of an authentic, self-directed life. But there are also significant New Age discourses and practices in the later work of Winifred Rushforth, as well as in the early ideological co-ordinates of the Wellspring Centre in Edinburgh, a successor organisation to the Davidson Clinic. While the model of 'Self-spirituality' is useful to understanding these varied phenom-ena, there are diverse trends and currents, which complicate any attempted univocal account of the psychotherapeutic spirituality which grows out of Scottish Christian psychotherapy.

R. D. Laing's mystical Self-spirituality

Laing's personal library demonstrates his interest in contemplative, mysti-cal experience, with titles such as Daniel Goleman's *The Varieties of Meditative Experience* (Sp Coll Laing 565), or Robert E. L. Masters's *The Varieties of Psychedelic Experience* (Sp Coll Laing 402). Laing also owned Alister Hardy's *The Spiritual Nature of Man* (Sp Coll Laing 1890), based on results from the 'Religious Experience Research Unit' at Oxford (Hardy 1979: vii), and even John M. Allegro's *The Sacred Mushroom and the Cross* (Sp Coll Laing 1051), which claims that primitive Christianity was a psychedelic mushroom cult. A key twentieth-century mystical theologian in the United Kingdom was Evelyn Underhill (1875–1941), whose lengthy and commercially successful book, *Mysticism* (1911), Laing owned in a 1960 reprint (Sp Coll Laing 1859). (As a measure of Underhill's success, it may be noted that Laing's copy was based on the 1930 twelfth edition, which by 1960 had already undergone eight reprints.) Laing's manuscript annotations on the back flyleaf show that he had acquired his copy by December 1964, and his underlining and other marks indicate that he closely read its first part on 'The Mystic Fact'. According to Underhill, in a passage marked by Laing, the mystic's experience consists in 'the finding of a "way out" or a "way back" to some desirable state in which alone they can satisfy their craving for absolute truth' (Underhill 1960: 3). For Underhill, the purest form of mystical experience is the mystic fusion, or 'Unitive State', described in a passage underlined and asterisked by Laing: 'Living union with this One ... is arrived at by an arduous psychological and spiritual process – the so-called Mystic Way – entailing the complete remaking of character and the liberation of a new, or rather latent, form of consciousness' (Underhill 1960: 81).

Underhill's discourse typifies the mysticism that Laing adopts in *The Politics of Experience*, his 1967 bestseller, where he argues that 'transcendental experience' is a mode of interior life prohibited in contemporary Western culture, despite being, in his view, 'the original well-spring of all religions' (Laing 1967: 112). In its account of a perennial philosophy transcending creed and culture, *Politics* offers a somewhat conventional mystical distinction between 'the phenomenal *ego*' and 'a non-phenomenal, eternal self' (Happold 1970: 20), as well as a further supposition that the 'organ or faculty' for 'discerning spiritual truth' is 'to a great extent atrophied and exist[s] only potentially in most men' (Happold 1970: 21). According to Laing, if the '"ego" is broken up, or destroyed (by the insurmountable contradictions of certain life situations, by toxins, chemical changes, etc.)' (Laing 1967: 115), then there may be a recovery of transcendental experience, accompanied by 'liberation and renewal' of the self (Laing 1967: 110) – a short-cut, as it were, along the 'Mystic Way'. By drawing upon the psychoanalytic tradition, Laing gives his own account of the mystical faculty's supposed atrophy, and the phenomenal ego's concomitant ascendancy. Contemporary socialisation suppresses or represses mystical experience: 'We live in a secular world. To adapt to this world the child abdicates its ecstasy' (Laing 1967: 118). Freud's great insight – Laing claims – is that 'the *ordinary* person is a shrivelled, desiccated fragment of what a person can be' (Laing 1967: 22) because of psychoanalytic processes such as 'repression, denial, splitting, projection, introjection and other forms of destructive action on experience' (Laing 1967: 23–4). As Daniel Burston explains, Laing argues in *Politics* that '[w]hat is repressed among normal people ... are not merely instincts (Freud), nor the memory of specific events or losses and the feelings and phantasies engendered by them, but whole modalities and possibilities of experience and relatedness to others' (Burston 2000: 105). Prime amongst these modalities, to Laing, is mystical experience.

By combining mystical theology and psychoanalytic theory, Laing provides a psychotherapeutically inflected form of what Paul Heelas calls New Age 'Self-spirituality' (Heelas 1996: 2), a contemporary non-traditional religiosity which holds sacred the cultivation of a higher, more authentic self. Although 'New Age' belief (as the term itself hints) was originally millenialist and apocalyptic, it was 'recast as a humanistic project of spiritual growth and self-realisation' during the 1960s (Sutcliffe 2003: 117). Heelas's account addresses this later, less rigorously bounded formation. His ideal type of New Age belief offers three focal characteristics (Heelas 1996: 18–20): (1) we are imperfect insofar as we are brainwashed or indoctrinated by mainstream socialisation; (2) perfection is reached via cultivation or breakthrough to the Higher Self, and replacement/displacement of the socialised ego; (3) the conventional ego may be overcome by some kind of spiritual technology or discipline. Self-spirituality thereby 'explains why life – as conventionally experienced – is not what it should be; it provides an account of what it is to find perfection; and it provides the means for obtaining salvation' (Heelas 1996: 18). The Laingian correspondences, as detailed above, are: (1) the destruction of experience via psychoanalytically theorised processes; (2) the credo of a fully experiencing self underlying the ego; (3) conventional psychotherapy, as well as the curative breakdown of so-called *metanoia* (whether spontaneous, or artificially induced by means such as LSD). In Laing's New Age discourse, the capacity for mystical experience both indicates and facilitates the subject's achievement of the Higher Self.

As the example of Diane Cilento indicates, Laing's theory and method were employed, and consumed, in the countercultural milieu by agents who were not mentally ill in any obvious clinical sense, but who were open instead to a technology of spiritual regeneration. According to Cilento, Connery was one of these consumers of Laing's services:

> On the first encounter, Laing gave Sean a tab of pure LSD, taking about a tenth of that amount himself. It was his standard procedure with patients he felt were emotionally blocked. No-one was privy to what happened over the next six hours but I believe that, with his enormous reserve and armouring, Sean resisted the drug. As a consequence, he had to go to bed for several days to recover. Still, it seems that this initial trip opened a Pandora's box. Suddenly, Sean began to remember challenging childhood scenes with his mother or father. Buried anger, victories or defeats came tumbling out without warning. (Cilento 2006: 235)

Connery has never provided his own narrative of the alleged encounter, and so Cilento's account must be treated with caution. He reappears, though, in the autobiography of the Irish author Edna O'Brien (b. 1930), where she recounts her experience of an acid trip with Laing. O'Brien takes LSD with Laing in London in May 1970 after being a patient of his for six months, and despite being advised by Connery that his trip with Laing had had 'its freight of terrors' (O'Brien 2013: 190). O'Brien's reasons for seeking therapy with Laing are definitely non-clinical: although she refers to her 'divided self', this seems to be a somewhat mundane sense of division between her solitary vocation as a writer and her entanglement in the London social scene (O'Brien 2013: 187). More pertinently, the trip offers greater intimacy with Laing, and the promise of enhanced creative powers: 'A secret part of me longed to be nearer to Laing and another part of me believed, from various literature I had read, that my dreams and therefore my writing would be enriched' (O'Brien 2013: 190). O'Brien's ambivalence towards Laing ('half Lucifer, half Christ' (O'Brien 2013: 183)) is clear. During her trip, Laing metamorphoses into 'a rat, an executive rat, trussed inside a suit with a collar and tie' (O'Brien 2013: 190). O'Brien's LSD experience defies easy summary, but the narrative imagery implies that she is, as it were, a woman giving birth to herself:

> At one point he [Laing] picked the huge gilt mirror off the wall and showed me my purple-faced, mad-eyed, gyrating self. I broke water as when I had given birth, cascades of it gushing out of me, and yet I could not feel any damp on the floor that I knelt on. (O'Brien 2013: 190)

Laing leaves O'Brien partway through her trip, so she is unattended in her flat until Sean Connery and the Canadian writer Ted Allan come round to check on her (O'Brien 2013: 191). They look after her until she retires to bed 'tired in body and in mind, having lived many lives in less than twenty-four hours' (O'Brien 2013: 192). O'Brien is eventually sent, to her annoyance, a large bill for Laing's services, which include his advice that her trip and subsequent flashbacks involve glimpses of her past lives (O'Brien 2013: 196). Despite these caveats, O'Brien identifies the trip as 'the dividing line in my life, between one kind of writing and another': 'I owed him [Laing] a debt; he had sent me packing with an opened scream, and that scream would become the pith of the novel I would write' (O'Brien 2013: 197).

Laing's celebration of *metanoia* was thus glossed within a countercultural framework that sought to configure LSD therapy (and psychosis) as a potentially curative journey of breakdown and breakthrough. Yet if one disregards the perennialist rhetoric, and the temporary availability of LSD as a spiritual technology, Laing's doctrines are clearly continuous with ideas propounded by an earlier Christianised psychotherapy (even if the latter could not anticipate the invention of a consumer technology for mystical experience). J. A. C. Murray's 1938 *An Introduction to a Christian Psycho-*

Therapy spells out very similar doctrines around three decades earlier, but within the framework of the reconfigured Christianity associated with the Davidson Clinic (which may explain Rushforth's hope that Laing would return to Scotland as its Medical Director (see p. 72)). Recall Murray's statement that '[j]ust as psychology has charted some of the dark regions of the unconscious mind, so also must a Christian psychology make straight the way for the Faith by adventuring a geography of the superconscious' (Murray 1938: 53). Murray's states of expanded consciousness (which even include psychoactive experiences induced by anaesthetics such as nitrous oxide (Murray 1938: 52)) are marshalled towards their culmination in mysticism: 'Such states of expanded consciousness are clearly nearest of all to that state, which is the especial property of religion, namely, the mystical consciousness of the unseen' (Murray 1938: 55). However, argues Murray, such experiences are systematically suppressed, with the collusion of conventional medical psychotherapy:

> The 'abnormal' who seeks cleansing and readjustment at the hands of the psycho-therapist, discovers in the process that the norm to which he is asked to remould his life is scaled well down to the average unimaginative specimen of the race, to whom vision is a fantasy, and conscience an encumbrance. Life is to be lived with the soft pedal on. (Murray 1938: 10–11)

Murray's proto-Laingian critique of 'normality' disparages 'the scientist whose own inner life has never touched even the hem of such phenomena' (Murray 1938: 10), and elaborates a musical metaphor for the supposed destruction of an irrefragable experiential realm. The conventional Freudian psychotherapist is a 'sublimated piano tuner. Such an one will achieve a certain harmony, but only at the cost of silencing part of the instrument, and even then, the overtones refuse to be stilled' (Murray 1938: 11); on the other hand, true normality 'is achieved when the man is rightly adjusted to God as well as to life, wholly attuned, not only to the still, sad music of humanity, but also to the echoes of eternity' (Murray 1938: 12).

Murray's discourse illuminates the extent to which Laing's *Politics* recycles such ideas, but tones down their Christian genealogy for his audience of countercultural consumers. In *Politics*, Laing argues that those who pass through the natural healing process of psychosis undergo a 'rebirth', encounter 'archetypal mediators of divine power', and eventually achieve a condition in which the ego is 'the servant of the divine' (Laing 1967: 101). This account of psychosis has been explored by Daniel Burston (Burston 2000: 106–8) and Andrew Collier – the latter perceives in *The Politics of Experience*, 'a sort of gnostic idea of an inner self imprisoned in the socially conditioned self and requiring deliverance' (Collier 1977: 184–5). Yet this model of rebirth is also inserted by Laing into a scriptural context. In the draft typescript of a lecture delivered in January 1966, entitled 'Religious experience and the role of organised religion' (Religious experience), Laing sets out his hypothesis that references to 'living water' in John 4: 10, and corresponding baptismal practices, are mythologised, objectified references to the experience of ego loss (the kind of psychic condition so explicitly valorised in *The Politics of Experience*). '[E]xternal water', he argues, is 'the outward and visible symbol' of 'a first level of the ego-loss consciousness, or ego-loss experience, whereby a person, in losing their ego and dying to their old self, becomes immersed in a state of fluidity and flux' (Religious experience: 11). Whatever the plausibility of Laing's scriptural exegesis, its underlying thesis is clear: the psychotic has hit unwittingly upon the lost essence of early Christian religious experience. The role of the therapist is therefore to assist in this conversion or rebirth, precisely because organised religion has lost its insight into the demythologised meaning of 'Living Water' (Religious experience: 10):

> it is essential for the fulfilment of one's humanity after the advent
> of Jesus Christ to die and to be reborn; and I suggest that this is
> what thousands of people are stumbling into, the original experience
> of Christianity. But they don't go to Christianity for any orientation,
> because they find no reference points, as it is mediated to them; and
> if they go to a priest, the priest will refer them to a psychiatrist, and
> the psychiatrist will refer them to a mental hospital, and the mental
> hospital will refer them to the electric shock machine. And if this is
> not our contemporary mode of crucifying Christ, what is? (Religious
> experience: 12)

Laing comes, at least for a time, to view psychotic experience as the manifestation of an authentic, early Christianity. He cannot, in his view, leave the madman to the ministrations of an uncomprehending clergy who are unable to demythologise the psychotic's experience, and who therefore refer him to the scientifically objectifying gaze of the conventional psychiatrist. The Laingian psychiatrist – so this lecture implies – must come forward to provide both guidance and community for these primitive Christians, who otherwise would be martyred with electro-convulsive therapy. Indeed, this is what Laing explicitly claims a few years earlier in his introduction to Morag Coate's *Beyond All Reason* (Coate 1964), a memoir of severe mental illness: 'I hope that theologians, priests and philosophers will see the relevance of this book to them, for here we are brought face to face with the nature of religious experience, albeit mad experience – yet never shorn of human meaning' (Laing 1964: viii). Coate's problem was not her psychotic experience per se, but rather her lack of spiritual guidance: 'If she had been more fortunate, she would have found her guru' (Laing 1964: x).

The practical conclusion from Laing's theories in the mid-1960s is that those who have experienced a baptismal immersion in ego-loss should make themselves available to guide and to commune with those who are undergoing this experience. Some such practical Christianity seems to partly inform Laing's close involvement with the founding of the Philadelphia Association in 1965 and the development of its associated therapeutic community at Kingsley Hall in London. Laing, in a 1975 lecture, explains retrospectively the name of the Philadelphia Association as an 'edifying illusion [*sic*] ... to the third chapter of the Book of Revelations; to the search of the Philadelphians who have been given the open door' (Philadelphia Association: 1). The religious significance of the building in which this open door could be found is striking. Kingsley Hall was originally 'a Baptist church known as Zion Chapel', before becoming an 'alcohol-free public house' that was named in honour of the Christian Socialist and novelist Charles Kingsley (1819–75) (Burston 1996: 78). In the early phase of the building's operation as a therapeutic community, it kept up an association with an '"evangelical black Christian group"', to which Laing 'was not at all averse to preaching on occasion' (Burston 1996: 79). During this time in his professional life, Laing seems to have seen himself 'as some sort of Christ figure' (Burston 1996: 89), who even tried to persuade Aaron Esterson – a Jew, and Laing's collaborator on *Sanity, Madness and the Family* (Laing and Esterson 1964) – to accept Jesus Christ 'into his heart' (Laing 1997: 123). To some extent, Kingsley Hall seems to have been an opportunity for Laing, and some of the residents, to play out his speculations on the original mystic philosophy of Christianity. The celebrated resident, Mary Barnes (1923–2001), for instance, was not directly under Laing's care, but used her stay at Kingsley Hall as a way of pursuing what Adrian Chapman has described as her 'unique version of countercultural Catholicism' in which she 'looks forward, in the end, to moving beyond illusory egoic consciousness into a state of all-encompassing heavenly union' like that promoted by Laing in *Politics* (Chapman 2018).

However, the latency of the Christian genealogy of the Self-spirituality promoted in *Politics* and other Laingian works meant that by the 1980s, Laing could also be an established New Age reference point. In 1982, for example, he corresponded with a US author and editor who invited him (Bates–Laing Correspondence) to write the foreword to an anthology to be called *Voices of New Age Experience*, presumably in homage to Laing's *The Voice of Experience* (Laing 1982). The synopsis and sample material for the (apparently unpublished) book indicate that it was a collection of interviews with people who felt they had undergone some *metanoia*-like process that had resulted in spiritual rebirth. Although Laing declined the invitation, he does not seem to have been hostile to New Age use of his work, having given, for instance, an interview in 1984 to Marc Barasch of *New Age Journal* (who subsequently invited Laing – without success – to write a further article for his periodical (Letter, Barasch to Laing, n.d.)). Barasch's interview (Barasch 1984) covers a variety of familiar themes within Laing's work (such as cultural conditioning and transcendental experience), and appears in an abundant New Age context, amongst articles on corporate whistle-blowing and Aboriginal art, and adverts for health foods, homeopathic remedies, biofeedback devices, massage tables, 'chi pants' and 'aura goggles'.

Yet Laing's New Age and mystical affinities would prove problematic as he attempted later in his career to draw upon the Scottish Christian organisational resources that he had exploited in the 1950s, before his relocation to London. In the early 1980s, Laing tried to renew his relationship with the Iona Community and to draw upon their shared discourse of corporate, incarnational theology. Although MacLeod had relinquished formal leadership of the Iona Community in 1967 (Ferguson 1990: 354), the incarnational and corporate ritual of communion was still prominent in the 1980s. For instance, a supplementary edition of the community's regular magazine, *The Coracle,* from this period (and preserved in the Laing archival materials) declares that '[t]he Iona Community was founded in the belief that we can't be Christians as individuals': 'People are being bidden to a "Great Feast" and the celebration is not just a celebration of human worth but of God's' (Iona Community). Laing's involvement in the 1980s with the Iona Community was at least partly motivated by his role in a protean project – variously called Sanctuary, St Oran's Trust, or simply Oran's Trust – which, according to its fundraising publicity, aimed to 'provide a range of sanctuaries and refuges for anyone who is suffering any form of mental distress' (Oran's Trust L98). Sanctuary seems to have formally begun around May 1984, when its company account was opened (Oran's Trust L127). An undated sheet of typescript, headed 'ST. ORAN' (Oran's Trust L113), shows that by latterly changing the project's name from Sanctuary to (St.) Oran's Trust, an affinity was intended with the Iona Community: 'St. Oran … was one of the companions, who with St. Columba, founded a community on Iona in the mid Sixth Century'; 'On the Isle of Oronsay … Oran founded a sanctuary where people in jeopardy might take refuge' (Oran's Trust L113). One of Laing's visits to Iona may have motivated this sense of affinity with St Oran: in an undated anecdote, Francis Huxley records how Laing, who 'had just come back from Iona', called at his home, and 'after a companionable silence told me he was, as it were, a reincarnation of St Odran [*sic*]' (Huxley 2005: 191).

Just over a year after his August 1983 visit to the Iona Community (recorded in *The Scotsman* (see p. 77)), Laing returned from 24 to 29 September 1984 to lead a week of seminars. In a typescript draft of the Iona Community Abbey Programme, sent to Laing for his approval, the seminar topic is billed as 'BODY, MIND AND SPIRIT': 'R. D. LAING, world-famous psychotherapist and writer will lead this exploration of the relationship between soul and body from the perspective of Christian and other religious traditions' (Programme: [3]). Laing was accompanied by a film crew who video-recorded his seminars, some interviews, and a promotional appeal for Sanctuary (as it was still called). In the latter, Laing refers to 'my old mentor, George MacLeod', and – rather grandiosely – invites 'the Scottish nation led by the churches of Scotland seriously to consider providing sanctuaries for ... people in great mental distress and confusion and terror' (Body, Mind and Spirit WE 8). In the seminar recordings, Laing compares Scotland unfavourably to England, claiming that he knows of no therapeutic communities in Scotland, and relating his proposed project to the 1960s Philadelphia Association community at Kingsley Hall (Body, Mind and Spirit WE 8). Given Laing's apparent re-reading of *Only One Way Left* in the 1980s, his citing of MacLeod's slogans is presumably deliberate. He uses the line (originally from St Teresa of Avila) 'Jesus Christ has no other hands but ours' (Body, Mind and Spirit WE8) – a sentence marked in his personal copy of *Only One Way Left* (MacLeod 1958: 108). He also repeats the well-worn assertion – found in *Only One Way Left* (MacLeod 1958: 63), as well as in Johnson's *Pastoral Ministration* (see p. 76) – that 'the word "healthy" has got the same root' as 'healthy, hale, whole, holy' (Body, Mind and Spirit WE9).

Despite his appeals to the Iona Community's founding theology, Laing antagonises his audience, many of whom feel that his seminars lack substantive content. In due course, the Reverend Donald N. Macdonald (*c*.1939–93), a former Deputy Leader of the Community, appears in response to the 'bad vibes' (Body, Mind and Spirit WE 10). Exactly how Macdonald and Laing first met is unclear, but, as well as appearing during Laing's seminars, Macdonald was also the officiating minister at the funeral of Laing's mother in November 1986 (Laing 1997: 227), and at the funeral service held for Laing in Glasgow after his death in 1989 (Laing 1997: 234). At the latter, Macdonald claimed that Laing had returned to the Church of Scotland during a 1986 visit to Iona (Laing 1997: 234). In 1993, Macdonald also incorporated a brief text by Laing into a collection of essays entitled *Voices from the Edge: Faith in a Post-Christian Scotland* (Macdonald 1993b).

Macdonald's autobiography, *The Less Travelled Way* (1993), provides further evidence that Laing's Self-spirituality was part of a longer Scottish and UK Christian history. Although Macdonald was born and raised in the Western Isles of Scotland in a Gaelic-speaking community, he was educated, like Laing, in the University of Glasgow, where he was similarly an enthusiastic participant in 'the Corporate Life', 'an existence beyond text books and classrooms' (Macdonald 1993a: 30–1). Like Laing (Laing 1998: 79), he attended in the 1950s one of the rallies led in Glasgow by the US evangelist, Billy Graham (1918–2018). Unlike Laing, Macdonald was successfully converted (Macdonald 1993a: 35). Macdonald studied for the ministry, and began a controversial career ministering to urban and inner-city parishes, while also working as a journalist in print, radio and television. His discourse exhibits the same theological contrast found in Laing's work. Much of his autobiography details work in the community demanded by an incarnational, corporate theology, and epitomised by a trope of communion, 'the Great Supper' (Macdonald 1993a: 43). Communion, for Macdonald, is a pastoral as well as a liturgical duty: he shares a drink with a gangster to establish an unofficial treaty limiting youth crime; he buys a drink for an old sailor who recalls a disastrous Second World War convoy; and while describing two extra worshippers at formal church Communion, an impoverished singer and a tramp, he exclaims, 'How I would have enjoyed a Supper with them. It might have turned out a True Thanksgiving' (Macdonald 1993a: 50). Yet, coupled with Macdonald's promotion of communion, is a distinct, Laing-tinged defence of extraordinary subjective experience – particularly of the so-called precognitive 'second sight' found in Scottish Gaelic folklore. Macdonald invokes Laing as 'perhaps the greatest Scottish intellectual of this century' (Macdonald 1993a: 84), and argues that 'transcendental and extra-sensory perceptions' (Macdonald 1993a: 82) comprise 'a dimension of our humanity that needs to be rescued and regained' (Macdonald 1993a: 85). As well as claiming to have psychically foreseen the 1993 wrecking of the *Braer* oil tanker in Shetland, Macdonald laments that 'the churches seem unable to mine' Scotland's supposed 'rich residual seam of transcendental need' (Macdonald 1993a: 74).

Macdonald interviews Laing towards the end of the 1984 Iona seminars. The interview, which was recorded both on video and audio tape, exhibits the tension between Laing's New Age mystical Self-spirituality and his competing allegiance to the communion paradigm. During his seminars, Laing has made comments consonant with the latter: 'Christ is among us, this Healthy Spirit is in us, ... whenever two or three people are gathered together in the name of Christ' (Body, Mind and Spirit WE 9). And, during his interview with Macdonald (which was also separately audio-recorded), Laing affirms his Christianity, describing himself as having completed (in Macdonald's phrase) a 'pilgrimage to faith again' (Macdonald Interview; Body, Mind and Spirit WE 10). Yet competing allegiances soon begin to appear. As Laing describes how the Gospels dispelled his teenage melancholia, he takes issue with Macdonald's vocabulary: Laing's declaration, 'that's not an assumption that's a direct experience' (Macdonald Interview; Body, Mind and Spirit WE 10), changes the terms of reference from belief or faith to mystical or spiritual experience. In due course, the technology of New Age Self-spirituality already seen, for instance, in the narratives of Cilento and O'Brien re-appears as Laing celebrates drug-induced transcendental (and discarnate) experience. Anyone who wants to know 'what an Out of Body Experience is like' can take 'katamine [*sic*; Laing means "ketamine"]' by finding a 'friendly vet', and determining the correct dosage by reading the psychedelic works of John Lilly (Macdonald Interview; Body, Mind and Spirit WE 10). Macdonald takes issue with Laing's spiritual claims for a *quantum sufficit* of horse tranquiliser, asking, in clear irritation, 'can you really say that a drug-induced experience like that is a real experience?', and describing it as far from 'a natural part of the human condition' (Macdonald Interview; Body, Mind and Spirit WE 10). An audience member (not visible to camera) far more directly expresses his or her disapproval by immediately and very audibly leaving the room.

Macdonald's criticism is not theologically naïve. The tendency to conflate mystical experience, hallucinogenic drug experience, and also psychotic experience, had been robustly criticised by theologians such as R. C. Zaehner (Zaehner 1957) in his rejoinder to Aldous Huxley's promotion of mescaline as a facilitator of mystical experience in *The Doors of Perception* (Huxley 1954). Furthermore, as these tensions on Iona indicate, Laing's brand of New Age mysticism could not easily harmonise with his other theological allegiances – for it was often implicitly, and sometimes explicitly, in tension with the paradigm of communion. Although MacLeod seemingly believed (like Laing's father) 'in the presence of angels' (Ferguson 1990: 321), he maintained that mysticism, such as Underhill's 'unitive experience' (MacLeod 1958: 153), was 'alien to the incarnation faith' (MacLeod 1958: 152). Since 'holiness is to be found in the encounters of daily life' (MacLeod 1958: 68), experiences such as mystic fusion are delusory: 'To be "lost in God", for the Christian, is not to enter some mystic trance but to be rightly involved in community' (MacLeod 1958: 63). Indeed, Laing was familiar with MacLeod's position. In his personal copy of *Only One Way Left*, he marks a passage in which MacLeod deprecates mystical experience: 'God is not directly discerned but mediated through other people; and that it is only at the level of fellowship that we can come to know God' (MacLeod 1958: 60). Laing is wedded both to MacLeod's theology and to mysticism – and the latter, according to Underhill, is 'in no way concerned with adding to, exploring, re-arranging, or improving anything in the visible universe' (Underhill 1960: 81).

This theological tension can also be extrapolated to a corresponding difficulty in Laing's psychiatry. Laing had – in theory, at any rate – a way of reconciling his New Age, mystical psychotherapeutic trajectory with his commitment to community and the supposed holiness of everyday life. This was via the principle of so-called '*epistemological experiential anarchy*' within the therapeutic community, by which one refused to trespass on the subjectivity of others so long as they, in turn, refrained from '*transgressive conduct*' (Laing 1998: 29). In practice, however, it was much harder to separate inner experience from outer action – or inaction. In Laing's Philadelphia Association community at Kingsley Hall in London during the 1960s, 'Basic functions like shopping, cooking, and cleaning up were done poorly, irregularly, and sometimes not at all' (Burston 1996: 80). This account is corroborated by Mary Barnes's narrative of her spiritual regeneration, which, as Adrian Chapman points out,

> presents a household beset by quite ordinary problems, despite its ostensibly experimental and radical focus, and despite the dangerousness of Barnes' plight. How do the bills get paid? Who is in charge? How far can one person be allowed to pursue their course if it troubles others? (Chapman 2018)

Had the Sanctuary project succeeded, it would likely have been beset by similar problems: a community, especially of the mentally ill, which accepted the psychedelic use of ketamine might well have found difficulty enforcing the washing-up rota. To borrow Zaehner's question to Huxley, 'if mescalin can produce the Beatific Vision here on earth', 'how on earth could a society composed exclusively of ecstatics possible be run?' (Zaehner 1957: 13).

Moreover, the tension between Laing and the Iona Community indicates a related concern about the political credentials of *metanoia*. In *Zone of the Interior* (1976), a thinly veiled satirical novel of Kingsley Hall, Clancy Sigal, a former resident, accuses the community of political accommodation to the age of consumer capitalism. Chapman explains how the narrator-protagonist Sid Bell, 'longs to go mad, to experience the truth that, supposedly, can be revealed only by schizophrenia', yet finds that

> [w]hen the epiphany occurs, far from being a moment of sublimity, it is one of bathos. The spirits and demons that Bell has been reading about and conjuring are nowhere to be seen. No arcane secrets are finally revealed. But Bell does meet God – and the deity is in the form of a trade unionist, an activist from the Industrial Workers of the World (the Wobblies), who tells Bell to quit focusing on high-falutin radicalism and return to the world of the everyday. (Chapman 2014a: 15)

Although first published in the USA in 1976, the novel did not appear in a UK edition until 2005, well after Laing's death in 1989. This was because of vague threats of legal action (Chapman 2014a: 15) regarding the novel's depiction of Laing as the grandiose 'Willie Last' leading, in Sigal's clumsy rendition of a Scottish accent, '"a Children's Crusade fightin' to retake th' Holeh Land of our Primal Unspoilt Selves"' (cited in Chapman 2014a: 21), and its critique of less savoury aspects of Kingsley Hall, such as sexual exploitation of female residents (Chapman 2014a: 19).

Rushforth and the Wellspring

At the same time as Laing moved to obscure the Christian genealogy of his spiritual psychotherapy, Winifred Rushforth's practice was expanding into a broader and explicitly 'New Age' spirituality (her 1983 book, *Something is Happening* is, for instance, subtitled *Spiritual Awareness and Depth Psychology in the New Age* (Rushforth 1983)). Analysis of Rushforth's activities reveals the way in which she used psychoanalytic psychotherapy to usher a declining Christian culture towards a mode of popularised vitalism. Those who were attracted to psychotherapeutically authorised biographical patterns of regeneration might be drawn onwards via practices of 'Self-spirituality' to a recognition of the cosmic purposiveness that, in Rushforth's view, pervaded all life and matter.

In the 1959 Davidson Clinic *Annual Report*, Rushforth presents an ideal type of the personal transformation wrought by psychoanalysis.

Rushforth remarks that analytic psychotherapy may relieve conversions and compulsions – 'asthma, skin disease, compulsive nail-biting, even duodenal ulcers' (*Annual Report* 1959: 6) – but then adds that '[w]e are working to liberate further dimensions of human personality, to increase the capacity for relationship and to set free the natural creative faculty in man' (*Annual Report* 1959: 6). The latter, for instance,

> may be through descriptive or imaginative writing, through musical composition or performance, through the ability to draw or paint, or to speak in public ... there is a quickening of life, a setting free of energy and an increase of happiness and contentment. (*Annual Report* 1959: 7)

Such supposed personal transformation could, of course, be comfortably accommodated within the Clinic's rhetoric of Christian psychotherapy. However, the self-transformation promised by the Clinic was also described in terms of contemporary spirituality. In the 1962 *Annual Report*, for instance, Rushforth approvingly recalls, even in the early days of the Clinic,

> a professional man coming to enquire 'Is it true that analysis leads to spiritual enlightenment?' and many years later at a casual meeting assuring me that his life had taken a new turn from the day he had begun a short analysis. (*Annual Report* 1962: 7)

The confluence of discursive Christianity, psychotherapy, and 'spiritual enlightenment' via analysis, certainly indicates that Rushforth and the Clinic were concerned with the liberation of a supposed higher self through spiritual discipline or technology. Moreover, Jane Darroch's testimony confirms the entanglement of the Clinic with the psychotherapeutic precursor to a New Religious Movement, when she recalls Rushforth's interest in what she calls 'Scientology':

> Scientology was in the air in the mid 1950s. Dr Rushforth underwent some training and used some of the techniques of the Scientologists judiciously with some of her patients. Mrs Christie [a lay therapist] became so enthusiastic about it that her attitude became incompatible with the analytic approach, and she left in 1957 to make it her main occupation. (Darroch 1973: 21)

Darroch is presumably referring to L. Ron Hubbard's earlier theory and practice of Dianetics, which proposed to rid the personality of traumatic memory traces known as 'engrams' which, it was held, remained active within the 'reactive mind', a part of the mind dedicated to immediate survival: 'The purpose of Dianetic therapy ... was to gain access to and locate engrams, and "erase" them from the reactive mind, thus eradicating their effects in the form of psychosomatic illness, emotional tension, or lowered capability' (Wallis 1976: 26). Rushforth's flirtation with Scientology no doubt lowered her credibility in medical eyes, but it reveals the Clinic's gradual expansion beyond the realm of strictly 'medical' psychotherapy. Like Laing in London, although with less celebrity, Rushforth and the Clinic were catering to consumers in search not of a cure for neurosis, but of transformative optimisation of the self. Rushforth herself was conscious of this expansion in their market in the late 1950s and the 1960s:

> Now a further and extremely important aspect of our work became prominent, which we saw as the emergence of the individual's potential. Doctors, ministers and clergy, teachers, even university professors and lecturers were asking for our help, not so much because they were aware of their neuroses, but rather they glimpsed that their creativity was blocked and their potential not fully realised. (Rushforth 1984: 132–3)

These managerial-professional consumers are the anonymous and uncelebrated equivalents of Laing's 'patients' from London's elite networks of cultural producers.

However, Rushforth's brand of psychotherapeutic spirituality shows something additional at work, namely a vitalism consistent with Heelas's more recent thesis that 'spirituality *is* life-itself, the "life-force" or "energy" which flows through all human life (and much else besides), which sustains life, and which, when experienced, brings all of life "alive"' (Heelas 2008: 27). Rushforth's vitalism no doubt drew on a modernist and proto-modernist European context that included the ideas and writings of Henri Bergson, Samuel Butler, George Bernard Shaw and D. H. Lawrence (Lehan 1992). There was also an unacknowledged affinity with the ideas of J. A. C. Murray, whose commodious concept of the unconscious describes it (in part) as 'the home of the instincts, and the seat of energy' (Murray 1938: 34). Although superficially Freudian, Murray's concept of unconscious 'energy' is actually of an 'elemental life-force, which, from the unconscious, and by means of its unknown faculties, keeps the body functioning' – an 'Energy, Libido, Life-force, Hormic Urge, or Elan Vital, as it has been variously labelled' (Murray 1938: 34–5). But apparently of greater importance for Rushforth was the work of Pierre Teilhard de Chardin (1881–1955), whose ideas she first encountered in the 1960s via the 1959 English translation of Teilhard's *The Phenomenon of Man* (Rushforth 1984: 136–7). 'For a time', testifies Rushforth, 'my thoughts were dominated by my longing to impart the truth contained in his teaching' (Rushforth 1984: 137) – this desire apparently led to a number of discussion groups being formed, as well as a 1969 conference at Scottish Churches' House in Dunblane on the subject of the Davidson Clinic's 'work in psychoanalysis, linked with Teilhard's teaching' (Rushforth 1984: 137). Julian Huxley's introduction to the English translation of *The Phenomenon of Man* describes Teilhard's account of 'the genesis of increasingly elaborate organization during cosmogenesis', progressing 'from atoms to inorganic and later to organic molecules', 'to cells, to multicellular individuals, to cephalized metazoa with brains, to primitive man, and now to civilized society' (Huxley 1959: 15). The 'all-pervading tendency' (Huxley 1959: 15) of complexification supposed by Teilhard allowed him to speculate, as Mary Midgley explains, on the eventual evolution of the 'Omega man',

> a future being, raised above us both spiritually and intellectually, whose destiny it is to complete the divine plan for this earth by perfecting it at the mental level – to add a nöosphere, or intellectual realm, to the living realm or biosphere (Midgley 2002: 83).

Teilhard's theory, which relies upon the idea of a linear direction to evolution, supposes that *Homo sapiens* is confronted with an imminent 'new domain of psychical expansion' (Teilhard 1959: 253).

Teilhard's work seems to have reawakened an enduring engagement with vitalism on Rushforth's part. Her longstanding vitalist commitments are apparent in an autobiographical reference to the work of her aunt and cousin, Isabella and Louisa Mears, 'on the translation of the *I Ching* (The Book of Changes)'; 'a book called *Creative Energy* was published in the early thirties at about the time of Aunt Isabella's death' (Rushforth 1984: 25). The Mears' book, *Creative Energy: Being an Introduction to the Study of the Yih King, or Book of Changes* (1931), shows a remarkable continuity with Rushforth's post-war vitalist spirituality, and may therefore have been more formative upon it than she publicly acknowledged. The Mears argue that the *I Ching*, although seemingly a manual of divination, in fact describes an intentionality directing a process of evolutionary orthogenesis. The Chinese authors of the *I Ching* intuited that

> the Scheme of Life made manifest in the world was the visible working out of a preconceived Plan. As they saw it, the Plan is being worked out partly through the agency of spiritual intelligences involved in it from the beginning, and then also partly through the agency of man. (Mears and Mears 1931: 18)

Homo sapiens (or 'man') was no accidental outcome of natural selection; rather '[l]iving "germs" were brought into existence that were destined, after millennia of generations, to become fully developed mankind of the sixth day of creation. Within each one Creative Energy surged unceasingly onward' (Mears and Mears 1931: 13). The *I Ching*'s authors, the Mears argue, were able to intuit this truth because, in effect, the Creative Energy, or 'cosmic soul-life' (Mears and Mears 1931: 13), bestowed upon some members of the human race a special sensitivity to religious truth (Mears and Mears 1931: 8–9).

Despite the significance of vitalism in Rushforth's later spiritualised psychotherapy, such ideas are not necessarily explicit. They are instead allowed to more indirectly permeate the discourses, attitudes and practices of Rushforth's associates and audience. Rushforth's obliqueness is typified by her choice of 'Sempervivum' as the name for one of the Davidson

Clinic's successor initiatives (see below). She explains how the 'flowering spikes' of sempervivum 'are evanescent and soon wither and might be likened to the life-span of the individual personality, but the plant itself is capable of almost unlimited growth' (Rushforth 1984: 141). Another metaphor inscribes into a central image both Christian and vitalist discourses. 'The Well' (Rushforth 1985b), a brief reflection first published in 1983 in the New Age periodical *New Humanity*, explores the various intertextual relations of this word and metaphor. 'What do we find at the bottom of the well?', asks Rushforth, 'A spring of water – *Ursprung-Quelle* – bubbling up from a deeper source. *Urgrund*, the ground of our being' (Rushforth 1985b: 150). She then indicates (somewhat imprecisely) a set of Judaeo-Christian scriptural antecedents, including Ezekiel 47, Ecclesiasticus 24: 31 (a deuterocanonical book), Isaiah 58: 11, and John 7: 37–8. The most important of these Christian allusions for Rushforth is the well at Samaria in John 4: 14: 'Anyone who drinks the water that I shall give will never be thirsty again; the water that I shall give will turn into a spring inside him, welling up to eternal life' (Rushforth 1985b: 151).

Rushforth's citations, however, do not necessarily indicate that she subscribes to a doctrine of personal immortality. Instead, the 'eternal life' springing up via psychoanalytic psychotherapy, and anticipated in Christian scripture, is to some extent the unceasing life process postulated by vitalism as the substance to which the living individual is 'accidental' (in an ontological, not aetiological sense). Rushforth therefore freely offers a variety of supposed vitalist equivalents from various traditions, including Jungian psychotherapy, Buddhism, Nietzsche's philosophy and Georg Groddeck's psychoanalysis (Rushforth 1985b: 150). Vitalist discourses were continued by Rushforth in dream groups that she ran for several years after the closure of the Davidson Clinic. The theoretical context is partly Jungian: Rushforth explains her view that '[d]reams take us into the collective unconscious'; 'The analogy is with the sea, the ocean with its mingling currents and waves; any one drop may touch any other' (Rushforth 1984: 162). Yet the Jungian collective unconscious is written into a larger narrative reminiscent of Teilhard's vitalism: 'one function of the unconscious is to unite individuals everywhere, regardless of geographical location' as '[g]radually the words we, us, ours, replace I, me, mine, and human life declares itself in unity' (Rushforth 1984: 164). This view clarifies Rushforth's peculiar and unelaborated statement in her 1973 address on the Davidson Clinic's closure: 'Analytic work is dynamic and, linked as it is with unconscious forces, cannot but survive and spread. I am bold enough to think it has evolutionary value, so today we are only slightly sad' (Rushforth 1984: 144). The unconscious here is not the Freudian personal unconscious, nor even the Jungian collective unconscious, but an evolutionary unconscious somehow underlying them – an entelechy which will eventually produce a new stage, or perhaps a 'New Age', in evolutionary development. Her leadership of dream groups allowed Rushforth to encode this vitalism into discourses and practices of the body. An anonymous manuscript entitled 'Holding hands with Winifred Rushforth' describes the groups further, and refers to a bodily, as much as psychic, discipline of supposed contact with the vitalist wellspring:

> she [Rushforth] would relax ... and 'plug in' to the Source ... Feeling God's energy flow in through her heart, abdomen, legs, through her whole body to the earth, to the poor, the sick, the depressed, to the rejected and to every living organism and thing. She emphasized how the energy must be received and freely given out ... which can then return to the Source, having completed its cycle. She emphasized that each one of us can tap this wonderful Source of energy at any and at all times. (Holding hands: 4)

Rushforth's practical encoding of her vitalism extended even beyond such ritualised activities. She seems also to have distributed cuttings of the symbolic plant sempervivum to at least some members of the networks that grew up around her various small group activities (Thomas Rodgerson, personal communication, 6 June 2011).

Given Rushforth's charismatic New Age leadership, it is perhaps unsurprising that the Davidson Clinic left behind three spiritually inflected legacy organisations: the Salisbury Centre, Sempervivum and Wellspring. These are described in a tribute to Rushforth *c.*1983 by Marcus Lefébure, a Roman Catholic monk active in the provision of counselling and psychotherapy in Edinburgh:

> the Salisbury Centre, at first a Sufi meditation centre which subsequently proved its vitality by opening up to become a meeting place for spiritual seekers of all kinds; Sempervivum, a movement and network of people concerned with creativity and all-round well-being, individual and social; and finally Wellspring, a psycho-therapeutic and counselling centre for individuals and groups and open to the Spirit. (How remember)

There are clear continuities with Rushforth and the Davidson Clinic in these three organisations, all of which are still in existence. The Salisbury Centre opened in 1973 in a large building originally owned and commercially let by the Davidson Clinic (Rushforth 1984: 142, *History – the Salisbury Centre*). The Centre continues as a focus in Edinburgh for the kind of spiritual 'holistic milieu' described by Linda Woodhead and Paul Heelas in their study of the town of Kendal (Heelas et al. 2005). Sempervivum has moved locations over the decades, but continues in much the same form, offering residential and non-residential participation in a variety of holistic workshops and activities that continue the ethos of the Davidson Clinic's popular Easter Summer Schools (*Sempervivum*, Rushforth 1984: 98). Wellspring was originally directed by Rushforth's daughter, Dr Diana Bates (Rushforth 1984: 168), and, as will be shown below, a syncretic psychotherapeutic spirituality was promoted by some key associates. However, the rhetoric of being 'open to the Spirit' is now marginal to Wellspring's current public face (*Wellspring Scotland*), and religious faith has not been explicit in its work or choice of practitioners (Bondi 2013: 681).

Counselling and spirituality: the dialogues of Hans Schauder and Marcus Lefébure

In the 1980s, the Edinburgh-based religious publishing house, T. & T. Clark, issued a short series of dialogues on the theory and practice of counselling. Billed as conversations 'between a Doctor and a Priest', the two discussants – both of whom lived and worked in Edinburgh – were Hans Schauder (1911–2001), a medically trained counsellor, and Marcus Lefébure (1933–2012), a Roman Catholic monk. The first volume of their dialogues, *Conversations on Counselling between a Doctor and a Priest: Dialogue and Trinity* (Lefébure 1982), was published in 1982. Lefébure was identi-fied as the 'Priest', but Schauder's identity was disguised by the pseudo-nym 'Martin Gregory' – his identity was, though, revealed in later editions and volumes, even though the pseudonym persisted in the text. In 1985, T. & T. Clark brought out a second volume, *Human Experience and the Art of Counselling: Further Conversations between a Doctor and a Priest* (Lefébure 1985), with a nominal third volume of *Conversations* appearing in 1990 (Lefébure and Schauder 1990), although it was in fact a revised compi-lation of the earlier dialogues. Finally, in 1987, a German-language text combining *Conversations* and *Human Experience*, and translated by Susanne Kerkovius, was published by the Swiss anthroposophical imprint, Geering, under the title *Lebensberatung: ein Weg zu Wandlung und Geborgenheit; ein anthroposophischer Arzt und ein katholischer Mönch im Gespräch* (*Life-counselling: A Path to Change and Security; An Anthroposophical Doctor and a Catholic Monk in Conversation*) (Lefébure and Schauder 1987).

A biographical sketch of Schauder may be gleaned from a brief obitu-ary published in 2001 in *The Scotsman* newspaper (Dawson and Kerkovius 2001), and from his biography (Franke [2002?]). Schauder, the 'Doctor' of the dialogues, was born in Vienna in 1911 to a non-observant Jewish family. As an adolescent, he was influenced by Adlerian individual psychology, which was then supplanted during his medical studies by anthroposophy. After the *Anschluss* of 1938, Schauder fled to Switzerland (where he completed his medical studies), before following his wife, Lisl, to Aberdeen. In late 1940, he joined Karl König at Camphill, near Aberdeen, where the latter was founding the first Camphill Community for the anthroposophical care of children with special needs. After a few years of involvement with Camphill, Schauder moved in 1944 to Garvald House, near Edinburgh, where he established a similar anthro-posophical institution (of which various offshoots and successor organi-sations still exist, albeit on a lesser scale than the Camphill Community movement). The strain of running Garvald House adversely affected Schauder's health, so he withdrew in 1949 to a medical consultancy role which he also extended to the Edinburgh Rudolf Steiner School. Rather than re-qualify to practise as a medical doctor, Schauder began to work in the 1950s as a counsellor, first for the Edinburgh Council of Social Service, then for Edinburgh's Saughton Prison, and latterly for the Samaritans. These positions were the foundation for Schauder's private counselling service, which he ran for several decades from his home in Edinburgh.

A partial biography of Marcus (also Pascal) Lefébure, the 'Priest' of the dialogues can be assembled from the various *Conversations*, and from his obituary in the Catholic theological journal *New Blackfriars* (Kerr 2012). Lefébure was born in London in 1933 to expatriate Viennese Catholic parents. He studied law in London, Cambridge and Paris before joining in 1958 the Dominican Order (also known as the Order of Preachers, and the Blackfriars), whereupon he acquired the new name 'Pascal' in observance of a longstanding tradition. After philosophical and theological studies at Hawkesyard Priory, and then Blackfriars Hall, University of Oxford, he edited the Catholic theological journal *New Blackfriars* from 1967–70. He moved to Edinburgh *c.*1970 to join the Dominicans' Catholic Chaplaincy at the University of Edinburgh, where he was both Assistant and, from 1974 to 1981, Head Chaplain. In 1978, he co-founded the Wellspring centre in Edinburgh, an organisation for the provision of counselling and psychotherapy. In the late 1970s, Lefébure met Schauder, to whom the Chaplaincy had occasionally sent students in need of counselling. The Schauder–Lefébure dialogues were based upon subsequent tape-recorded conversations which took place in Schauder's home in Edinburgh *c.*1979–84. After leaving the Chaplaincy (and the Order) *c.*1985, Lefébure remained active in counselling and psychotherapy, with connections to the Lincoln Clinic in London, and to Wellspring, where he returned from 1991 until his retirement in 2000.

The Schauder–Lefébure dialogues emerged in the 1980s, a period when counselling expanded greatly, in part because of cutbacks to the welfare state under neoliberalism. Counselling in Scotland had previously been rather a modest enterprise: the first recognisable counselling came from voluntary organisations offering marriage guidance in the immediate postwar period (Bondi 2006: 248–9). However, the erosion of the post-war consensus in the 1960s, and the eventual arrival of the Thatcher government in the late 1970s, began 'a period of resurgence for the third sector' (Bondi 2013: 677) which included the provision of counselling sponsored by Christian religious organisations. These influential voluntary organisations included the Catholic Marriage Advisory Council (later Scottish Marriage Care), a variety of enterprises sponsored by the Church of Scotland (epitomised by the Tom Allan Centre in Glasgow), as well as more ecumenical initiatives (Bondi 2013: 678–9). The ethos of the Christian-sponsored organisations established between the mid-1960s and the mid-1980s was one of voluntary service and free provision (Bondi 2013: 679). Volunteers, most of them female, were recruited from church members, but services were offered regardless of the client's creed (if any), and the counselling thereby obtained was essentially indistinguishable from that offered in secular third-sector contexts (Bondi 2013: 679). Counselling, whether sponsored by secular or religious organisations, offered support to persons in distress who were not mentally ill, and had an egalitarian and voluntarist ethos (Bondi 2013: 673).

The Schauder–Lefébure dialogues are particularly interesting because they emerge in a period early in the professionalisation of counselling in the United Kingdom, which was to gather momentum in the 1990s (Bondi 2013: 681). They attempt to articulate a spiritual foundation for counselling theory and practice, and eclectically combine a variety of materials, including Christian religious philosophy as well as theories of psychoanalysis, psychotherapy and counselling. Although the dialogues are intended primarily for an audience of counsellors, they also address a readership interested in 'spirituality'. This term is used by Lefébure in his author's questionnaire to assist T. & T. Clark in marketing the dialogues, where he states that '[i]mplicit throughout the books ... is the idea that counselling or, more largely, true human dialogue, is a modern locus for spiritual striving and growth' (*Human Experience*). He refers to an anticipated readership of

> [t]hose interested in the deeper issues of counselling, in spirituality especially in a contemporary setting invested with much energy, in the inter-relationship between the modern profession of counselling and the ancient search for spirituality, followers of Rudolf Steiner, and generally open-minded and intelligent seekers. (*Human Experience*)

The anticipated readership therefore seems in part to consist of spiritual 'seekers' as described by Robert C. Fuller:

> Forsaking formal religious organizations, these people have instead embraced an individualized spirituality that includes picking and choosing from a wide range of alternative religious philosophies. They typically view spirituality as a journey intimately linked with the pursuit of personal growth or development. (Fuller 2001: 6)

Although Fuller's analysis draws on US culture and society, spiritual seekership is a phenomenon found also in the UK context, as has been noted by Colin Campbell in his description of a 'common ideology of seekership' in which 'individuals ... frequently travel rapidly through a wide variety of movements and beliefs' (Campbell 1972: 123).

The Schauder–Lefébure dialogues consistently argue that the evocation of spiritual experience is essential to counselling; in so doing, they traverse a variety of spiritual and religious positions, enacting within the text a kind of spiritual 'pick and mix' which extracts presumed truths from larger intellectual and cultural traditions. For instance, personalism and mysticism are syncretically woven by Schauder and Lefébure into supposedly equivalent non-Western discourses, thereby creating a spiritual doctrine pertaining to no single organised religion. *Human Experience* ends with a 'Concluding personal postscript on counselling and friendship' authored by Lefébure. Lefébure introduces the work of John Macmurray, and his 'seminal intuition that "the unit of the personal is not the 'I' but the 'you and I'." ... We are insufficient to our sole selves' (Lefébure 1985: 131). Schauder and Lefébure see such intersubjective personalism as a cross-cultural philosophy. The latter, for instance, argues that the personalist thesis, '*being human intrinsically involves a reference to a second*', is paralleled in Chinese thinking, and is likely a 'perception recurring time and again in divers [*sic*] settings' (Lefébure 1985: 79) – Lefébure then specifically refers to the nineteenth-century idealist philosopher T. H. Green, and to the twentieth-century Thomistic legal philosophy of John Finnis (Lefébure 1985: 80).

Schauder inserts counselling within personalism by describing the former as '*Gespräch*', German for 'discussion' or 'conversation', but specifically defined by Schauder as 'a truly human dialogue, where people raise fundamental questions, exchange basic impressions, and where they both grope for some kind of direction' (Lefébure 1982: 26). Lefébure elsewhere concurs, asserting that '*Gespräch*, the dialogue, between counsellor and client is only a particular but a crystallised and disciplined version of any truly human communication' (Lefébure 1985: 6). Although Schauder and Lefébure wonder if there is some 'element of reciprocity which exists between equal friends and which does not exist between counsellor and client' (Lefébure 1982: 33), their hesitations do not preclude the supposed spiritual experience arising in counselling's intersubjective personalist dialogue. Lefébure explains that *Gespräch* invites a presence akin to the Holy Spirit, 'the deeper one allows oneself to go into a relationship', the greater 'the mysterious presence of some third thing ... somehow personal, a breath, a breathing that is like an inspiration as well as a grace' (Lefébure 1982: 95). Counselling, as a particular form of such encounter, turns out to be 'the human figure of some more eternal face-to-face' (Lefébure 1982: 95).

Such vocabulary indicates Lefébure's eclectic deployment of Martin Buber's philosophy, as further articulated in a concluding epigraph to *Conversations*, a passage from Buber's *I and Thou*: 'Every particular *Thou* is a glimpse through to the eternal *Thou*; by means of every particular *Thou* the primary word addresses the eternal *Thou*' (M. Lefébure *Conversations* 96). Such theological personalism was an established tradition in the twentieth-century British scene. Similar ideas could be found in Macmurray, and also in another Scottish theologian, John Baillie (1886–1960). The latter argues that knowledge of other persons is 'a primary and original mode of consciousness' that is 'not inductively derived' from experience

(Baillie 1939: 213–14). As Donald S. Klinefelter explains, this distinct personalist transcendental *a priori* requires for Baillie that the epistemological issues in theology be reformulated: 'Our primary religious knowledge', for Baillie, 'is not a knowledge of true propositions but of *realities*' (Klinefelter 1977: 417). Lefébure's reference to a 'mysterious presence' in the *Gespräch* employs an identical mode of argument: knowledge of the 'eternal thou' is putatively an empirical interpersonal relationship rather than an inference from experience of the self or objective world.

The personalist theological thesis that 'in each genuinely relational event there is "a breath of the eternal Thou"' (Smith 1966: 33) additionally leads Schauder to synthesise personalist religious experience with a kind of perennialist mysticism. (Of the two discussants, he is particularly syncretic, claiming in his biography that '[a] universal religious approach has developed for me which ... entails mutual attraction and penetration of the religions in supplementing one another' (Franke [2002?]: 74)). Schauder invites Lefébure to analogise the counselling relationship with the 'spiritual path' (Lefébure 1982: 75). There are, according to Schauder, seven stages in the counselling relationship, which map onto 'the four basic stages of the spiritual path' (Lefébure 1982: 75). Schauder, who conceives the four stages as common to Buddhism, Hinduism and Christianity (Lefébure 1982: 62), summarises them:

> first, a moral training or the *via purgativa* ...; secondly, the stage of meditation, which then proceeds into the third stage of contemplation or illumination or intuitive knowledge ...; and, fourthly, the stage of liberation, of union, where we are able to enter something which is completely beyond our ordinary self. (Lefébure 1982: 75)

Of particular importance is the terminus of the spiritual path, in which, according to Schauder, there is an encounter with a 'presence' that 'will begin to permeate you' in what is 'spiritually speaking, communion' (Lefébure 1982: 70).

The dialogues present counselling as a discipline that cultivates spiritual experiences of contact, and even fusion with, a higher personal reality, in a process that is (supposedly) amenable to conceptualisation from a variety of religious and philosophical positions, including non-European traditions. In order to further secure and develop their account of counselling as essentially spiritual, Schauder and Lefébure negotiate with the legacy left to counselling by psychoanalysis. The dialogues confront the problem of reconciling the Freudian account of the sexual instincts and their vicissitudes with religious traditions that have often valorised sexual abstinence. One straightforward compromise offered by the dialogues is to acknowledge that while celibacy as a spiritual discipline may be praiseworthy it is fundamentally an act of supererogation of which only a few are capable (Lefébure 1985: 123). The two discussants also tentatively present the institutional Christian correlation between spirituality and celibacy as naïvely objectifying in its focus upon physiological abstinence rather than inner detachment. Asian religions, proposes Lefébure (rightly or wrongly), are more clear-sighted: 'the masters of the West couch their insight in terms of ... behaviour, whereas the Eastern texts speak directly about an inner attitude of mind' (Lefébure 1985: 108); 'the gradual overcoming of "cravings" and appetites is about ... the detachment that liberates the ... inner state of mind that has been called devotion in the traditions of both West and East' (Lefébure 1985: 109).

This emphasis on what one might call 'inner celibacy' (which seems a concept open to abuse) is accompanied by a modification to so-called psychoanalytic 'transference', defined by Lefébure with admirable clarity as 'the tendency ... to see people in the present as if they were figures from the past, especially very significant figures, and so to relive the love, hates, reactions and overreactions, dependencies etc. of the past here and now' (Lefébure 1985: 63). Lefébure agrees that transference occurs in the counselling relationship, but argues that certain transference phenomena show that 'what people are secretly looking for, beyond the figures of people they've missed, like a father or a lover', is the 'true image of man as made in the likeness of God' (Lefébure 1985: 68). As Francis Grier notes, psychoanalysis has typically required that '[a]doration and idealisation ... be replaced by the realistic, non-narcissistic, critical perception of the real qualities of the other person' (Grier 2006: 161). But Schauder and Lefébure argue that the counsellor should resist idealisation only in order to 'return that power back to the client' (Lefébure 1985: 70) so that he or she finds the capacity for self-transcendence (the 'image of god') within him- or herself. The counsellor thereby spiritually renews the client's capacity for personal growth and, indeed, moral betterment.

The Schauder–Lefébure dialogues aim also to neutralise the mechanistic Freudian model of sexual libido by translating Freud's quasi-hydraulic terminology (Gellner 1985: 105–12) into a vitalist teleological framework amenable to their account of personal growth and development within counselling. Both discussants agree that counselling is 'future orientated' (Lefébure 1985: 26) since it helps the client to 'release the energies of life that are directed to the future' (Lefébure 1985: 29). Schauder offers a metaphor drawn from the local geography of Cramond, a small coastal settlement on the outskirts of Edinburgh:

> the little harbour was usually clogged with various bits of debris ... Every now and then, however, the river [Almond] would gain power and sweep away a great deal of all this deposit from the past out into the sea ... If we can only help people to release the energies of life that are directed to the future, most of the blockages in the way will simply be swept away. (Lefébure 1985: 29)

This future orientation, however, *prima facie* contradicts the psychoanalytic emphasis on regression and recapitulation – on working through the 'there and then' that still affects the 'here and now'. Schauder attempts a solution with the notion of '*ungelebtes Leben,* unlived life, ... a life or a period of life which has not been lived through' (Lefébure 1985: 38) – a concept perhaps related to Erich Fromm's existential-psychoanalytic account of the destructiveness that supposedly arises from '*unlived life*', namely 'the block-age of spontaneity of the growth and expression of man's [*sic*] sensuous, emotional, and intellectual capacities' (Fromm 1960: 158). According to Schauder, unlived life can weigh upon the present to the extent that the client must return to earlier possibilities, and effect a reconciliation with them – even just 'the very fact that he has expressed the need and realised the problem may resolve it' (Lefébure 1985: 40). Such accommodations of psychoanalysis allow Schauder and Lefébure to rework Freudian drive theory so that what is therapeutically released is no longer fixated libido, but instead the creative, spiritual flow of universal life through the individual: for Lefébure, 'the therapist's essential function is to enable the release of this stream of life by raising the sluice-gate or removing the obstacle in the way of its natural flow' (Lefébure 1985: 32).

By such indications, the Schauder–Lefébure dialogues reconceive psychoanalytic theory and practice as hospitable to their evolving account of the spiritual essence of counselling. The resulting synthesis relies on an implicit vitalism to strip psychoanalysis of its mechanistic causality, while also using spiritually reworked psychoanalytic concepts to describe the presumed process of personal growth and development facilitated by counselling. Although provisional in their spirit, the dialogues clearly argue that various forms of spiritual experience are central to the counselling relationship. By connecting counselling with a cosmic life process, Schauder and Lefébure offer a thesis with some affinity to the unchurched religiosity of the immensely influential person-centred counselling developed by Carl Rogers (1902–87). Even though Rogers had abandoned his earlier connection – via study at Union Theological Seminary (Fuller 2006: 231) – with organised Christianity, his theory nonetheless maintained that 'energies from a higher metaphysical dimension enter into, and exert causal influence upon, our inner lives' (Fuller 2006: 232). For Rogerian counselling, the client's renewed participation in the process of cosmic evolution elicits 'an innate, biologically grounded impulse toward whole-ness and self-actualization' (Fuller 2006: 231).

However, although Schauder and Lefébure depict counselling and psychotherapy as essentially spiritual, their dialogues are reflexively conscious of and resistant to the Self-spirituality phenomenon identified by Heelas, and later amplified in the spiritual revolution thesis developed with Woodhead. Admittedly, the Schauder–Lefébure dialogues focus on subjectivised, experiential elements of religion such as the perceived personal presence of the Divinity in the counselling relationship. The dialogues also relate such supposed spiritual phenomena to a psychotherapeutic and psychoanalytic concern with the facilitation of personal growth and self-integration. Nonetheless, the Schauder–Lefébure dialogues do not univocally affirm Self-spirituality. Instead, the dialogues challenge the authorisation in counselling of spontaneous subjective experience – as Erich Fromm, for instance, asserts that in 'psychoanalysis' (a term which he uses very flexibly), the analysed personality regains autonomy by an 'immediate, unreflected grasp of reality, without affective contamination and intellectualization', a condition that is putatively identical with Buddhist enlightenment (Fromm 1986: 100).

Lefébure contends that the ideal of immediate experience is mistakenly accepted and authorised within counselling. He argues that cultural pre-understandings inescapably inform even our most inward experiences, and that the counsellor should in fact be understood as a bearer of traditions that may stimulate the client's growth and development, providing the latter has sufficient trust or faith in the therapeutic relationship. The dialogues thus challenge Self-spirituality by critiquing the emphasis on unmediated interiority within counselling, and by presenting counselling (in the Schauder–Lefébure mode, at any rate) as oppositional to contemporary forms of subjectivity. One line of attack exploits a Gadamerian response to person-centred counselling (and to existential psychotherapy). Lefébure cites Carl Rogers's dictum from *On Becoming a Person* (1954) that '"[t]he touchstone of validity is my own experience"' (Lefébure 1985: 88), but immediately counters that 'reliance on experience above all, in the spirit of Erich Fromm and Carl Rogers, is at the very least logically incoherent' (Lefébure 1985: 89). Reliance on experience is a 'shibboleth of modernity' apparent in the many people who 'are saying that they rely on experience to guide them through life rather than any code or tradition or the advice of others' (Lefébure 1985: 87). Such reliance is logically incoherent, he argues, because cultural pre-understandings inform and mediate our apparently 'immediate' experience. Alluding to Cardinal Newman's defence of prejudice and Gadamer's philosophical hermeneutics, Lefébure argues for 'the frank and willing acceptance of some pre-guidance, some tutoring and directing of our projects, prejudice in the etymological sense of pre-judice, pre-judgement, *Vorverständnis* or pre-understanding' (Lefébure 1985: 90). We are, by our very nature, given 'an *initial* and initiating acceptance of the tradition and the moral code' (Lefébure 1985: 92).

If 'experience' is a 'shibboleth of modernity' for Schauder and Lefébure, then the point – at least in part – is that obedience to supposed 'experience' is a norm both in contemporary society and in some forms of spirituality (a norm of both the 'permissive society' and 'at a more esoteric level … the Aquarian age' (Lefébure 1985: 87)). It is also a psychotherapeutic norm embedded within a tradition exemplified by Fromm's *The Art of Loving* (1956) and Rogers's *On Becoming a Person* (both texts cited by Lefébure), and also (as mentioned above) Fromm's *Psychoanalysis and Zen Buddhism* (1960), as well as Laing's *The Politics of Experience* (1967) and *The Voice of Experience* (1982). Indeed, Laing's work may be regarded as the *reductio ad absurdum* of the psychotherapeutic authorisation of subjective experience, since it led Laing to affirm the veridicality of all kinds of peculiar beliefs, purely because of the intense conviction with which they were held – re-incarnation was, for instance, one of these subjectively authorised doctrines (Laing 1982: 99), as Edna O'Brien's acid trip indicates (see p. 98). The fetishisation of experience as a source of intuitive self-authorising knowledge was also mocked by Sigal in *Zone of the Interior*. 'When a patient is so sure she came fr' another planet', announces Willie Last (the thinly veiled Laing), 'th' integrity of her statement slices my rationality off at th' knees' (Sigal 2005: 206).

Moreover, the Schauder–Lefébure dialogues have an additional implicit response to the authorisation of subjectivity central to models of Self-spirituality. The counsellor, according to Lefébure, is akin to the Thomistic 'wise and kindly "doctor", teacher' (Lefébure 1985: 75) in that he or she may make moral demands upon the client, precisely because '[a] system of law is ... a stimulus to growth, *not* its contradiction and thwarting' (Lefébure 1985: 76). The Schauder–Lefébure dialogues here draw upon a theological tradition in which faith (in God, others, tradition) facilitates a personal or spiritual development that is precisely *not* mandated by subjective experience: 'living initially out of trust is not irrational ... We ... believe in order to understand, trust in order to become convinced, presume in order to experience' (Lefébure 1985: 90). John Macmurray's Adlerian-informed formulation of this paradigm (see p. 45) was certainly familiar to Lefébure, who cites Macmurray's description of it as 'the rhythm of withdrawal and return' (Lefébure 1982: 44). For Macmurray, the prototypical form of withdrawal and return is found in the mother–child relation. The child subjectively experiences the mother's gradual withdrawal of care as abandonment, but – in the ideal case – overcomes this subjective certainty by its faith in the goodness of the mother's intentions. Trusting in the mother, the child embarks upon a process of growth and self-formation, 'acquiring and exercising the skill to do for himself [*sic*] what the mother refuses any longer to do for him' (Macmurray 1961: 89). After each stage of growth is completed, the child understands that what was experienced as abandonment was in fact an expression of love – to borrow Lefébure's phrase, it has had to 'trust in order to become convinced'. In this model of development, subjective experience may be revealed as unworthy of authority once one has acquired a more developed psychological or spiritual condition.

Admittedly, this moralism in the Schauder–Lefébure dialogues is tempered by their revival of another mode of reasoning that has often been neglected within modern philosophy, namely casuistry. Schauder, who perhaps has less investment in the Catholic theological and philosophical tradition, responds that

> there are cases in which individuals have to go against the traditional morality in the interests of their own growth, and in which at best they

live with the conflict until they have a sense of moral intuition from deep within, from the wisdom of the higher self. (Lefébure 1985: 81–2)

Lefébure assents, indicating a continuity between casuistry in counselling and in pastoral work: 'we have to be uncompromising on principle and infinitely flexible on application. This is the real pastoral skill, so that what you are talking about is as it were the secular equivalent of this pastoral skill' (Lefébure 1985: 92). Nonetheless, the liberation of the 'higher self' in the dialogues clearly differs from that proposed in Heelas's model of New Age Self-spirituality, in which 'experiences of the "Higher Self"' refer to the 'inner realm, and the inner realm alone ... the source of authentic vitality, creativity, love, tranquillity, wisdom, power, authority' (Heelas 1996: 19). The Schauder–Lefébure dialogues therefore invite reflection on sociological models which depict spirituality as essentially subjectivised. Giuseppe Giordan explains, for instance, that

[t]he concept of spirituality ... not only focuses on the relationship between institution and personal experience, but also places these two aspects in hierarchical form thus legitimising the relationship with the sacred, no longer from the point of view of obedience to external authority but instead centralising the freedom of the individual. (Giordan 2007: 170)

Heelas argues that the 'Self-ethic' (Heelas 1996: 23) in spirituality extends beyond merely personal preference in modes of the sacred; instead, subjectivisation is generalised so that 'what lies within – experienced by way of "intuition", "alignment" or an "inner voice" – serves to inform the judgements, decisions and choices required for everyday life. The "individual" serves as his or her own source of guidance' (Heelas 1996: 23). This Self-spirituality model serves as the basis for Heelas's later work with Linda Woodhead on the supposed 'spiritual revolution' in Western religiosity. They argue that spirituality is something more than merely the subjectivisation of the sacred (as, say, the spiritual quest for a personally satisfying and convincing mode of sacred life, one that may remove the individual from traditional modes and organisations). Spirituality is, they maintain, the sacralisation of the search for authenticity *in toto*. Heelas and Woodhead therefore contrast the supposed emphasis on overall personal authenticity in spirituality with what they regard as the prescription of traditional roles in organised religion: '"the massive subjective turn of modern culture" favours and reinforces those (subjective-life) forms of spirituality which resource unique subjectivities and treat them as a primary source of significance, and undermines those (life-as) forms of religion which do not' (Heelas et al. 2005: 78). To enter 'the holistic milieu' – the places and spaces of spirituality – is thus to enter a context which 'help[s] people live out their own interior lives in their own unique ways' (Heelas et al. 2005: 13).

But to what extent is the proposed connection between spirituality and the 'cultivation of unique individuality' (Heelas et al. 2005: 14) an *a posteriori* discovery, and to what extent is it an artefact born of *a priori* suppositions? The Schauder–Lefébure dialogues anticipate Stef Aupers and Dick Houtman's argument that scholarship on spirituality may overlook the way in which 'individualism operates as a socially sanctioned obligation of personal authenticity' (Aupers and Houtman 2006: 218). To clarify Aupers and Houtman's point, consider Heelas and Woodhead's hypothetical example of 'subjective life' authorisation, whereby I no longer slot myself 'into the role of a dutiful daughter and a loving and caring wife and mother' who disregards 'feelings of exhaustion, unhappiness and periodic disgruntlement' (Heelas et al. 2005: 2); instead, I 'heed those subjective states, ... by altering my life in ways that better suit my own unique needs, desires, capabilities and "relationalities"' (Heelas et al. 2005: 3). This example both occludes the normativity of subjective authorisation (the self mysteriously chooses to authorise subjectivity – along with millions of other Western selves), and the discursive mediation of 'subjective states' (why does the self report experiences of 'unhappiness' and 'disgruntlement' rather than feelings of guilt and inadequacy?). Christopher Bunn and Matthew Wood argue that an evidential bias in sociology of spirituality has tended to conceal problems in models that take the 'subjective turn' as definitive of spirituality: 'the research methods commonly employed hinder such investigation, being strongly oriented to texts, especially of a published nature', whereas 'ethnographic study ... would help to situate discourses of self-authority in people's broader practices and interactions' (Wood and Bunn 2009: 289).

Part of the challenge of the Schauder–Lefébure dialogues to subjectivised models of spirituality is a reflexivity that problematises the opposition between traditionally mandated 'life-as' and wholly interior 'subjective-life'. This is particularly pronounced in the adoption by Schauder and Lefébure of a personalist theory in which what appears to be ego-alien (to be 'life as' rather than 'subjective life') may nonetheless be incorporated into the self by an intersubjective leap of faith which impels a process of personal development and transformation. Perhaps, as Bunn and Wood argue, texts such as the Schauder–Lefébure dialogues are relatively uncommon in explicitly critiquing supposed self-authority from within the discourses of spirituality. However, an additional, more fundamental difficulty – un-noted by Wood and Bunn – arises from the broadly structuralist-functionalist approach epitomised by Heelas and Woodhead in the spiritual revolution thesis. They suppose that those who participate in spirituality, and thereby enter the holistic milieu, do so because they require a form of the sacred functional for modern, subjectivised forms of life: it is a 'Durkheimian principle that people are more likely to be involved with forms of the sacred which are "consistent with their ongoing beliefs and values"' (Heelas et al. 2005: 78). A definition of spirituality in terms of such functional predicates is, though, also a substantive or material definition (or definition by negation, at any rate), since it *a priori* excludes any spirituality that critically thematises the concept of 'inner', subjective authority. The counselling theorised within the Schauder–Lefébure dialogues (and seemingly practised by Schauder) is a spirituality that is intentionally in conflict with the subjective turn in modern culture. Further evidence would be required from, for instance, Schauder's clients in order to show how explicit or effective this ambition was, but the intention in the Schauder–Lefébure dialogues is clear.

To invite a less functionalist, more conflictual sociology of contemporary spirituality on the basis of the Schauder–Lefébure dialogues may seem capricious, especially given the existence of an additional research base that insists on the ideological function of spirituality. Jeremy Carrette and Richard King, in their Marxist commentary on spirituality, regard the psychologisation of religion (in, for instance, Abraham Maslow's theories of religious experience (Carrette and King 2005: 75)) as a precondition to the production of spiritual ideologies that legitimate and maintain late, consumer capitalism. In their uncompromising assessment, 'The psychological turn provided the intellectual platform for the corporate takeover of religion by facilitating the incorporation of religious traditions into the capitalist worldview' (Carrette and King 2005: 27). The resulting 'capitalist spirituality', in their view, legitimates and promotes values and behaviours such as social atomism, selfishness, the primacy of business interests, the instrumentalisation of others, consumerism, and the use of pacifying psychological techniques (Carrette and King 2005: 21–2). Nor are Carrette and King alone in this analysis: Aupers and Houtman similarly perceive an ideological function in the apparent 'elective affinity between the post-industrial service sector and New Age spirituality' (Aupers and Houtman 2006: 217).

Nonetheless, at least one of the discussants in the Schauder–Lefébure dialogues emerged from a context of British left politics. In his editorials from 1967–70 for *New Blackfriars*, Lefébure (then known as Pascal Lefébure) envisages a general process of social evolution or creativity, a kind of vitalist Marxism: 'a system based on competitive demand and profit' is an 'evolutionary cul de sac', whereas 'working for a co-operative, socialist world welfare state' is a 'regathering for the forward élan of life' which 'assumes the form of a shaking out of all our relationships and their recasting to a more universal and fraternal design' (Lefébure 1967: 116). Given this background to Lefébure's spiritual seeking, it is unsurprising that the Schauder–Lefébure dialogues propose a spiritualised counselling that in some ways resembles what Carrette and King call '[t]he renunciatory spiritualities of Asia, such as Hindu yoga, the various Buddhist traditions, and early Taoist philosophy' (Carrette and King 2005: 120). There is, as has been shown, a clear sense in which Schauder and Lefébure are, like these traditions as described by Carrette and King, 'seek[ing] to develop "other-directed" ethical ideals such as compassion and consideration for others by dissolving the fantasies of an autonomous individual self at the centre of our world' (Carrette and King 2005: 120). Such substantive political critique means that, rather than being the 'capitalist spirituality' condemned by Carrette and King, the Schauder–Lefébure dialogues resemble more the 'progressive spirituality' identified by Gordon Lynch in his discussion of the ideology of the 'progressive milieu', which consists of those 'individuals, organizations and networks across and beyond a range of religious traditions that are defined by a liberal or radical approach to religious belief and/or a green or left-of-centre set of political attitudes and commitments' (Lynch 2007: 10).

The 'doctor and the priest' of the Schauder–Lefébure dialogues may therefore be identified as amongst those '"organic intellectuals" whose life and work is embedded within the social structures and relationships of the progressive milieu, and who represent its leading intellectual edge' (Lynch 2007: 41). By gesturing to a left politics and to a model of counselling informed by vitalism, Schauder and Lefébure share with progressive spiritual ideology an identification of 'the divine as the energy that vitalizes the universe and that is the motivating force behind all that gives life and health' (Lynch 2007: 47). Indeed, such vitalist motifs are now regarded as fundamental to spirituality by Heelas, who has moved beyond the Self-spirituality and spiritual revolution paradigms to insist that, '[f]or participants, spirituality *is* life-itself, the "life-force" or "energy" which flows through all human life (and much else besides)' (Heelas 2008: 27). Precisely this meaning was coded into the term 'Wellspring' as originally employed within the Davidson Clinic. Lefébure alludes to Rushforth in the dialogues when he discusses 'the mysterious presence of some third thing' in the counselling relationship: 'what is revealed in … the innermost core … of dialogue and reciprocal duality … is, in Dr. Winifred Rushforth's fine phrase, the truth at the bottom of the well – … the mystery underlying the wellspring' (Lefébure 1982: 95). This 'wellspring' ideology may not have remained operative in the history of Wellspring itself, but certainly in the view of one of the organisation's founders, counselling leads to the 'truth at the bottom of the well, the individual wellspring's very reservoir' (Lefébure 1985: 53). Though it may be tempting to theorise the 'wellspring' metaphor solely in terms of access to a higher (or deeper) self, it also points, via vitalism, to a more co-operative and social vision of the self: the individual wellspring is a surface manifestation of a deeper, living connection between persons.

Yet, although the Schauder–Lefébure dialogues problematise Self-spirituality, they appear to have had little or no enduring effect upon the context of Scottish counselling. As Bondi notes (Bondi 2013: 681), Wellspring's counselling practice now has no particular religious or spiritual affiliation beyond the motivations of a few practitioners. Unlike the Davidson Clinic's other successors, the Salisbury Centre and Sempervivum, Wellspring has lost (and perhaps never really had) any essential connection with the holistic milieu. One important factor is undoubtedly the decline of the 'intrinsically religious clinical space' (Bondi 2013: 677) that had been offered by the Davidson Clinic. As Bondi explains, even church-sponsored counselling organisations offered (in theory at least) a secular space to consumers who in the main had no affiliation to organised religion:

> none of these organisations claimed to offer 'Christian counselling'; nor did they claim to be offering counselling that differed significantly from any imagined secular variant. A factor underlying this shift away from an explicitly Christian version of psychotherapy in the 1940s was that Scotland had changed in the intervening years from a neo-Durkheimian environment in which Christian affiliation was very much the norm to a post-Durkheimian one in which such affiliation could not be taken for granted ... In this more differentiated urban environment, any services designed to reach beyond congregations needed to present themselves in new ways. (Bondi 2013: 679)

The 'clinical space' of counselling therefore became secularised. Lacking even an underlying religious organisation, the spiritualised counselling of Lefébure and Schauder was merely an idiosyncratic discourse that, at best, dissolved into the wider holistic milieu.

Counselling training also became more professionalised during the 1990s, eroding the religious ethos of earlier organisations (Bondi 2013: 681–2), and establishing various de facto professional protocols, even though counselling and psychotherapy were not eventually to be regulated by the Health Professions Council (now known as the Health and Care Professions Council). Amongst these boundary definitions was an emerging professional prohibition on the direct giving of advice (Bondi 2013: 673) which has also spread even into consciously spiritual contexts. (William West, for instance, repudiates a model of the psychotherapist as 'something of a wise man', 'akin to a spiritual teacher or elder of the community who could offer sound advice' (West 2000: 38).) This de facto ban on giving advice is another factor mitigating against the Schauder–Lefébure dialogues, which frankly offer moral instruction as a stimulus to the client's growth and development. Lefébure's 1996 article, 'Who will count as a counsellor?: gleanings and tea-leaves', seems conscious of this narrowing of the professional boundaries of counselling: he announces his intention 'to sound the alarm' (Lefébure 1996: 15) given (he believes) that 'the momentum towards national organisation and therefore professionalisation of psychological care is unstoppable' (Lefébure 1996: 12). He anticipates 'the corresponding development of at least two national registers, possibly one somehow amalgamated national register, outside of which it will become illegal to practise as a psychotherapist/counsellor' (Lefébure 1996: 14). Although statutory regulation of counselling has not (so far) come into force in the United Kingdom (which currently prefers voluntary self-regulation), Lefébure was presumably concerned at the implications for his eclectic theory and practice.

A further probable factor in the historical inefficacy of the Schauder–Lefébure model is the account of gender which the dialogues initially promoted (and eventually repudiated). Bondi notes a feature of 'church-sponsored counselling centres' was that 'the majority of the volunteer counsellors who were trained and who delivered counselling were women' (Bondi 2013: 679). Indeed, this also seems to be true not only of counselling, but of the holistic milieu: Woodhead argues that the latter is disproportionately female because 'it makes use of resources traditionally drawn upon by women – religion and the nurturing care of other women – in order to move beyond traditional activities and the roles they entailed' (Woodhead 2007: 124). Yet the Schauder–Lefébure dialogues were only latterly responsive to the needs of female practitioners and clients, and offered initially the almost extinct narrative of woman as 'angel in the house'. In the 1990 edition of *Conversations*, Lefébure explains that while the earlier editions of 1982 and 1985 contained 'a chapter on "Woman and man"', 'Our own later hesitations about it were reinforced by comments from outside', so that he and Schauder 'decided to omit it altogether' (Lefébure and Schauder 1990: xvi). The 'hesitations' were probably due to its manifestly sexist pronouncements on the 'complementary' natures of men and women (Lefébure 1982: 55). Schauder asserts, for instance, that 'a woman is according to her psychic being given to confabulation, she can invent her own truth' (Lefébure 1982: 55), and argues that a woman without a man to look up to, will become 'absolutely indigestible, aggressive, self-dependent, self-righteous, or whatever' (Lefébure 1982: 46). Schauder also positions women in the waning role of 'angel in the house' when he asserts that something 'radiates' from his wife and daughter, 'a positive balm for me, the very thing I've been missing and of which I feel I've been depleted' (Lefébure 1982: 58). Women are innately more spiritual than men; their 'incarnation is less dense and less intense, is much more *spiritually* open' (Lefébure 1982: 53). Lefébure amplifies this idea by gendering the Thomistic distinction between '*intellectus* and *ratio*, roughly intuitive understanding and discursive reasoning in the sense of ratiocination, working out': 'if we equate the intuitive with the feminine quality and the ratiocinative with the masculine quality then what the woman has to give the man is this more spiritual, synchronic intuition' (Lefébure 1982: 56). Implicit in this argument, is the idea that women, by virtue of their putative greater capacity for *intellectus*, are closer to angels since the latter know entirely by apodictic insight: 'the human being, precisely as human being, as distinct from the angel, does not have an immediate and simple perception of the truth' (Lefébure 1982: 56).

Conclusion

Steven Sutcliffe criticises the field of New Age studies for its 'entrenched essentialism' (Sutcliffe 2006: 295), and uses Pierre Bourdieu's concept of the *habitus* (the 'customary, routinized attitudes and practices' of everyday life (Sutcliffe 2006: 298)), to argue that '[s]o-called "new age religion" is ... more fruitfully conceptualised as a popular *habitus* within majority ethnic cultures' (Sutcliffe 2006: 302). 'Popular religion', states Sutcliffe, 'consists in pragmatic adaptation to and supplementation of normative religious orders by various non-elite constituencies of practitioners, both subaltern and middle ranking' (Sutcliffe 2006: 301). When understood as popular religion, argues Sutcliffe, '*sui generis* new age cults and *gurus* begin to look more like an outgrowth from secularized and globalized Protestant cultures' (Sutcliffe 2006: 301). The continuities between Laing's practice of psychedelic *metanoia* and the earlier discourses of Christian psychotherapy promulgated by Murray and the Davidson Clinic clearly indicate this genealogy. Laing was a 1960s guru of countercultural London who offered a technology for spiritual renewal and rebirth that perpetuated earlier discursive Christian narratives of regeneration and rebirth through psychotherapy. Indeed, the narrative was appealing even to lapsed Roman Catholics such as Edna O'Brien as well as to consumers from secularising majority Protestant cultures. Rushforth's activities further substantiate and elaborate Sutcliffe's argument. What Rushforth brought to Christianity, psychotherapy and vitalism, was not a rigorous theoretical contribution, but instead a discursive and practical translation of her worldview into the *habitus* via signifiers such as the 'wellspring', symbolic objects such as the sempervivum plant, and ritual practices such as the dream groups. While Heelas may insist on a clear distinction between Christian and New Age spirituality (Heelas 2008: 27–8), this view cannot be sustained: Rushforth's 'New Age' was (to echo Sutcliffe's words) a popular outgrowth from a secularised Protestant culture, an offshoot in which the life narratives of discursive Christianity were continued via psychoanalytic psychotherapy, and grafted into a vitalist cosmology. The discourses and practices of the Davidson Clinic's Christian psychotherapy, and the parallel discourses of Rushforth's vitalist healing, thus exemplify precisely the pragmatic adaptation and supplementation of normative religiosity identified by Sutcliffe. Nor should it be assumed that the development of 'New Age' psychotherapeutic popular religion necessarily involves the attenuation of Christian political engagement. As the Schauder–Lefébure dialogues show, there have been oppositional strands which are conscious of, and resist, the accusation that the spirituality (and counselling) are, or should be, functional for the normative cultivation of individuality in post-war consumer capitalism.

Conclusion

Refer to the intertwined theories, practices, actors and organisations examined in this monograph as 'Scottish Christian psychotherapy'. What, then, was Scottish Christian psychotherapy?

It began in the late nineteenth and early twentieth centuries when psychology consolidated as a distinct discipline, and as psychoanalytic psychology challenged the somatic orthodoxy of psychiatry in Scotland and the United Kingdom. Psychology, like anthropology, claimed partial jurisdiction over a domain of the human in which religion and theology had long been authoritative. The radical critique of religion offered by Freudian psychoanalysis stimulated psychological and clinical experts who, like most of the population in Scotland and the United Kingdom, were affiliated to one of the various organised Christian denominations. As Freudian ideas and practices were imported into Scotland, and into the wider United Kingdom by Scots, they were modified not only by domestic psychological ideas, but also by post-Darwinian programmes of evolutionary inquiry into the validity and future direction of Christianity – represented by, for instance, Biblical higher criticism and comparative anthropology. These traditions included a riposte to Social Darwinism in which natural history was conceptualised as a Providential design leading to the evolution of higher mammals, and then to human societies which embodied the supposed maternal values of altruism and self-sacrifice celebrated in Christian wisdom.

The inter-war years saw an intense period of innovation as psychoanalytic and psychotherapeutic practitioners and theorists explored the implications of such traditions for psychoanalytic ideas, and vice versa. Innovators such as Suttie, Macmurray and Fairbairn critiqued and revised what they saw as the fundamentally asocial model of the psyche presumed by Freud, while offering their own accounts of psychopathology that laid more explanatory and therapeutic weight on personal, or 'object' relationships. Psychoanalytic and psychotherapeutic concepts and methods were seen explicitly by figures such as Crichton-Miller as a way to discover, preserve and reinvigorate the supposed imperishable core to Christianity: the religion was seen primarily as a progressive social movement that sought to promote loving fellowship within a putatively universal community. Such ideas proceeded partly from existing intellectual traditions that theorised interpersonal communion as the fundamental social bond, but they were also fostered by organisational contexts, such as the Tavistock Clinic, and Fairbairn's isolated private practice, which permitted a more eclectic, scep-

tical and selective attitude to psychoanalytic orthodoxy. The Adlerian tradition became a particularly fruitful source of ideas for a psychotherapy
oriented towards social relationships, and towards an emerging welfare
state.

The heyday of Scottish Christian psychotherapy continued into the
1950s. The Davidson Clinic, as a charitable organisation outside the NHS,
marketed Christian psychotherapy to Scottish consumers, including clergy,
who appreciated its refurbishment of Christian life narratives, as well as
the additional insight into pastoral care and organisational life. Laing's
psychiatry fruitfully explored a variety of Christian traditions, including the domestic incarnational and corporate theology of MacLeod and
the Iona Community, the existential theology that was being imported
and translated into Glasgow, and the mystical theology represented by
Underhill. Yet Christian psychotherapy could not establish a secure niche
in the psychological and medical professions, and gradually found itself
being eroded, or displaced into alternative contexts. These determinants
are well represented by the Church of Scotland's Special Commission
on Spiritual Healing. The Commission's 1958 Report set firm limits on
healing ministry, even within the Church's great alignment, in light of
the Baillie Commission, with the welfare state. Spiritual healing (which
extended to psychological and psychosomatic therapeutics) was complementary to the work of medical and psychological specialists, and should
prioritise spiritual wellbeing, particularly reconciliation to the will of God;
it should not dabble in areas beyond the competence of the average minister. Specialised areas of professional interest were also identified, such
as hospital chaplaincy, where teamwork with medical experts could be formally pursued in an organisational setting. The rhetoric around 'miracles
of healing', such as those supposedly offered by the Davidson Clinic's psychotherapy, became much more subdued, and representatives of spiritual
healing, such as the Davidson's former Governor and Christian psychotherapist, J. A. C. Murray, were displaced into marginal organisations such
as the Fellowship of Christian Healing. Laing's ongoing project to recast
himself as the 'angel in the house' who preserved Christian life-narrative
discourses could prosper better in countercultural organisations such as
Kingsley Hall, which was hospitable to his grandiose self-image.

The cultural and social decline in organised Christianity during the
1960s was also crucial. Secularisation, and the concomitant growth in non-
traditional spirituality, worked further changes on Christian psychotherapy
as life-narrative patterns of regeneration and rebirth were grafted into a
wider syncretic and perennialist New Age spirituality that freely adopted
ideas and practices from a variety of sources, including world religions and
New Religious Movements. The underlying narratives remained remarkably similar, but could be offered to consumers whose spiritual needs were
not accommodated by the orthodoxies of declining Christendom. Elite
consumers underwent transformative *metanoia* in the countercultural 1960s

context presided over by Laing. In Edinburgh, the Davidson Clinic, and its Rushforth-inspired successors, offered regenerative contact with the universal 'wellspring' that was held to underlie authentic religious and spiritual life. As well as going underground in New Age Self-spirituality, Scottish Christian psychotherapy found refuge in the model of counselling promoted in the 1980s by Schauder and Lefébure, who offered a syncretic spiritual counselling which also reflexively distanced itself from the author- isation of subjective experience. Nonetheless, this was a temporary refuge: the Schauder–Lefébure model was relegated to a historical footnote as the professionalisation of counselling consolidated an essentially secular theory and practice, even where underwritten by Christian organisations.

The history of Scottish Christian psychotherapy has been crucially shaped by a number of processes, most prominently: the ongoing rationalisation of Christianity; the diffusion of psychological expertise; the 'subjective turn'; the United Kingdom's transition to majority secularism (accompanied by the growth in New Age spirituality); and the professionalisation of caring occupations. Christianity looked to psychology, and particularly psychoa- nalysis and psychotherapy, as an instrument of rationalisation during an era when the psychological disciplines were permeating cultural and organi- sational life. The fruitful alliance between psychotherapy and Christianity offered Christian life-narrative patterns of rebirth and regeneration that were useful for the new, post-war era of subjectivisation, in which an 'inner' standard of authenticity displaced ascriptive criteria (sex, ethnicity, class, etc.) in the shaping of personal identity. This alliance was, however, eroded by secularisation, which increasingly displaced Christian psychotherapy into the holistic milieu, where it offered a popular, syncretic religiosity of the self. Moreover, professionalisation repeatedly displaced Christian psychotherapy from its various organisational niches, whether in psycho- therapy, ministry or counselling.

Trailing threads and missing 'voices'

Naturally, this monograph has left unexplored a number of figures and ini- tiatives connected with Scottish Christian psychotherapy. The investigation in the preceding chapters has been largely framed by a national context, focusing on developments within Scotland, or led by Scottish agents outside Scotland. Inevitably, the discussion must be incomplete, and leave behind trailing threads that could be pursued further, whether with reference to Scotland, the United Kingdom or a broader, transnational context.

Macmurray's religious philosophy, for instance, casts a long shadow within Scotland and the United Kingdom. His Gifford Lectures appear in the bibliography to the Glaswegian psychiatrist Aaron Esterson's *The Leaves of Spring* (1970), in which Esterson (1923–99) pursues in detail one of the case studies that he and Laing developed in *Sanity, Madness and the Family* (1964). In the second part of *The Leaves of Spring*, which explains the principles of Esterson's analysis, Macmurray's distinction between mechanical, organic and personal explanation is invoked, as well as his thesis that persons are essentially persons in relation (Esterson 1970: 185–201). The work of the English (Leeds-based) psychotherapist, academic and Congregational minister H. J. S. [Harry] Guntrip (1901–75) in object relations psychoanalysis is also consciously within the parameters of Macmurray's thought. In *Personality Structure and Human Interaction* (1968), Guntrip, who was analysed extensively by Fairbairn and later by D. W. Winnicott, aligns Macmurray's 'definition of the sphere of religion as the sphere of human relationships' with Fairbairn's 'fundamental concern with "object relationships" as the substance of human living' (Guntrip 1961: 253). In *You and Your Nerves* (1951), originally broadcast on BBC Radio as a series of ten talks, Guntrip uses Macmurray's personalist philosophy to argue that 'belief in God ultimately springs from the fact that it is the very essence of human nature to be a person, and to need and seek personal relationships' (Guntrip 1951: 103). An explicit integration of Fairbairn, Macmurray, and additionally Suttie, has been systematically developed by Graham S. Clarke, who is professionally associated with the Centre for Psychoanalytic Studies at the University of Essex. Clarke argues in his monograph *Personal Relations Theory: Fairbairn, Macmurray and Suttie*, that the tradition which runs through these thinkers, and which he identifies as distinctively Scottish, should be used to develop a Kuhnian normal science paradigm that could unify psychoanalytic research (Clarke 2006). The diligent work of J. D. Sutherland (1905–91), Fairbairn's former student and analysand, in connection with centres such as the Menninger Foundation in Topeka, Kansas, has carried object relations theory to American climes. In the USA, Fairbairn's legacy has been preserved, and developed, by figures such as Jill and David Scharff (e.g. Scharff and Scharff 2005), while in South America the *Asociación Psicoanalítica Argentina* shelters a Fairbairn special interest group, 'Espacio Fairbairn' (Campi et al. 2014). There is also continuing contemporary interest within Scotland in the ramifications of a personal relations approach to psychotherapy and counselling (e.g. Cullen et al. 2014, Kirkwood 2012).

As well as leaving certain connections unexplored, this monograph has also been able to exploit only a limited range of testimony (both conceivable and actual) to the actions, organisations and ideologies contained in its narrative. The geographical emphasis of the preceding chapters must be acknowledged: the examination of a Scottish context concentrates on developments in Scotland's most highly populated city, Glasgow, and the nation's capital, Edinburgh. This focus on the central belt of Scotland neglects developments in other urban locations. Aberdeen, for instance, would yield to further investigation, particularly of developments after Adler's death in the city in 1937. These include the work of David Cairns (1904–92), Professor in Practical Theology, and W. Malcolm Millar (1913–96), Professor of Mental Health, under whose supervision the Australian minister Francis Macnab (b. 1931) undertook doctoral work in Kingseat Mental Hospital, near Aberdeen. The foreword to Macnab's subsequent monograph *Estrangement and Relationship* (1966) is provided by R. D. Laing; and in the text itself, Macnab characterises the theological issue at stake as one of corporate salvation (Macnab 1966: xiii). Macnab's subsequent career as a minister of the Uniting Church in Australia involved the founding in 1961 in Melbourne of the Cairnmillar Institute (named after Cairns and Millar), which continues to offer psychotherapeutic and counselling services and training. As well as neglecting other Scottish urban centres, this monograph has also said little about developments in Scotland's extensive rural hinterland, including the Highlands and Islands. The Shetland-born psychiatrist Ronald A. Sandison (1916–2010) was a pioneer in LSD-therapy at Powick Hospital in Worcestershire during the 1950s and 1960s, and returned to Shetland from 1975 to 1982 to improve psychiatric services on the island (Sessa 2010). Sandison's collocation of Christianity and psychotherapy is readily apparent in his writings: he refers, for instance, to 'a fundamental issue for group analysts', namely 'the way in which we understand the "other worldly" or the spiritual when it manifests itself in the group' (Sandison 1984: 248).

Many of the professions relevant to this investigation were male-dominated for much of the period under examination. This means there are only tantalising glimpses of female professional agents such as Jane Isabel Suttie, who seems likely to have had a far greater influence upon the object relations tradition than the existing record can securely evidence. The problem persists with respect to the large female constituency who became interested in psychoanalytic and psychotherapeutic ideas during the interwar period. This group appears in attendance at Alexandra Adler's lectures in Edinburgh in 1937, given shortly after her father's death in Aberdeen. According to *The Scotsman* newspaper, 'she addressed a large audience, in which women preponderated, in the British Medical Association Hall' (Adler's beliefs 1937). Although the evidence and testimony surrounding the Davidson Clinic helps to provide a more balanced representation, it prefers elite female practitioners, such as the Tavistock-trained Rushforth, or her colleague Margaret Allan, who also received analysis at the Tavistock, and was closely involved in the formation of the Scottish Pastoral Association (Darroch 1973: 6–7). Almost nothing is known about Jean Neillands, who (according to Darroch) 'later became one of our best analysts', and who in the early days of the Davidson Clinic 'was taking her first patient in her spare time, while continuing to work in the office of British Rail' (Darroch 1973: 9).

The narrative in this monograph is dominated by the voices of the middle and professional classes, as represented by medical doctors, academics and clergy. Moreover, many of the key actors (for example, Suttie, Rushforth, Fairbairn) came from securely middle and upper-middle-class backgrounds, and even a 'lad of pairts' (an upwardly mobile educated male) such as Laing entered the professional classes from a lower-middle-class background. Their testimony only indirectly and infrequently records class differences and antagonisms. Rushforth's 1933 child-rearing manual, *The Outstretched Finger*, proclaims that 'if Peace is to come in our time we must lay the foundation for it in our dealings with the future citizen in his nursery' (Rushforth 1933: 20). Yet Rushforth's social world is one in which the middle-class mother can delegate childcare to appropriately enlightened nurses, nannies, ayahs and boarding schools (for example, Rushforth 1933: 14, 19–20, 50–3). Gerson correctly identifies a gendered domestic ideology in the object relations worldview, whereby '[w]omen are defined by their potential or actual motherhood and accordingly are relegated to a single, if important, role' (Gerson 2009b: 388). But this underlying patriarchal worldview is ameliorated by Rushforth's class position: the well-off mother can be released back to her professional duties by a household that pays for childcare and boarding school. A similar obliviousness to class difference is apparent in Jane Darroch's memoir of the Davidson Clinic, which offers a harmonious vision of disinterested beneficence whereby the lower classes are offered variable fees (rather than a higher income):

> 'My charwoman has been so much better since she went to the Davidson Clinic.' So said a friend of mine recently, while another friend told me of a young honours graduate who had benefited greatly through going there. For over thirty years the Davidson Clinic has been a place where the bus conductor, the charwoman, the joiner, the clerkess, the minister, the doctor, the poet, the housewife – everyone of every social and educational level – could receive individual help and understanding, based on the discoveries of Freud and Jung, at a fee graded to suit his or her income and in many cases free. (Darroch 1973: 5)

Yet as Rushforth's testimony indicates, the working-class population could be suspicious of a clinic that remained outwith the National Health Service, and therefore seemed to endorse the principle of charitable support for healthcare. During a fundraising drive (a 'flag day') on the streets of Edinburgh in the early years of the NHS, she was confronted over this issue: 'The fact that we charge fees was brought up against us and one gentleman said "Na, Na, I would not contribute to a Tory organisation". We wonder whether he has a Tory inside him whom he is ready to project on to anything' (Rushforth 1985a: 170). Skilled men, though, had been particularly hostile to pre-NHS flag days on grounds of political principle (Hayes 2012: 642–3), psychoanalytic explanations for their intransigence notwithstanding.

Although there are colonial settings in the narrative of this monograph, indigenous perspectives are poorly represented, largely because of a lack of easily accessible sources. The New Zealand Association of Psychotherapists during the time of Bevan-Brown's leadership, for instance, seems entirely oblivious to the Maori population. There are, of course, occasional glimpses of the subaltern, refracted through the testimony of the settler population. For instance, Rushforth's various narratives contain recollections of her time in India, where she refers to a 'cross-fertilisation occurring between the Indian culture and our own' (Rushforth 1984: 55). She elaborates this hybridity as a recognition of indigenous psychological 'wisdom':

> [o]ne day on visiting the children's ward I found a Telengu woman, the hospital dhobin, sitting cradling one of these infants on her thighs as she sat cross-legged in the sun. I suggested she should put the child into the cot; she indignantly asked, 'Did I not know that children needed to be fondled, to be in touch with the body of the mother or whoever could act as substitute?['] I recognised her wisdom, and this incident impressed me deeply. (Rushforth 1962: 4099)

Was Rushforth genuinely provoked to question the 'taboo on tenderness'? This encounter might have articulated views she already held, or be retrospectively narrated as a vindication of psychotherapy from a latterly authorised voice. What appear to be counterflows of indigenous knowledge are perhaps better understood as raw material for Rushforth's Orientalism, which is particularly clear in her assimilation of world religions to her vitalist worldview:

> In my childhood and youth we were sending missionaries to the East to spread the Christian gospel, and today, strangely, they have nearly all been recalled. Now streaming in from India, China, Tibet, Japan and Thailand too, we get the different schools teaching us the ways of meditation, other ways of approaching the great Source. (Rushforth 1983: 139)

A similar Orientalism is apparent in Schauder's blithe assimilation of so-called 'Hinduism' to Christian mysticism. His 'universal religious approach' simplifies the complex historical and cultural reality of Asian religions. For Richard King, '"Hinduism" is ... a Western-inspired abstraction' (King 1999: 98) that has constructed a unitary religion analogous to Christianity through, for instance, a 'textualization' that seized upon and valorised analogues to the Judaeo-Christian scriptures (King 1999: 101), and a correlated perennialist agenda that 'emphasize[d] the "mystical" nature of Hindu religion by reference to the "esoteric" literature known as the Vedānta, the end of the Vedas – namely the Upaniṣads' (King 1999: 119).

Finally, the patient or client voice has been marginal to this investigation. Where such testimony has been employed, it is largely mediated through the testimony of others (for example, in case reports or analogous narratives), or it is a first-person narrative of ostensible success – such as Edna O'Brien's narrative of her acid trip, or the various endorsements assembled for the purposes of the Davidson Clinic. Counter-narratives from patients and clients have been harder to obtain. Sigal's *Zone of the Interior* (Sigal 2005) is one prominent exception, but is clearly a literary artefact produced by an elite agent. Psychiatric historiography is much more advanced in this area of 'history from below', with a stronger sense of the methodological need for patient testimony (for example, Davies 2001), exemplified in UK-focused research using nineteenth-century asylum patient letters (Beveridge 1998) and oral-history investigation of aversive therapies for homosexuality in the NHS during the 1950s and 1960s (Dickinson et al. 2012). However, excluding biographical and literary memoir, there has been far less historiographic work done to identify and capture testimony from patients and clients (as opposed to providers) in the realms of psychotherapy, counselling and spiritual care. There is little from the patient or client voice that equals, for instance, the dual client-analyst viewpoint in Harry Guntrip's frank, albeit fragmentary, first-person account of his lengthy analysis with Fairbairn, which lasted from 1949 to 1960 (Hazell 1996: 74). Guntrip gently criticises the Edinburgh analyst for his formal manner, and rigidly intellectualised approach to therapy, illustrated in the interior space of the consulting room:

> The set-up of the consulting room itself creates an atmosphere which has meaning. Fairbairn lived in the country and saw patients in the old Fairbairn family house in Edinburgh. I entered a large drawing room as waiting room, furnished with beautiful valuable antiques, and proceeded to the study as consulting room, also large with a big antique bookcase filling most of one wall. Fairbairn sat behind a large flat-topped desk, I used to think 'in state' in a high-backed plush-covered armchair. (Guntrip 1994a: 355)

The sense of distance in the clinical space between the upper-middle-class Fairbairn, and Guntrip (the son of a struggling shopkeeper (Hazell 1996: 1–10)) is readily apparent in this vignette, but is the kind of meaning that remains unexplored in Hazell's psychoanalytic biography, which draws upon the 'eleven exercise books of 200 pages each' in which Guntrip recorded his analysis (Hazell 1996: 74), and which remain for consultation in the Menninger Clinic Archives.

Christianity, psychotherapy and the science–religion relationship

As well as illuminating a specific national confluence of psychotherapy and Christianity, this book's investigation of Scottish developments also provides a detailed case study that can inform conceptualisation of the relationship between psychology and religion. The historian Graham Richards outlines three main perceived relationships between psychology and religion: (i) religion is seen as essentially impervious to psychological investigation, which cannot invalidate or scientifically encroach upon religious belief and conduct; (ii) religion and psychology are seen as complementary or even partially identical activities that address the spiritual core to religious life; (iii) religion is (in part or whole) valid only as a folk psychology which will be supplanted by its scientific successor (Richards 2011: 141–9). These three perceived relationships between psychology and religion resemble the synoptic taxonomy of the relationship between science and religion proposed by the theologian Ian G. Barbour. According to Barbour, there are four possible relationships between these two endeavours: conflict, independence, dialogue and integration (Barbour 1990, ch. 1). *Conflict,* equivalent to Richards's third category, is represented by the confrontation between scientific materialism (abetted by reductionism) and biblical literalism (strictly, literalism and inerrancy) where both claim to make 'rival literal statements about the same domain': 'the victor, whichever it is, swallows the vanquished' (Barbour 1990: 4). For proponents of *independence* (equivalent to Richards's first category), each of science and religion 'has its own distinctive domain and its characteristic methods that can be justified on its own terms … there are two jurisdictions and each party must keep off the other's turf' (Barbour 1990: 10) – existential theology, for example, insists on a distinction 'between the realm of personal selfhood and the realm of impersonal objects' (Barbour 1990: 12). *Dialogue* refers to 'indirect interactions between science and religion involving boundary questions and methods of the two fields' (Barbour 1990: 16) – and is equivalent to the complementarity found within Richards's second category. Thus, according to Barbour, in the boundary relationship between Christianity and Western science, the latter has imported a (now latent) Christian presupposition regarding 'the contingency and intelligibility of nature' (Barbour 1990: 17) which enables the empirical investigation of a world amenable to human cognition. *Integration* (the remainder of Richards's second category) brings together 'the content of theology and the content of science' (Barbour 1990: 23), ranging from natural theology's evidence of design in nature, to reformulation of science and religion in light of each other (such as Teilhard's evolutionary cosmology (Barbour 1990: 183–5)), to a thoroughgoing 'inclusive metaphysics' (Barbour 1990: 24). Barbour's taxonomy, unlike Richards's, is explicitly evaluative: he regards conflict as mistaken, and independence as limited because it fails to recognise 'the possibility of constructive dialogue and mutual enrichment' (Barbour 1990: 16). Science and religion are therefore ushered towards dialogue and integration.

If Barbour's scheme is applied to the history of Scottish Christian psychotherapy, then dialogue and integration are apparently the most relevant categories. The category of independence is largely irrelevant, since none of the actors, ideologies and organisations studied within this monograph understand themselves as self-sufficient autarkies located within either 'psychotherapy' or 'Christianity'. Laing's use of existentialism, for instance, is intended to dialogically enrich the psychiatric understanding of psychotic patients, and even offers integration when psychosis is taken to reveal the essence of early Christian experience. Some of the encounter between Christianity and psychotherapy elaborated in this monograph can indeed be modelled (albeit imprecisely) along the lines of a conflict in which psychotherapy attempts to annexe Christianity (Richards's third category). Suttie's invitation to 'exploit the resources of religious belief and feeling for the promotion of mental health and social harmony' seems to indicate a psychological rationalisation of Christian tradition, even though there is a positive evaluation of the faith (Emotional Development: 4). But most of the interaction between Christianity and psychotherapy revealed by this monograph understands itself as dialogue or integration, with the former tending to be the academically and professionally authorised relationship.

Fairbairn, for instance, authorises a complementary, dialogic relationship between psychotherapy and religion. In his 1958 address to an audience of clergy, Fairbairn characterises religion as 'the earliest and original form of psychotherapy', tracing a genealogy whereby '[p]sychotherapy as such may be said to have developed out of religion as the result of an attempt to establish the cure of psychological troubles on a scientific basic' (Fairbairn 1994f: 363). But Fairbairn does not see psychotherapy as the rational inheritor that agonistically supplants the Christian care of souls: 'The concrete problems with which religion and psychotherapy deal have much in common, albeit the two disciplines deal with these problems in different ways; the approach of psychotherapy being characteristically medical, whereas the approach of religion is characteristically spiritual' (Fairbairn 1994f: 363). Although he compares psychotherapy with 'the forgiveness of sins and the casting out of devils' (Fairbairn 1994f: 364), this is clearly an analogy. Fairbairn leaves room for a separate 'priestly function of absolution and exorcism' (Fairbairn 1994f: 364), as well as 'an ordinary spiritual approach' in pastoral care (Fairbairn 1994f: 365): these would be unsuited, though, for patients who have 'an element of morbidity' that requires properly psychotherapeutic remedy (Fairbairn 1994f: 364). A similar view on the complementarity of psychotherapy and religion is promoted in the same year by Fairbairn's analysand, Harry Guntrip, in response to criticisms of psychotherapy made in the Christian *British Weekly* by the theologian John G. McKenzie (see Fergusson 2012: 301). McKenzie's stentorian excursus on the limitations of psychotherapy contends that psychotherapists 'know that love is the greatest psychotherapeutic agent; but they can neither give nor receive, as Freud knew' – 'The only thing that can dissolve guilt feelings is the forgiveness of God' (McKenzie 1958). Guntrip responds by stating that psychotherapy can and should offer parental love to the patient precisely so that he or she can be relieved of 'pathological guilt':

> The therapist seeks to bring this diseased pseudo-moral guilt into the fullest consciousness, not that the patient may seek forgiveness for it, but that he may get rid of it, grow out of it. The mental field is now clear for the development of a healthy moral sense. (Guntrip 1994b: 402)

Guntrip's confidence that 'the psychotherapist cannot dissolve *real* guilt' draws a border that establishes a complementary priestly function of absolution like that indicated by Fairbairn (Guntrip 1994b: 403).

Fairbairn's address to clergy was delivered on 8 May 1958 (Birtles and Scharff 1994: 481), just a few weeks before the General Assembly of the Church of Scotland considered the Report on Spiritual Healing which also sought, through inter-professional dialogue, to consensually 'define the various '"zones" of therapeutics' (Church of Scotland General Assembly 1958: 918) across somatic medicine, psychological medicine and healing ministry. If there were any modern-day miracles, concluded the Report, then (whatever the Davidson Clinic might proclaim) their divine provenance was unknowable: clear-cut healing miracles are knowable only 'in the healing ministry and methods of Jesus' which are distinguished by 'a sense of sheer spiritual power, authority, and confidence' (Church of Scotland General Assembly 1958: 911). The minister's core function is not to request miraculous intervention in particular cases, but rather to promote reconciliation with the will of God and continued faith in face of death, disease, and other 'personal problems – doubts, fears, guilts, hopes, and aspirations' (Church of Scotland General Assembly 1958: 918). Psychological and psychosomatic healing might thereby incidentally occur, but 'the amateur should guard against over-simplifying the plight of a patient whose malady has been competently diagnosed as a psychoneurotic state, a condition which calls for skilful handling' (Church of Scotland General Assembly 1958: 917).

A dialogue defining mutually recognised borders is later elaborated in John R. Wilson's 1973 article (based on a 1969 conference paper) on the distinction between the three realms of 'pastoral care, pastoral counselling and psychotherapy' (Wilson 1973). Wilson was probably psychoanalysed within the integrationist ambience of the Davidson Clinic, but his view on the relationship between Christianity and psychotherapy is recognisably a dialogue promoting complementarity and mutual enrichment. Wilson repudiates the contention that Christianity is essentially impervious to, and wholly independent of, psychoanalytic psychology:

> Much has been written about the relationship between psychodynamics and the Christian faith, and many presume a dichotomy between them. This I cannot accept. I get upset when people say that as I am a Christian I must deal with the soul and spiritual matters rather than the mind and psychological matters. (Wilson 1973: 205)

However, Wilson does not accept an integration or fusion of psychotherapy with Christianity, for he distinguishes the spiritual and the mental as 'two models of the world', and identifies a basic need 'for the relationship between theological and psychological concepts to be worked out so that the Christian can deal with a coherent set of concepts to sustain him in his work' (Wilson 1973: 205). Much of the article concerns different professional requirements in pastoral care, pastoral counselling and psychotherapy, with particular emphasis on increased training as the psychodynamic approach impinges further on practice: psychotherapists need a training 'far longer and more rigorous' than the pastoral counsellor or pastoral worker (Wilson 1973: 192). Wilson's views on the relationship between theology and psychotherapy indicate that the latter functions properly when it brings about the psychological health that can facilitate Christian belief and practice, and that religion is misused when it substitutes for a scientific (psychological) relationship to troubled persons. Wilson testifies that his experience of psychoanalytic psychotherapy while a parish minister allowed him to 'come closer to human need without undue anxiety', demonstrating how '[t]he whole range of possible relationships are extended, and so are the experiences one can mediate' (Wilson 1973: 198). Before this personal transformation (which leads him out of the clergy and into his role as 'Counsellor for Students at a College of Education' (Wilson 1973: 203)), Wilson's pastoral care involved the application of moralistic and Scriptural bromides to his parishioners:

> One dished out prefabricated prescriptions for persons which were quite rightly rejected, as were those 'Words of God', the texts from scripture, thought to be appropriate to the occasion, which I am sure were employed not so much to help the person, as to bolster up the shaky condition of the helper. (Wilson 1973: 195)

The dialogic model was reinforced in a Scottish context in 1982, when the Scottish theologian Alastair Campbell (b. 1938) reviewed *Tight Corners in Pastoral Counselling* (Lake 1981), a collection of essays by Frank Lake (1914–82), the founder of Clinical Theology, and – like Laing and Rushforth – an exponent of theological-psychotherapeutic fusion (see p. 93). Campbell's frankly disparaging review was published in *Contact*, founded in 1960 as the journal of the Scottish Pastoral Association. It appeared a few days before Lake's death, and prompted a 'pained, if vigorous response' from Lake, who was Campbell's friend, and indeed a key sponsor of *Contact* (Lyall 2010: 154). Lake's reply was published in the subsequent issue alongside a conciliatory letter from Campbell, addressing the deceased Lake (Lyall 2010: 154). Although the interpersonal context was no doubt painful, this sharp exchange is informative because, as Graham Richards has noted, the issue of the relationship between psychology and religion was often 'debated in such a mutually respectful, civilised and non-confrontational manner that no thoroughgoing analysis of the broad picture of the relationship could emerge' (Richards 2011: 142). Campbell's review, and Lake's reply, express openly the rise of a professionally authorised dialogic model that pushed Lake's integrative Christianised psychotherapy into the realms of popular practice. Campbell tackles directly Lake's interest in the alleged pathogenic effects of intra-uterine experience, a causal relationship supposedly revealed in the practice of Primal Integration Therapy, which was applied in residential workshops held by the Clinical Theology Association: 'Subjects in these workshops are taken back to the very earliest period – conception itself – and through the use of guided fantasy are encouraged to re-live the primal experience of the foetus in the mother's womb' (Campbell 1982: 25). Campbell's blunt assessment is that '[m]uch of the discussion of "primal experiences" seems both epistemologically confused and of dubious theological relevance' (Campbell 1982: 25). With regard to the supposed scientific status of Lake's claims, Campbell employs verification and falsification as criteria for scientific rationality: 'So far as epistemology is concerned, Dr. Lake seems to be making statements which are impossible to substantiate (or refute), yet for which he claims the status of scientific fact' (Campbell 1982: 25). But nor are Lake's claims theological. Campbell diagnoses 'a failure to tackle the basic issues of theological methodology' that 'leaves the religious language in the book in a state of profound disarray' (Campbell 1982: 26). A consequence of 'this theological unevenness' is a

> lack of clarity about pastoral care and pastoral counselling. Are 'clinical theologians' the same, or different, from pastoral counsellors? What is the distinction, if any, between pastoral care and pastoral counselling? Who should offer pastoral care and/or pastoral counselling? How does primal therapy (or any other psychotherapeutic method) relate to pastoral work? (Campbell 1982: 26)

In his reply, Lake states that the review characterises his work as a 'record of scientific and theological bumbling' (Lake 1982: 27). He defends his research on foetal experience as 'a reliable map of early foetal life' built up inductively using reports from 'well over 90%' of a cohort of 1,200 participants in Clinical Theology workshops (Lake 1982: 28). These results, Lake insists, are 'scientifically-established facts, genuinely open to nullification' (Lake 1982: 28). With regard to his supposed misuse of theological terms, Lake defends his right to a separate, yet putatively consistent technical vocabulary: 'So long as the sense of the word is accurately preserved, why should not two definitions be allowed?' (Lake 1982: 28). Nor are Campbell's remarks about professional boundaries relevant to the project of Clinical Theology: 'The reviewer takes me to task several times for unclarity in defining the boundaries between "pastoral counselling", "pastoral care" and "non-professional helping". I do not work in a church setting, where it may remain important to make such distinctions' (Lake 1982: 29).

A contemporary Scottish authorisation of a dialogic relationship between psychotherapy and Christianity is articulated by the theologian David Fergusson, who argues that 'the relationship between psychotherapy and theology was jeopardized by attempts to achieve a premature integration or synthesis' (Fergusson 2013: 8). These attempts arose because the 'religious roots and motivation of several key practitioners led to an enthusiasm to reach a single discourse of therapeutic theology or equally theological psychotherapy' (Fergusson 2013: 8). On one hand, 'there was a tendency to pour religion into the moulds that had been created by psychotherapeutic theories' (Fergusson 2013: 8), while, on the other, the 'appropriation of psychotherapy [by religion] could be similarly eclectic and amateurish' (Fergusson 2013: 8). Fergusson concludes that theology and therapy 'represent different domains with their own descriptive terms and methods of evaluation' (Fergusson 2013: 9): 'The relationship is one in which partial analogies and links can be made, but with an awareness of the different conceptualities that are employed. These are neither reducible one to another, nor capable of full systematic integration' (Fergusson 2013: 9). Fergusson's position condenses the Barbour-informed rhetoric of inter-disciplinary dialogue which has increasingly demarcated theology from therapy, despite the partial integration attempted by some elements of Scottish Christian psychotherapy. The term 'boundary work' was created by Thomas F. Gieryn to characterise the imaginary mapmaking which, at key historical moments, distinguishes science from non-science in professional ideology (Gieryn 1983: 791–3), including the 'ideological demarcations of disciplines, specialities or theoretical orientations *within* science' (Gieryn 1983: 792). As Gieryn notes, 'boundary-work excludes rivals from within by defining them as outsiders with labels such as "pseudo", "deviant", or "amateur"' (Gieryn 1983: 792) – a point illustrated by Fergusson's characterisation of the integration of theology and therapy as 'eclectic and amateurish' (Fergusson 2013: 8).

The model articulated by Fergusson and others is widely authorised. In their 2002 handbook, *Psychology for Christian Ministry*, Fraser Watts, Rebecca Nye and Sara Savage raise 'the broader question of the relative "authority" of theology and psychology in pastoral counselling', proposing that '[t]he basic issue is whether theology and psychology ought to be regarded as two autonomous disciplines that are in dialogue with each other in the context of pastoral studies, or whether one ought to be subordinate to the other' (Watts et al. 2002: 199). Their preferred model for pastoral counselling is the former – a dialogue between counselling psychology and theology, in which neither discipline absorbs, overlaps with, or subordinates the other. They are, like Fergusson and Campbell, accordingly sceptical of what they call 'integrationist approaches' such as Frank Lake's 'Clinical Theology', which, they contend, 'approaches the relationship of psychology and theology in a way that often seems to fuse them, rather than keeping them distinct but exploring the links between them' (Watts et al. 2002: 199). This model of the relationship between psychotherapy and theology as a dialogue across a boundary is clearly embedded in the literature of pastoral theology. David Lyall, for instance, when discussing pastoral counselling, argues that while the discipline must inevitably 'draw upon the insights of one or more of the secular psychotherapies', '[w]hat the pastoral counsellors must not do is fall into an uncritical acceptance of such assumptions; rather they must bring to them a critique based upon a Christian understanding of what it means to be human' (Lyall 2001: 15). Such rhetoric is elaborated in Deborah van Deusen Hunsinger's metaphor of the 'bilingual fluency' of the pastoral counsellor in which 'theology would not need to be psychologized, nor psychology theologized. Nor would it be necessary to unify them conceptually or to integrate them systematically' (van Deusen Hunsinger 1995: 6).

However, it would be misleading to suppose that attempted integration between psychotherapy and religion has been consigned to the past. Daniel A. Helminiak, for instance, robustly criticises the contemporary project (largely North American, it seems) of theistic psychology and psychotherapy represented by, amongst others, P. Scott Richards and Allan E. Bergin. Helminiak rebukes this putative psychological subdiscipline for its tendency to define 'the psychology of religion and spirituality as inextricably linked to theism' (Helminiak 2010: 52), and also to 'consistently and expressly erase the lines between academic and professional specializations' so that 'psychology, philosophy, and theology are seemingly the same discipline' (Helminiak 2010: 53). As a consequence, theistic psychology, in Helminiak's view, deals in a hypostatised and falsely universalised 'generic theism' (Helminiak 2010: 68–9) insulated from the expert interrogation of professional theology (Helminiak 2010: 54). Helminiak characterises theistic psychology as science corrupted into non-science by an invasion of US popular piety, amplified by respect for 'belief' construed as religious identity. Theistic psychology promotes the 'audacious insistence that the first premise of anyone's religious argument is immune to criticism' and further assumes that 'everyone has a theology' (Helminiak 2010: 54), whether one's theism is conscious or not. Helminiak is particularly critical of theistic psychology's contention that psychology must accommodate theism by recognising divine intervention as a causal explanation for phenomena such as healing and extraordinary insight (Helminiak 2010: 59, 63–5). Instead, argues Helminiak, providential naturalism 'allows for both scientific explanation and for belief in an involved Creator-God' (Helminiak 2010: 60):

> God cares for creation not by constantly intervening to adjust the original creation and its particularities, as supernaturalism, occasionalism, and the theistic psychologists would have it, but by having established and by sustaining an overall order in which all particularities, because they function within this given order, work eventually toward the good. (Helminiak 2010: 61)

God may still choose to intervene (whether through scientifically inexplicable singular occurrences, or providential sequences of accidental causation), but caution should be exercised in any claims to have identified miraculous happenings (Helminiak 2010: 61–2).

Projects that integrate psychotherapy with religion and theology continue, though, to the present day. Isabel Clarke's work on psychosis revisits the Laingian claim that madness partially overlaps with authentic religious experience. In a rhetorical reversal, she criticises the so-called 'discontinuity model' for its attempt to clearly separate psychosis from spiritual experience:

> The starting point for this enquiry is the observation of overlap between the phenomenology of religious/spiritual and psychotic experience, and the prevalence of religious/spiritual themes in the pre-occupations of those diagnosed with psychosis. The old paradigm tended to assume that psychosis was mimicking spiritual experience – or was it the other way round? At all events, the agenda was to find a way to distinguish them. The new agenda takes this overlap/area of identity at face value. (Clarke 2010b: 101)

The arguments of Clarke and her affiliates draw upon a broad range of discourses, including post-empiricist philosophy of science (she offers a Kuhnian 'new paradigm'), as well as contemporary neuroscience, the expertise by experience of service users, and cultural psychiatry (Clarke 2010a *passim*). A debate that might seem to have closed after the decline of so-called 'antipsychiatry' has therefore been re-opened by newer arguments that challenge the territorial demarcation of psychology and spirituality. The US psychologist and Mad Pride activist, Seth Farber (b. 1951), makes a striking call in his 2012 book, *The Spiritual Gift of Madness*,

> to all those who are mad, or just heretics, to commit ourselves to a utopian or messianic-redemptive vision, to a realization of the kingdom of heaven, of God/Goddess, the divine life on Earth, as the basis for a new, spiritually informed political activism. (Farber 2012: 391)

Farber's manifesto defies easy summary, given its multiple theoretical and practical affiliations, which include a significant debt to the Indian guru Sri Aurobindo (1872–1950), whose vision of continuing spiritual evolution informs Farber's identification of the mad as a messianic political vanguard (Farber 2012: 362–80). Farber certainly owes much to the countercultural Laing of the 1960s. He criticises mental health activism for having neglected Laing's thesis that 'the mad were *superior* in certain important respects to normal people' by being 'more sensitive and spiritually aware' (Farber 2012: 6–7). Were the Mad Pride movement to recuperate 'the vision and sense of mission that provided the basis of its original inspiration' it would become, in Farber's view, the mobilising force for a political and spiritual vanguard composed of formerly pathologised 'prophets who will help to make the messianic vision a force within history' (Farber 2012: 34).

Many mental health experts are sympathetic to mad activism, which extends through mental patient consumerism, to the libertarian assertion of mad rights, to the demand for recognition of 'madness' as an identity (Miller 2018). Yet Farber has been criticised by the clinical psychologist and historian of psychotherapy, Daniel Burston, who remarks that

[w]hile mad people need hope and must often rebuild their shattered self-esteem in the process of recovery, telling people who are
profoundly disturbed that they are on the verge of a spiritual epiphany
that will point the way for the rest of us is not necessarily the best way
to do this, and may be counter-therapeutic. (Burston 2013: 332)

Nor does Farber appear to have any significant endorsement from within
organised Christianity, which is presumably equally wary of his unequivocal
claim that '[t]he mad have spiritual proclivities – "dangerous gifts" – that
reflect an unusual capacity for spiritual experience' (Farber 2012: 124).
Yet Farber illustrates how one strand of Scottish Christian Psychotherapy
has become detached from its national context and taken root in the
contemporary neoliberal USA. His discourse and practice are redolent of
the fusion of psychotherapy with religion, spirituality and countercultural
politics promoted by Laing. Madness is an exalted state of mystical insight
that, if properly cultivated, results in a radical regeneration of the self.
Moreover, the authentically mad are the prophetic vanguard of a politically radical utopian movement. This neo-Laingian discourse persists in the
relatively unregulated and informal domain of the Mad movement; Farber
laments what he sees as professionalised activism in, for instance, the formation of NGOs that seek improved, service-user focused mental health
care (Farber 2012: 10).

Despite the temptation to present the current relationship between psychotherapy and Christianity as one of (say) mature and respectful dialogue, the historical reality continues to be rather more complex, dynamic
and protean. The history explored by this book is one in which boundaries
are repeatedly drawn, erased and redrawn, and relationships reconfigured,
across nominally religious domains of ritual, myth, doctrine, ethics, organisation and subjective experience, and across nominally psychotherapeutic
domains of nosology, diagnosis, aetiology and therapeutics. The recent
inter-professional account of this relationship (as explored above) tends,
however, to rely (consciously or not) upon the widely disseminated model
of the science–religion relationship developed by Barbour. Yet this model
has limitations. Geoffrey Cantor and Chris Kenny query whether, as
Barbour seems to presume, the typology of conflict, independence, dialogue and integration is necessarily comprehensive and historically universal (Cantor and Kenny 2001: 766) – 'conflict', for instance, 'could not have
been an actors' category at any time before about 1870' (Cantor and Kenny
2001: 767). Moreover, the categories of 'science' and 'religion' are used
'as distinct classes with fixed, temporally independent, and self-evident
meanings. This is particularly irksome for the historian of science who
investigates in detail the diachronic and synchronic alterations in both the
extension and intension of these continually transforming terms' (Cantor
and Kenny 2001: 771). As noted above, the fourfold taxonomy, at least
in Barbour's usage, also implies an evaluative hierarchy and evolutionary

progression – 'a pilgrim's progress starting with Conflict, briefly engaging Independence, and finally finding haven either in Dialogue or preferably in some form of Integration' (Cantor and Kenny 2001: 768). Furthermore, the typology is extrapolated from the primacy of conflict: 'Not only does this term set his agenda, but it also biases our understanding by introduction of language often associated either with internal religious discord or with warfare' (Cantor and Kenny 2001: 769). To elaborate Cantor and Kenny's point, note that Barbour's fourfold typology might otherwise be expressed with unity/holism as the primary reality, and the other categories as deviations: for instance, holism (integration), discontinuity (dialogue), mutual impermeability (independence), factionalism (conflict).

The spatial imaginary in Barbour's model is also problematic. According to Cantor and Kenny, Barbour's foundational metaphor represents the science–religion relationship cartographically in terms of a primary territorial rivalry:

> We can envisage his taxonomy as a form of mapping in which both science and religion are represented by bounded regions projected onto the page. Thus *Independence* is represented by the total separation of the two regions – S[cience] and R[eligion] – neither touching nor intersecting. *Dialogue* involves some contact, perhaps along a common boundary, while with *Integration* there is significant overlap and merging. (Cantor and Kenny 2001: 776)

This cartographical and territorial relationship is inadequate when set against historical reality, such as that of seventeenth-century science-religion in which 'boundaries between different forms of knowledge were very fluid and were a recurrent source of conflict' (Cantor and Kenny 2001: 773). Cantor and Kenny conclude that 'the static maplike relationships that Barbour envisages are inadequate to portray the dynamic engagements between science and religion' (Cantor and Kenny 2001: 778): 'Relationships of Conflict, Independence, Dialogue and Integration occur only between highly specific features of both science and religion' (Cantor and Kenny 2001: 777).

One can apply this kind of critique to the relationship between Christianity and psychotherapy explored in this monograph. The fluidity of the term 'religion' is well exemplified by the dominance of Macmurray's religious philosophy, which licenses the term 'religion' to characterise the promotion of fellowship between persons (of which psychotherapy is putatively one branch), yet which also neglects or suspends doctrinal positions such as theism or personal immortality. As Colin Kirkwood puts it, discovering the work of John Macmurray in the 1980s allowed him to 'entertain the idea that belief in God might not be the core of religion' (Kirkwood 2012: 3). From the perspective of actors informed by Macmurray's ideas, such as the New Zealand Association of Psychotherapists in the 1950s, we have neither a conflictual victory in which philosophy and psychotherapy swallow religion, nor even strictly an integration, but rather the restoration, at a higher level of rationality, of an original lost unity of theory and practice. Moreover, such fluidity of the signifier 'religion' is complemented by contestations and multiplicity within psychology itself. Barbour's typology tends to elevate physics and biology as typical sciences, and is heavily reliant upon the Kuhnian notion of a 'paradigm', composed of 'a research tradition, the key historical examples through which the tradition is transmitted, and the metaphysical assumptions implicit in the fundamental concepts of the tradition' – a key example being Newtonian mechanics (Barbour 1990: 51). But psychology – unlike physics – has never had a phase of development based around a commonly accepted paradigm, despite the pretensions of psychological schools such as behaviourism, which sought to imitate the natural sciences by offering laws relating publicly-observable behavioural phenomena (e.g. Watson 1913). As Sonu Shamdasani explains,

> At the outset, psychologists sought to emulate the form and formation of established prestigious sciences, such as physics and chemistry. This emulation – or simulation – took different forms. Central to it was the conception that psychology should also be a unitary discipline. Yet very quickly, the proliferation of variously styled psychologies demonstrated that there was little consensus as to what could be considered the aims and methods of psychology. (Shamdasani 2003: 5)

For many commentators, such emulation would be entirely misguided. Mark W. Lipsey concludes that psychology 'is neither preparadigmatic nor postparadigmatic, it is misparadigmatic' (Lipsey 1974: 409). Psychology has therefore freely investigated matters that might seem (on a territorial model) to be the province of theology, such as introspective reports that attest to religious experience. As Graham Richards notes, William James in *The Varieties of Religious Experience*, his Gifford lectures of 1901–2, proposes to treat as veridical the reports of those who 'claim to have had a direct and unmediated encounter with another, transpersonal, power' (Richards 2011: 33).

An important factor in this monograph's historical narrative is variation in loci for the authorisation of religion, and particularly in the pre-eminence of experiential authorisation, a locus which is open to inquiry from theologians, psychotherapists, and indeed those who recognise no such professional division. The pre-eminent 'integrationists' (or perhaps holists) Rushforth and Laing prefer, at least at certain points in their careers, a psychological and experiential authorisation of religion. Rushforth offers a model of contact through psychotherapeutic practice with the wellspring underlying all religion. The countercultural Laing is similarly experiential, locating the authorisation of religion in experiences of *metanoia*, whether spontaneous, drug-induced or spiritually cultivated. Religion tends in both these figures to be conceived as ultimately authorised by subjective experiences amenable to psychological identification and clarification. This 'integration' of psychotherapy with religion and theology is motivated by a perceived obsolescence in other sources of authorisation for religion, such as doctrine, scripture, various forms of revelation, philosophical knowledge, natural theology, and the customary power of social institutions and traditions, including ritual observance. Where these other sources of authority re-enter the contexts inhabited by figures such as Rushforth and Laing, they are reinterpreted as psychologically grounded. Textual criticism is used (or misused) to demonstrate the supposed psychological meanings of scriptural passages ('living water'); rituals such as communion, healing and baptism are presented as essentially psychotherapeutic in their meaning; the organisational life of the early church is re-interpreted as that of a therapeutic or clinical community; Providence smiles on the Davidson Clinic's healing ventures; natural history reveals the evolution of a mentally superior form of human life as explicated by Teilhard; and so on. Within this complex of interacting ideas, texts, interpretations, narratives, practices and organisations, there arise further psychotherapeutic-religious adornments. Personal immortality may be reconfigured as the salvation in this world of a finite life lived authentically, and the sting of death eased further by doctrines such as reincarnation (Laing) or dissolution of the individual into a single underlying life process (Rushforth). Moralism is dissolved by diagnoses of ethical and organisational elements of Christianity as psychopathological (for example, sexual moralism as a defence mechanism), and replaced by a higher, more abstract commitment to authenticity, or truth to self. Nosological and diagnostic categories such as psychosis, hallucination and delusion can be pre-emptively dissolved by interpretative work such as Laing's, which ushers the experiences, words and actions of psychotic patients back into the realm of intelligible behaviour. Moreover, biomedical therapeutics (such as neuroleptic pharmaceuticals) that might negate supposed religious experience can be opposed precisely on the grounds of their insensitivity to spiritual realities.

Historically speaking, the relationship between psychotherapy and Christianity is not one of historical progress towards a stage of mature dialogue between disciplinary fields that resist integration. The progressivist narrative is a rhetorical obstacle to historical insight and invites the errors enumerated by Cantor and Kenny. In thinking of Christianity and psychotherapy as elaborated in this monograph, it is important to acknowledge the limitations in Barbour's cartographical model of a territorial relationship between rival powers. At particular points in their respective careers, Laing and Rushforth would have seen themselves not as 'integrating' Christianity and psychotherapy, but as opposing the diremption of authentic and wholesome spiritual life, experience and fellowship, into lifeless compartments amenable to professional administration and factionalism. Recall Laing's proclamation in 1966 that 'thousands of people are stumbling into [psychosis], the original experience of Christianity':

But they don't go to Christianity for any orientation, because they find no reference points, as it is mediated to them; and if they go to a priest, the priest will refer them to a psychiatrist, and the psychiatrist will refer them to a mental hospital, and the mental hospital will refer them to the electric shock machine. And if this is not our contemporary mode of crucifying Christ, what is? (Religious experience: 12)

As the work of Isabel Clarke and Seth Farber shows, this kind of challenge to the dialogic model, and its presuppositions, endures to the present day.

Archival Sources

The list below is arranged alphabetically by name of person or organisation. Items are identified by the short title form used in citations.

Association of Social Workers. GB 152 SWK. Modern Records Centre, University Library, University of Warwick, Coventry, CV4 7AL.
Emotional Development. Lectures (4) by Dr Ian D. Suttie, given February 1933. Emotional development in the early years. MSS.378/ASW/B/7/5/8.

Quasi-archival sources relating to the Davidson Clinic. Edinburgh and Scottish Collection, Central Library, 7–9 George IV Bridge, Edinburgh, EH1 1EG.
Annual Report. Davidson Clinic Annual Report, 1941–71. Y RC 343.
Davidson Clinic Bulletin, Nos 1–85, July 1946 – July 1967. Y RC 343.
  [References to *Bulletin* articles are given in Works Cited.]

Papers of William Ronald Dodds Fairbairn, psychiatrist and psychoanalyst. MSS.50100–50251. National Library of Scotland Archives and Manuscripts Collections. George IV Bridge, Edinburgh EH1 1EW.
Letters of, to or concerning William Ronald Dodds Fairbairn relating to his publication *Psychoanalytic Studies of the Personality,* 1951–1955. MS.50105.
Letter, Hempsons Solicitors to Fairbairn, 22 June 1953. MS.50105(69–120).
Letter, Fairbairn to Hempsons Solicitors, [24 June 1953]. MS.50105 (69–120).
Letter, Hempsons Solicitors to Fairbairn, 30 September 1954. MS.50105(121–156).
Letter, Jock [Sutherland] to Fairbairn, 22 September 1954. MS.50105(121–156).
Letter, Hempsons Solicitors to Fairbairn, 14 October 1954. MS.50105(121–156).

Library of William Ronald Dodds Fairbairn. Centre for Research Collections, Main Library, University of Edinburgh, George Square, Edinburgh, EH8 9LJ.
Fairbairn.S.108. Geddes, Patrick and J. Arthur Thomson ([1911]), *Evolution,* London: Williams and Norgate.

The Geoffrey Gorer Archive. SxMs52. University of Sussex Library Special Collections. The Keep, Woollards Way, Brighton, BN1 9BP.
SxMs52/3 Book Reviews.
Gorer Review. Fairbairn, W. R. D. *Psychoanalytic Studies of the Personality.* SxMs52/3/4/3/5.

R. D. Laing Collection. MS Laing. Special Collections Department, Library, University of Glasgow, Glasgow, G12 8QE.
Celebration. Transcript of a talk given by R. D. Laing entitled 'Psychotherapy as celebration'. Delivered in October 1983 at the Queen's Hall, Edinburgh, under the sponsorship of Wellspring. Published in the first issue of the newsletter *Wellspring*, Summer, 1984, pp. 6–10. Printed text, with pencil emendations by R. D. Laing. MS Laing A1.
Philadelphia Association. Lecture entitled 'What is the Philadelphia Association?' 11.12.1975. Photocopy of typescript. MS Laing A78.
Religious Experience. Draft of a lecture entitled 'Religious experience and the role of organised religion' given at N.A.M.H., 7 Jan. 1966. Typescript. Papers of Ronald David Laing. MS Laing A393.
Ministers' Group. Minutes of the meetings of the Ministers' Group, Southern General Hospital, Glasgow by R. D. Laing. 1956. Typescript. MS Laing DS90.
Bates–Laing Correspondence. Letter from Dorothy Bates to R. D. Laing. New York. 11 October 1982. Enclosing an outline of a manuscript entitled *Voices of New Age Experience* and asking Laing to consider writing an introduction. Typescript. With reply from R. D. Laing. [London] 15 January 1983. Carbon copy of typescript. MS Laing GB661–3.
Correspondence Rushforth–Laing. Five letters from Winifred Rushforth to R. D. Laing. Edinburgh. 1964–5. Includes an invitation to Laing to take over as Director of the Davidson Clinic in Edinburgh. ms. With four replies from R. D. Laing. [London] 1964–5. Carbon copy of typescript. MS Laing GR71–80.
Elements. Notes concerning Elements for an Autobiography by R. D. Laing. Patmos, Monday 29.7.68. Manuscript. MS Laing K1.
Notebook. R. D. Laing: Notebook and partial diary covering Laing's stay at the military hospitals at Netley and Catterick, January 1952 – June 1953. With later annotations by R. D. Laing made in August, 1981. Manuscript. MS Laing K14.
Oran's Trust. Letters and documents relating to Oran's Trust (later renamed Sanctuary). 1984–5. MS Laing L96–127.
Laughing Man. Transcript of interview with R. D. Laing for the magazine *Laughing Man.* Published under the title 'Sparks of Light' in *Laughing Man* vol. 5, no. 2, 1984. Typescript. MS Laing L138.
Letter, Barasch to Laing, n.d.. Letter from Marc Barasch to R. D. Laing. Undated. Regarding an interview with Laing published in the *New Age Journal.* Typescript. MS Laing L238/71.

Letter, Lake to Laing, 28 June 1963. Letter from Dr Frank Lake to R. D. Laing. 28 June 1963. Confirmation that Laing's visit to and participation in the Clinical Theology Centre's conference at Scargill House in Yorkshire was a great success. Typescript. MS Laing L316/4.

Letter, Lake to Laing, 19 September 1964. Letter from Dr Frank Lake to R. D. Laing. 19 Sept. 1964. Regarding Laing's address to the International Congress and Social Psychiatry. Handwritten. MS Laing L316/5.

Programme. Programme for the Iona Community. Spring and Autumn Programme 1984. Includes leaders' briefing sheet and timetable. Typescript. MS Laing L411/3. [Page numbers are inferred.]

Glaswegian guru. Glaswegian guru turns his mind to Iona by Lorn MacIntyre. 12 August 1983. *The Scotsman*. Printed text. Copy of original. MS Laing T93.

Iona Community. What is the Iona Community? *Coracle Supplement*. [Iona, 1985]. MS Laing T105.

Macdonald Interview. Audio recording of an interview between R. D. Laing and Donald Macdonald, Iona Community. 1984. R. D. Laing [his life, family and the city of Glasgow]. Interview intended for radio broadcast. WB16.

Body, Mind and Spirit. R. D. Laing and the Iona Community Programme. Body, Mind and Spirit [Theme]. Colour. JVC [VHS] video cassettes. MS Laing WE8–10.

Personal Library of R. D. Laing. Special Collections Department, Library, University of Glasgow, Glasgow, G12 8QE.

Sp Coll Laing 402. Masters, Robert E. L. ([1967]), *The Varieties of Psychedelic Experience*, London: Blond.

Sp Coll Laing 565. Goleman, Daniel (*c.*1977), *The Varieties of Meditative Experience*, New York: Dutton.

Sp Coll Laing 646. MacLeod, George F. (1958), *One Way Left: Church Prospect*, Glasgow: Iona Community.

Sp Coll Laing 1051. Allegro, John M. (1970), *The Sacred Mushroom and the Cross: A Study of the Nature and Origins of Christianity within the Fertility Cults of the Ancient Near East*, London: Hodder & Stoughton.

Sp Coll Laing 1859. Underhill, Evelyn (1930), *Mysticism: A Study in the Nature and Development of Man's Spiritual Consciousness*, 12th rev. edn, London: Methuen.

Sp Coll Laing 1890. Hardy, Alister (1979), *The Spiritual Nature of Man: A Study of Contemporary Religious Experience*, Oxford: Clarendon Press.

John Macmurray Papers. Gen. 2162, E.2003.36. Centre for Research Collections, Main Library, University of Edinburgh, George Square, Edinburgh, EH8 9LJ.

Christian apologetic. The Christian apologetic in the modern world.

Contribution to the Conference on the Preparation of the Ministry, York, 2–6 April 1929. Printed. 20pp. Gen 2162.2.27.

Personal and social. The personal and the social. Fifth paper given on 5 June 1934, 8–9.45, and 6 June, morning, at the conference entitled, 'The Church, the State and the World Order', 4–6 June 1934. Typescript, dated 22 May 1934. 5pp. Gen 2162.2.29.

Fear and faith, Faith and love. To Save from Fear. Four Lent talks. BBC transcripts of broadcasts, 12–20 February 1964. (1. Fear and faith; 2. Faith and love; [3. missing]; 4. The world today.) Typescript. 17pp. Gen 2612.2.38, 1 & 2.

Modern world. Religion in the modern world. Typescript and MS. 25pp. and 19pp. n.d. Gen 2162.2.40.1.

New Zealand Association of Psychotherapists: Records. MS-Group-0936. Alexander Turnbull Library, Wellington, New Zealand.

Bevan-Brown cv. Dr M. Bevan-Brown [curriculum vitae of Maurice Bevan-Brown]. Manuscript. Papers relating to the history of the Association. 98-209-2/18.

Collection relating to Winifred Rushforth, Coll-1260. Centre for Research Collections, Main Library, University of Edinburgh, George Square, Edinburgh, EH8 9LJ.

Minute Book. Davidson Clinic Minute Book (1938–45). ms. Box 1.

Summer School 1949. Programme for Summer School, 'The Contribution of Psychotherapy to the Life of the Community in Medicine, in Education and in Religion', 28 July – 3 August 1949. Box 1.

Easter School 1951. Programme for Easter School 'Psychology and Health', 28 March – 3 April 1951. Box 1.

St Paul's search. St Paul's search for identity (Sermon preached in St Bride's Church on 2 August 1964), JRW [John R. Wilson]. Box 1 [pages are un-numbered in this document; page references are to inferred page numbers].

Holding hands. Holding hands with Winfred Rushforth, author unknown. ms. Box 4.

How remember. How should we remember her, Marcus Lefébure. Box 4.

Rushforth cv. Curriculum vitae of Dr Winifred Rushforth. Typescript. Box 4.

Summary of conversation. 'Summary of conversation of Duke of Rothesay [i.e. Prince Charles] and Winifred [Rushforth]', author unknown. Typescript. Box 9.

Papers of T. & T. Clark. Correspondence of T. & T. Clark 1963–94. Acc. 11792. National Library of Scotland Archives and Manuscripts Collections. George IV Bridge, Edinburgh EH1 1EW.

Human Experience. Lefébure, *Human Experience*, 1981–6. Acc. 11792/29.

Works Cited

Abrahamson, D. (2007), 'R. D. Laing and long-stay patients: discrepant accounts of the refractory ward and "rumpus room" at Gartnavel Royal Hospital', *History of Psychiatry*, 18, 2, 203–15.

'Adler's ashes found in Edinburgh' [Online]. Available at <https://www.theguardian.com/uk/2011/apr/10/alfred-adler-ashes-found-edinburgh> [last accessed 17 July 2019].

'Adler's beliefs' (1937), *The Scotsman*, 22 June, 14.

Adler, A. (1918), *The Neurotic Constitution: Outlines of a Comparative Individualistic Psychology and Psychotherapy*, trans. B. Glueck and J. E. Lind, London: Kegan Paul, Trench, Trubner.

Adler, A. (1928), *Understanding Human Nature*, trans. W. B. Wolfe, London: Allen & Unwin.

Adler, A. (1938), *Social Interest: A Challenge to Mankind*, trans. J. Linton and R. Vaughan, London: Faber & Faber.

Alexander, S. (1998), 'Psychoanalysis in Britain in the early twentieth century: an introductory note', *History Workshop Journal*, 45, 135–43.

Allan, R. S. (1950), 'Testimony to psychotherapy', in M. Bevan-Brown, *The Sources of Love and Fear*, 76–88.

Anderson, J. W. (1981), 'The methodology of psychological biography', *The Journal of Interdisciplinary History*, 11, 3, 455–75.

Andrews, J. (1998), 'R. D. Laing in Scotland: facts and fictions of the "Rumpus Room" and interpersonal psychiatry', in M. Gijswijt-Hofstra and R. Porter (eds), *Cultures of Psychiatry*, Amsterdam: Rodopi, 121–50.

Anonymous (1951), 'An American looks at the Clinic', *Davidson Clinic Bulletin*, 21, 11–15.

Anonymous (1953), 'By what power this healing?: a further report on a ministry being restored to the Church', *Life and Work*, 8, 88 (April), 84.

Anonymous (1957), 'Healing through prayer', *Life and Work*, 12, 136 (April), 90.

Anonymous (1961), 'The Christian Fellowship of Healing', *Life and Work*, 16, 185 (July), 176.

Atkinson, J. J. (1903), *Primal Law*, London: Longmans, Green and Co.

Aupers, S. and D. Houtman (2006), 'Beyond the spiritual supermarket: the social and public significance of New Age spirituality', *Journal of Contemporary Religion*, 21, 2, 201–22.

Baillie, J. (1939), *Our Knowledge of God*, Oxford: Oxford University Press.

Barasch, M. (1984), 'The New Age interview: R. D. Laing', *New Age Journal*, September, 58–63, 85–6, 89.

Barbour, I. G. (1990), *Religion in an Age of Science: The Gifford Lectures 1989–1991: Volume 1*, London: SCM.

Bartlett, F. C. (1995), *Remembering: A Study in Experimental and Social Psychology*, Cambridge: Cambridge University Press.

Beattie, H. J. (2003), '"The repression and the return of bad objects": W. R. D. Fairbairn and the historical roots of theory', *International Journal of Psychoanalysis*, 84, 5, 1171–87.

Beattie, H. J. (2016), 'W. R. D. Fairbairn and the problem of homosexuality: a study in psychoanalytic prejudice', *The Psychoanalytic Quarterly*, 85, 4, 889–928.

Bediako, G. M. (1997), *Primal Religion and the Bible: William Robertson Smith and his Heritage*, Sheffield: Sheffield Academic Press.

Beidelman, T. O. (1974), *W. Robertson Smith and the Sociological Study of Religion*, Chicago: University of Chicago Press.

Bell, M. (2004), *The Pioneers of Parents' Centre: Movers and Shakers for Change in the Philosophies and Practices of Childbirth and Parent Education in New Zealand*, Doctor of Philosophy in Education, Victoria University of Wellington.

Benedict, R. (1935), *Patterns of Culture*, London: Routledge.

Bevan-Brown, M. (1950), *The Sources of Love and Fear*, New York: Vanguard.

Bevan-Brown, M. (1956), *The Foundations of Mental Health*, Christchurch, New Zealand: Caxton.

Bevan-Brown, M. (1961), *Mental Health and Personality Disorder*, Christchurch, New Zealand: Dunford.

Beveridge, A. (1998), 'Life in the asylum: patients' letters from Morningside, 1873–1908', *History of Psychiatry*, 9, 36, 431–69.

Beveridge, A. (2011), *Portrait of the Psychiatrist as a Young Man: The Early Writing and Work of R. D. Laing, 1927–1960*, Oxford: Oxford University Press.

Beveridge, C. and R. Turnbull (1989), *The Eclipse of Scottish Culture: Inferiorism and the Intellectuals*, Edinburgh: Polygon.

Birtles, E. F. and D. E. Scharff (eds) (1994), *From Instinct to Self: Selected Papers of W. R. D. Fairbairn. Volume II: Applications and Early Contributions*, Northvale, NJ: Jason Aronson.

Bliss, S. (2010), 'The "internal saboteur": contributions of W. R. D. Fairbairn in understanding and treating self-harming adolescents', *Journal of Social Work Practice*, 24, 2, 227–37.

Bloor, D. (1991), *Knowledge and Social Imagery*, 2nd edn, Chicago: University of Chicago Press.

Boardman, P. (1978), *The Worlds of Patrick Geddes: Biologist, Town Planner, Re-educator, Peace-warrior*, London: Routledge & Kegan Paul.

Bondi, L. (2006), 'The changing landscape of voluntary sector counselling in Scotland', in C. Milligan and D. Conradson (eds), *Landscapes of Voluntarism: New Spaces of Health, Welfare and Governance*, Bristol: Policy, 247–65.

Bondi, L. (2013), 'Between Christianity and secularity: counselling and psychotherapy provision in Scotland', *Social & Cultural Geography*, 14, 6, 668–88.

Bondi, L. (2014), 'On Freud's geographies', in P. Kingsbury and S. Pile (eds), *Psychoanalytic Geographies*, Farnham: Ashgate, 57–72.

Bos, J., D. W. Park and P. Pietikainen (2005), 'Strategic self-marginalization: the case of psychoanalysis', *Journal of the History of the Behavioral Sciences*, 41, 3, 207–24.

Bottome, P. (1957), *Alfred Adler: Apostle of Freedom*, 3rd edn, London: Faber and Faber.

Bowlby, J. (1988), 'Foreword', in I. D. Suttie, *The Origins of Love and Hate*, London: Free Association, xv–xviii.

Brown, C. G. (1992), 'A revisionist approach to religious change', in S. Bruce (ed.), *Religion and Modernization: Sociologists and Historians Debate the Secularization Thesis*, Oxford: Clarendon Press, 31–58.

Brown, C. G. (2006), *Religion and Society in Twentieth-Century Britain*, London: Longman.

Brown, C. G. (2009), *The Death of Christian Britain: Understanding Secularisation 1800–2000*, 2nd edn, London: Routledge.

Brown, S. J. (1994), 'The social ideal of the Church of Scotland during the 1930s', in A. R. Morton (ed.), *God's Will in a Time of Crisis: A Colloquium Celebrating the 50th Anniversary of The Baillie Commission*, Edinburgh: Centre for Theology and Public Issues, 14–31.

Bruce, S. (2002), *God is Dead: Secularization in the West*, Oxford: Blackwell.

Brunton, W. (2003), 'The origins of deinstitutionalisation in New Zealand', *Health and History*, 5, 2, 75–103.

Brunton, W. (2011), 'The Scottish influence on New Zealand psychiatry before World War II', *Immigrants & Minorities*, 29, 3, 308–42.

Bultmann, R. (1955), 'The problem of hermeneutics', *Essays Philosophical and Theological*, London: SCM, 234–61.

Bultmann, R. (1956), *Primitive Christianity in its Contemporary Setting*, trans. R. H. Fuller, London: Thames and Hudson.

Bultmann, R. (1957), *History and Eschatology: The Gifford Lectures 1955*, Edinburgh: Edinburgh University Press.

Bultmann, R. (1984a), 'New Testament and mythology: the problem of demythologizing the New Testament proclamation', trans. S. M. Ogden, in S. M. Ogden (ed.), *New Testament and Mythology and Other Basic Writings*, London: SCM, 1–43.

Bultmann, R. (1984b), 'On the problem of demythologizing', trans. S. M. Ogden, in S. M. Ogden (ed.), *New Testament and Mythology and Other Basic Writings*, London: SCM, 95–130.

Burnham, J. C. (2006), 'The "New Freud Studies": a historiographical shift', *The Journal of the Historical Society*, 6, 2, 213–33.

Burston, D. (1996), *The Wing of Madness: The Life and Work of R. D. Laing*, Cambridge, MA: Harvard University Press.

Burston, D. (2000), *The Crucible of Experience: R. D. Laing and the Crisis of Psychotherapy*, Cambridge, MA: Harvard University Press.

Burston, D. (2013), 'Seth Farber. *The Spiritual Gift of Madness: The Failure of Psychiatry and the Rise of the Mad Pride Movement* [Review]', *Journal of the History of the Behavioral Sciences*, 49, 3, 331–3.

Buss, M. J. (1999), *Biblical Form Criticism in its Context*, Sheffield: Sheffield Academic Press.

Cameron, J. L., R. D. Laing and A. McGhie (1955), 'Patient and nurse: effects of environmental changes in the care of chronic schizophrenics', *The Lancet*, 266, 6905, 1384–6.

Campbell, A. (1982), '*Tight Corners in Pastoral Counselling* by Frank Lake [Review]', *Contact*, 74, 25–6.

Campbell, C. (1972), 'The cult, the cultic milieu and secularization', in M. Hill (ed.), *A Sociological Yearbook of Religion in Britain · 5*, London: SCM, 119–36.

Campi, M., A. Besuschio, L. Oswald, I. S. De Basili and R. M. Basili (2014), 'Fairbairn in Argentina: the "Fairbairn Space" in the Argentine Psychoanalytic Association (APA)', in G. S. Clarke and D. E. Scharff (eds), *Fairbairn and the Object Relations Tradition*, London: Karnac, 101–13.

Cantor, G. and C. Kenny (2001), 'Barbour's fourfold way: problems with his taxonomy of science–religion relationships', *Zygon: Journal of Religion and Science*, 36, 4, 765–81.

Carrette, J. and R. King (2005), *Selling Spirituality: The Silent Takeover of Religion*, London: Routledge.

Chapman, A. (2014a), 'Into the zone of the interior: a novel view of anti-psychiatry', *PsyArt*, 18, 14–24.

Chapman, A. (2014b), '"Knots": drawing out threads of the literary Laing', *PsyArt* [Online], 18, 323–39.

Chapman, A. (2015), 'Dismemberment and the attempt at re-membering in R. D. Laing's *The Bird of Paradise*', *Literature and Medicine*, 33, 2, 393–418.

Chapman, A. (2018), '"May all be shattered into God": Mary Barnes and her journey through madness in Kingsley Hall', *Journal of Medical Humanities*. Available at https://doi.org/10.1007/s10912-018-9517-1 [advance online publication].

Chryssides, G. D. (2012), 'The New Age', in O. Hammer and M. Rothstein (eds), *The Cambridge Companion to New Religious Movements*, Cambridge: Cambridge University Press, 247–62.

Church of Scotland General Assembly (1958), 'Report of the Commission on Spiritual Healing', *Reports to the General Assembly with the Legislative Acts*, 909–30.

Cilento, D. (2006), *My Nine Lives*, London: Viking.

Clarke, G. S. (2006), *Personal Relations Theory: Fairbairn, Macmurray and Suttie*, London and New York: Routledge.

Clarke, G. S. (2018), *Thinking through Fairbairn: Exploring the Object Relations Model of Mind*, London: Karnac.

Clarke, G. S. and D. E. Scharff (eds) (2014), *Fairbairn and the Object Relations Tradition*, London: Karnac.

Clarke, I. (ed.) (2010a), *Psychosis and Spirituality: Consolidating the New Paradigm*, 2nd edn, Chichester: Wiley-Blackwell.

Clarke, I. (2010b), 'Psychosis and spirituality: the discontinuity model', in I. Clarke (ed.), *Psychosis and Spirituality: Consolidating the New Paradigm*, 2nd edn, Chichester: Wiley-Blackwell, 101–14.

Clydesdale [Pseud.] (1955), 'Cured by faith? experiences of a minister in healing', *Life and Work*, 10, 120 (December), 309.

Coate, M. (1964), *Beyond All Reason*, London: Constable.

Cohen, A. P. (2004), 'Review: *Scots' Crisis of Confidence*', *Scottish Affairs*, 49 (First Series), 1, 160–2.

Collier, A. (1977), *R. D. Laing: The Philosophy and Politics of Psychotherapy*, Hassocks: Harvester.

Collins, K. (2008), 'Joseph Schorstein: R. D. Laing's "rabbi"', *History of Psychiatry*, 19, 2, 185–201.

Conford, P. (2008), '"Saturated with biological metaphors": Professor John Macmurray (1891–1976) and the politics of the organic movement', *Contemporary British History*, 22, 3, 317–34.

Cook, F. (1945), *Ex-Servicemen Talk It Over: A Group Discussion on War Neurosis*, Christchurch, New Zealand: J. W. Baty.

Cook, P. S. (1996), 'The early history of the New Zealand Association of Psychotherapists and the related movement for primary prevention in mental health: some recollections', *Australian and New Zealand Journal of Psychiatry*, 30, 3, 405–9.

Costello, J. E. (2002), *John Macmurray: A Biography*, Edinburgh: Floris.

Craig, C. (2003), *The Scots' Crisis of Confidence*, Edinburgh: Big Thinking.

Crichton-Miller, H. (1924), *The New Psychology and the Preacher*, London: Jarrolds.

Crossley, N. (1998), 'R. D. Laing and the British anti-psychiatry movement: a socio-historical analysis', *Social Science & Medicine*, 47, 7, 877–89.

Crossley, N. (2006), *Contesting Psychiatry: Social Movements in Mental Health*, London: Routledge.

Cullen, K., L. Bondi, J. Fewell, E. Francis and M. Ludlam (eds) (2014), *Making Spaces: Putting Psychoanalytic Thinking to Work*, London: Karnac.

D. A. (1973), 'To the Davidson Clinic: an appreciation', in J. Darroch (ed.), *The Davidson Clinic 1939–1973*, Edinburgh: Bishop & Sons, 28–9.

Damousi, J. and M. B. Plotkin (2009), 'Introduction', in J. Damousi and M. B. Plotkin (eds), *The Transnational Unconscious: Essays in the History of*

Psychoanalysis and Transnationalism, Basingstoke: Palgrave Macmillan, 1–16.

Darroch, J. (1973), *The Davidson Clinic 1939–1973*, Edinburgh: Bishop & Sons.

'Davidson Clinic' (1943), *The Scotsman*, 5 February, 3.

Davidson, R. (2009), 'Psychiatry and homosexuality in mid-twentieth-century Edinburgh: the view from Jordanburn Nerve Hospital', *History of Psychiatry*, 20, 4, 403–24.

Davies, K. (2001), '"Silent and censured travellers"? patients' narratives and patients' voices: perspectives on the history of mental illness since 1948', *Social History of Medicine*, 14, 2, 267–92.

Dawson, A. and S. Kerkovius (2001) 'Dr Hans Schauder', *The Scotsman*, 27 September, 14.

'Death Of Dr Adler' (1937), *The Scotsman*, 29 May, 17.

Deed, M. (1969), 'Attitudes of four religiously-oriented psychoanalysts', *Pastoral Psychology*, 20, 4, 39–44.

Dickinson, T., M. Cook, J. Playle and C. Hallett (2012), '"Queer" treatments: giving a voice to former patients who received treatments for their "sexual deviations"', *Journal of Clinical Nursing*, 21, 9/10, 1345–54.

Dicks, H. V. (1970), *Fifty Years of the Tavistock Clinic*, London: Routledge and Kegan Paul.

Dobbs, T. M. (2008), 'Transformation in psychoanalysis and religion as "persons in relationship": the influence of John Macmurray', *Psychoanalytic Inquiry*, 28, 5, 590–8.

'Dr William Kraemer' (1983), *The Times*, 11 January, 10.

Drever, J. (1948), 'Psychotherapy in Edinburgh', *The Scotsman*, 21 May, 4.

Drummond, H. (1884), *Natural Law in the Spiritual World*, London: Hodder & Stoughton.

Drummond, H. (1894), *The Lowell Lectures on The Ascent of Man*, London: Hodder & Stoughton.

Esterson, A. (1970), *The Leaves of Spring: A Study in the Dialectics of Madness*, London: Tavistock.

Fairbairn, W. R. D. (1994a), 'Addendum', *Psychoanalytic Studies of the Personality*, London: Routledge, 133–6.

Fairbairn, W. R. D. (1994b), 'Autobiographical note', in E. F. Birtles and D. E. Scharff (eds), *From Instinct to Self: Selected Papers of W. R. D. Fairbairn. Volume II: Applications and Early Contributions*, Northvale, NJ: Jason Aronson, 462–4.

Fairbairn, W. R. D. (1994c), 'Endopsychic structure considered in terms of object relationships', *Psychoanalytic Studies of the Personality*, London: Routledge, 82–136.

Fairbairn, W. R. D. (1994d), 'Object-relationships and dynamic structure', *Psychoanalytic Studies of the Personality*, London: Routledge, 137–51.

Fairbairn, W. R. D. (1994e), *Psychoanalytic Studies in the Personality*, London: Routledge.

Fairbairn, W. R. D. (1994f), 'Psychotherapy and the clergy', in E. F. Birtles and D. E. Scharff (eds), *From Instinct to Self: Selected Papers of W. R. D. Fairbairn. Volume II: Applications and Early Contributions*, Northvale, NJ: Jason Aronson, 363–7.

Fairbairn, W. R. D. (1994g), 'The repression and the return of bad objects (with special reference to the "war neuroses")', *Psychoanalytic Studies of the Personality*, London and New York: Routledge, 59–81.

Fairbairn, W. R. D. (1994h), 'A revised psychopathology of the psychoses and psychoneuroses', *Psychoanalytic Studies of the Personality*, London: Routledge, 28–58.

Fairbairn, W. R. D. (1994i), 'Schizoid factors in the personality', *Psychoanalytic Studies in the Personality*, London: Routledge, 3–27.

Farber, S. (2012), *The Spiritual Gift of Madness: The Failure of Psychiatry and the Rise of the Mad Pride Movement*, Rochester, VT: Inner Traditions.

Ferenczi, S. (1926), *Further Contributions to the Theory and Technique of Psycho-Analysis*, trans. J. I. Suttie, London: Hogarth.

Ferguson, R. (1988), *Chasing the Wild Goose*, Glasgow and London: Fount Paperbacks and Collins.

Ferguson, R. (1990), *George MacLeod: Founder of the Iona Community*, London: Collins.

Fergusson, D. (2012), 'Persons in relation', *Practical Theology*, 5, 3, 287–306.

Fergusson, D. (2013), 'Theology and therapy: maintaining the connection', *Pacifica*, 26, 1, 3–16.

Fergusson, D. A. (1992), *Bultmann*, London: Geoffrey Chapman.

Fielding, M. (2012), 'Education as if people matter: John Macmurray, community and the struggle for democracy', *Oxford Review of Education*, 38, 6, 675–92.

Forrester, J. and L. Cameron (2017), *Freud in Cambridge*, Cambridge: Cambridge University Press.

Franke, H. W. ([2002?]), *Hans Schauder: Vienna – My Home: Recollections Collected and Recorded by Horst Werner Franke*, Edinburgh: Privately published by Agathe Dawson.

Freud, S. (1955), 'Totem and taboo: some points of agreement between the mental lives of savages and neurotics', trans. J. Strachey, in J. Strachey (ed.), *The Standard Edition of the Complete Psychological Works of Sigmund Freud: Volume XIII (1913–1914): Totem and Taboo and Other Works*, London: Hogarth and the Institute of Psycho-analysis, 1–162.

Freud, S. (1961), 'The future of an illusion', trans. J. Strachey, in J. Strachey (ed.), *The Standard Edition of the Complete Psychological Works of Sigmund Freud: Volume XXI (1927–1931): The Future of an Illusion: Civilisation and its Discontents: and Other Works*, London: Hogarth Press and the Institute of Psycho-analysis, 1–56.

Fromm, E. (1960), *The Fear of Freedom*, London: Routledge and Kegan Paul.

Fromm, E. (1986), *Psychoanalysis and Zen Buddhism*, London: Unwin.

Fuller, R. C. (2001), *Spiritual, but not Religious: Understanding Unchurched America*, New York: Oxford University Press.

Fuller, R. C. (2006), 'American psychology and the religious imagination', *Journal of the History of the Behavioral Sciences*, 42, 3, 221–35.

Geddes, P. and J. A. Thomson (1889), *The Evolution of Sex*, London: Walter Scott.

Geddes, P. and J. A. Thomson ([1911]), *Evolution*, London: Williams and Norgate.

Gellner, E. (1985), *The Psychoanalytic Movement: Or the Coming of Unreason*, London: Paladin.

Gergen, K. J. (1973), 'Social psychology as history', *Journal of Personality and Social Psychology*, 26, 2, 309–20.

Gergen, K. J. (1985), 'The social constructionist movement in modern psychology', *American Psychologist*, 40, 3, 266–75.

Gerson, G. (2004), 'Object relations psychoanalysis as political theory', *Political Psychology*, 25, 5, 769–94.

Gerson, G. (2009a), 'Culture and ideology in Ian Suttie's theory of mind', *History of Psychology*, 12, 1, 19–40.

Gerson, G. (2009b), 'Ian Suttie's matriarchy: a feminist utopia?', *Psychoanalysis, Culture & Society*, 14, 4, 375–92.

Gieryn, T. F. (1983), 'Boundary-work and the demarcation of science from non-science: strains and interests in professional ideologies of scientists', *American Sociological Review*, 48, 6, 781–95.

Giordan, G. (2007), 'Spirituality: from a religious concept to a sociological theory', in K. Flanagan and P. C. Jupp (eds), *A Sociology of Spirituality*, Farnham: Ashgate, 161–80.

[Gorer, G.] (1953) '*Psychoanalytic Studies of the Personality* by W. Ronald D. Fairbairn' [Review]. *The Listener*, 12 March, 443.

Granek, L. (2010), 'Grief as pathology: the evolution of grief theory in psychology from Freud to the present', *History of Psychology*, 13, 1, 46–73.

Grier, F. (2006), 'Reflections on the phenomenon of adoration in relationships, both human and divine', in D. M. Black (ed.), *Psychoanalysis and Religion in the 21st Century: Competitors or Collaborators?* London: Routledge, 154–72.

Gunn, G. S. (1952), 'The cure of souls: work of the Davidson Clinic', *Life and Work*, 7, 84 (December), 258.

Guntrip, H. (1951), *You and Your Nerves: A Simple Account of the Nature, Causes and Treatment of Mental Illness*, London: Allen and Unwin.

Guntrip, H. (1961), *Personality Structure and Human Interaction: The Developing Synthesis of Psychodynamic Theory*, London: Hogarth and the Institute of Psycho-analysis.

Guntrip, H. (1994a), 'Analysis with Fairbairn and Winnicott: (how complete a result does psycho-analytic therapy achieve?)', in J. Hazell (ed.), *Personal Relations Therapy: The Collected Papers of H. J. S. Guntrip*, Northvale, NJ: Jason Aronson, 351–69.

Guntrip, H. (1994b), 'Can the therapist love the patient?', in J. Hazell (ed.), *Personal Relations Therapy: The Collected Papers of H. J. S. Guntrip*, Northvale, NJ: Jason Aronson, 399–404.

Happold, F. C. (1970), *Mysticism: A Study and an Anthology*, London: Penguin.

Hardy, A. (1979), *The Spiritual Nature of Man: A Study of Contemporary Religious Experience*, Oxford: Clarendon Press.

Hawkins, M. (1997), *Social Darwinism in European and American Thought, 1860–1945: Nature as Model and Nature as Threat*, Cambridge: Cambridge University Press.

Hayes, N. (2012), 'Did we really want a national health service? hospitals, patients and public opinions before 1948', *The English Historical Review*, 127, 526, 625–61.

Hazell, J. (1996), *H. J. S. Guntrip: A Psychoanalytical Biography*, London: Free Association.

Heard, D. (1988), 'Introduction: historical perspectives', in I. D. Suttie, *The Origins of Love and Hate*, London: Free Association, xix–xl.

Hechter, M. (1975), *Internal Colonialism: The Celtic Fringe in British National Development, 1536–1966*, London: Routledge and Kegan Paul.

Heelas, P. (1996), *The New Age Movement: The Celebration of the Self and the Sacralization of Modernity*, Oxford: Blackwell.

Heelas, P. (2008), *Spiritualities of Life: New Age Romanticism and Consumptive Capitalism*, Oxford: Blackwell.

Heelas, P., L. Woodhead, B. Seel, B. Szerszynski and K. Tusting (2005), *The Spiritual Revolution: Why Religion is Giving Way to Spirituality*, Oxford: Blackwell.

Heidegger, M. (1962), *Being and Time*, trans. J. Macquarrie and E. Robinson, Oxford: Blackwell.

Helminiak, D. A. (2010), '"Theistic psychology and psychotherapy": a theological and scientific critique', *Zygon: Journal of Religion and Science*, 45, 1, 47–74.

Henderson, I. (1952), *Myth in the New Testament*, London: SCM.

Hinshelwood, R. D. (1995), 'Psychoanalysis in Britain: points of cultural access, 1893–1918', *The International Journal of Psycho-Analysis*, 76, 1, 135–51.

History – The Salisbury Centre [Online]. Available at <https://www.salisburycentre.org/about-us/history/> [last accessed 25 July 2019].

Hoffman, M. (2004), 'From enemy combatant to strange bedfellow: the role of religious narratives in the work of W. R. D. Fairbairn and D. W. Winnicott', *Psychoanalytic Dialogues*, 14, 6, 769–804.

Hugh Crichton-Miller: A Personal Memoir by his Friends and Family (1961), Dorchester: Friary Press.

Huxley, A. (1954), *The Doors of Perception*, London: Chatto & Windus.

Huxley, F. (2005), 'Shamanism, healing and R. D. Laing', in S. Raschid (ed.), *R. D. Laing: Contemporary Perspectives*, London: Free Association, 185–203.

Huxley, J. (1959), 'Introduction', in P. T. D. Chardin (ed.), *The Phenomenon of Man*, London: Collins, 11–28.

Ireland, W. I. (1965), 'The ministers' group', *Davidson Clinic Bulletin*, 75, 6–10.

Itten, T. and C. Young (eds) (2012), *R. D. Laing: 50 years since The Divided Self*, Ross-on-Wye: PCCS.

Iverach, J. (1894), *Christianity and Evolution*, London: Hodder & Stoughton.

Jaspers, K. (1963), *General Psychopathology*, trans. J. Hoenig and M. W. Hamilton, Manchester: Manchester University Press.

Johnson, P. E. (1955), *Pastoral Ministration*, London: James Nisbet.

Jones, J. D. F. (2001), *Storyteller: The Many Lives of Laurens van der Post*, London: John Murray.

Kerr, F. (2012), 'Comment: in memoriam Marcus Lefébure', *New Blackfriars*, 93, 1047, 503–4.

King, F. T. (1932), *Feeding and Care of Baby*, London: Macmillan.

King, R. (1999), *Orientalism and Religion: Postcolonial Theory, India and 'The Mystic East'*, London and New York: Routledge.

Kirkpatrick, F. G. (2005), *John Macmurray: Community beyond Political Philosophy*, Lanham, MD: Rowman & Littlefield.

Kirkwood, C. (2012), *The Persons in Relation Perspective: in Counselling, Psychotherapy and Community Adult Learning*, Rotterdam: Sense.

Klinefelter, D. S. (1977), '"Our knowledge of God" in the theology of John Baillie', *Scottish Journal of Theology*, 30, 5, 401–27.

Kohut, T. A. (1986), 'Psychohistory as history', *The American Historical Review*, 91, 2, 336–54.

Kraemer, W. (1951), 'The Christian label', *Davidson Clinic Bulletin*, 20, 1–6.

Kraemer, W. P. (1954), 'Homosexuality', *British Medical Journal*, 1, 4876, 1443.

Kuhn, P. (2014), 'Subterranean histories: the dissemination of Freud's works into the British discourse on psychological medicine, 1904–1911', *Psychoanalysis and History*, 16, 2, 153–214.

Künkel, F. (1929), *Let's Be Normal!: The Psychologist Comes to His Senses*, trans. E. Jensen, New York: Ives Washburn.

Künkel, F. (1936), *What It Means to Grow Up: A Guide in Understanding the Development of Character*, trans. B. Keppel-Compton and H. Niebuhr, London and New York: Charles Scribner's.

Künkel, F. (1938), *Character, Growth, Education*, trans. B. Keppel-Compton and B. Druitt, Philadelphia: Lippincott.

Künkel, F. (1949), *In Search of Maturity: An Inquiry into Psychology, Religion, and Self-Education*, New York: Scribner's.

Kuper, A. (2005), *The Reinvention of Primitive Society*, 2nd edn, Abingdon: Routledge.

Laing, A. (1997), *R. D. Laing: A Biography*, London: HarperCollins.

Laing, R. D. (1964), 'Introduction', in M. R. A. Coate (ed.), *Beyond All Reason*, London: Constable, vii–x.

Laing, R. D. (1965), *The Divided Self: An Existential Study in Sanity and Madness*, Harmondsworth, Middlesex: Pelican.

Laing, R. D. (1967), *The Politics of Experience and the Bird of Paradise*, London: Penguin.

Laing, R. D. (1970) 'Religious sensibility', *The Listener*, 23 April, 536–7.

Laing, R. D. (1982), *The Voice of Experience*, London: Allen Lane.

Laing, R. D. (1998), *Wisdom, Madness, and Folly: The Making of a Psychiatrist 1927–57*, Edinburgh: Canongate.

Laing, R. D. and A. Esterson (1964), *Sanity, Madness and the Family: Volume I: Families of Schizophrenics*, London: Tavistock.

Lake, F. (1966), *Clinical Theology: A Theological and Psychiatric Basis to Clinical Pastoral Care*, London: Darton, Longman & Todd.

Lake, F. (1981), *Tight Corners in Pastoral Counselling*, London: Darton, Longman and Todd.

Lake, F. (1982), '[Letter to Editor of *Contact* responding to review of *Tight Corners in Pastoral Counselling*]', *Contact*, 75, 27–9.

LaMothe, R. (2008), 'John Macmurray's philosophy of community and psychoanalysis', *Contemporary Psychoanalysis*, 44, 4, 581–603.

Lefébure, M. (ed.) (1982), *Conversations on Counselling between a Doctor and a Priest: Dialogue and Trinity*, Edinburgh: T. & T. Clark.

Lefébure, M. (ed.) (1985), *Human Experience and the Art of Counselling: Further Conversations between a Doctor and a Priest*, Edinburgh: T. & T. Clark.

Lefébure, M. (1996), 'Who will count as a counsellor?: gleanings and tea-leaves', in R. Bayne, I. Horton and J. Bimrose (eds), *New Directions in Counselling*, London: Routledge, 5–15.

Lefébure, M. and H. Schauder (1987), *Lebensberatung: ein Weg zu Wandlung und Geborgenheit; ein anthroposophischer Arzt und ein katholischer Mönch im Gespräch*, trans. S. Kerkovius, Dornach: Geering.

Lefébure, M. and H. Schauder (1990), *Conversations on Counselling between a Doctor and a Priest*, 3rd edn, Edinburgh: T. & T. Clark.

Lefébure, P. (1967), 'Comment', *New Blackfriars*, 49, 571, 115–16.

Lehan, R. (1992), 'Bergson and the discourse of the moderns', in F. Burwick and P. Douglass (eds), *The Crisis in Modernism: Bergson and the Vitalist Controversy*, Cambridge: Cambridge University Press, 306–29.

Lipsey, M. W. (1974), 'Psychology: preparadigmatic, postparadigmatic, or misparadigmatic?', *Science Studies*, 4, 4, 406–10.

Livingstone, D. N. (2014), *Dealing with Darwin: Place, Politics, and Rhetoric in Religious Engagements with Evolution*, Baltimore: Johns Hopkins University Press.

Lockhart, A. (2010), 'The "Parson's Clinic": religion and psychology at the interwar Tavistock Clinic', *History and Philosophy of Psychology*, 12, 2, 11–24.

Long, A. A. (2002), *Epictetus: A Stoic and Socratic Guide to Life*, Oxford: Clarendon Press.

Lyall, D. (1991), 'Introduction: Clinical Theology in Context', in C. Christian (ed.), *In the Spirit of Truth: A Reader in the Work of Frank Lake*, London: Darton, Longman and Todd.

Lyall, D. (2001), *Integrity of Pastoral Care*, London: Society for Promoting Christian Knowledge.

Lyall, D. (2010), '*Contact/Practical Theology* at fifty: beacon or mirror for a changing discipline?', *Practical Theology*, 3, 2, 151–61.

Lynch, G. (2007), *The New Spirituality: An Introduction to Progressive Belief in the Twenty-First Century*, London: I. B. Tauris.

MacAllister, J. (2014), 'Education for personal life: John Macmurray on why learning to be human requires emotional discipline', *Journal of Philosophy of Education*, 48, 1, 118–36.

Macdonald, D. N. (1993a), *The Less Travelled Way*, Tigharry, North Uist: Mitchell Media.

Macdonald, D. N. (ed.) (1993b), *Voices from the Edge: Faith in a Post-Christian Scotland*, Tigharry, North Uist: Mitchell Media.

McGeachan, C. (2013a), 'Needles, picks and an intern named Laing: exploring the psychiatric spaces of Army life', *Journal of Historical Geography*, 40, 67–78.

McGeachan, C. (2013b), '(Re)remembering and narrating the childhood city of R. D. Laing', *Cultural Geographies*, 20, 3, 269–84.

McGeachan, C. (2014a), '"The world is full of big bad wolves": investigating the experimental therapeutic spaces of R. D. Laing and Aaron Esterson', *History of Psychiatry*, 25, 3, 283–98.

McGeachan, C. (2014b), '"Worlding" psychoanalytic insights: unpicking R. D. Laing's geographies', in P. Kingsbury and S. Pile (eds), *Psychoanalytic Geographies*, Farnham: Ashgate, 89–101.

McGeachan, C. (2016), '"Do you have a frog to guide you?": exploring the "asylum" spaces of R. D. Laing', in D. Kritsotaki, V. Long and M. Smith (eds), *Deinstitutionalisation and After: Post-War Psychiatry in the Western World*. Cham, Switzerland: Palgrave Macmillan, 195–213.

McGeachan, C. (2017), 'The ghosts of the refractory ward: R. D. Laing and (re)configuring psychiatric spaces of care', in C. Nord and E. Högström (eds), *Caring Architecture: Institutions and Relational Practices*, Newcastle upon Tyne: Cambridge Scholars Publishing, 111–26.

McIntosh, E. (2011), *John Macmurray's Religious Philosophy: What it Means to be a Person*, Farnham: Ashgate.

McIntosh, E. (2015), 'Why we need the arts: John Macmurray on education and the emotions', *Educational Philosophy and Theory*, 47, 1, 47–60.

McKenzie, J. (1952), 'A ministry in healing: is the Church recovering a lost power?', *Life and Work*, 7, 75 (March), 59.

McKenzie, J. G. (1958) 'Limitations of psychotherapy', *British Weekly*, 6 March, 13.

MacLeod, G. ([1944]), *We Shall Re-Build: The Work of the Iona Community on Mainland and on Island*, Glasgow: The Iona Community.

MacLeod, G. F. (1958), *Only One Way Left: Church Prospect*, Glasgow: The Iona Community.

McLeod, H. (2007), *The Religious Crisis of the 1960s*, Oxford: Oxford University Press.

Macmurray, J. (1930), *Today and Tomorrow: A Philosophy of Freedom*, London: BBC.

Macmurray, J. (1935a), *Freedom in the Modern World*, 2nd edn, London: Faber & Faber.

Macmurray, J. (1935b), *Reason and Emotion*, 2nd edn, London: Faber & Faber.

Macmurray, J. (1938a), *The Clue to History*, London: Student Christian Movement.

Macmurray, J. (1938b), 'A philosopher looks at psychotherapy', *Individual Psychology Medical Pamphlets*, 20, 9–22.

Macmurray, J. (1961), *Persons in Relation*, London: Faber & Faber.

Macnab, F. A. (1966), *Estrangement and Relationship: Experience with Schizophrenics*, Bloomington, IN: Indiana University Press.

Macquarrie, J. (1955), *An Existentialist Theology: A Comparison of Heidegger and Bultmann*, London: SCM.

Macquarrie, J. (1960), *The Scope of Demythologizing: Bultmann and his Critics*, London: SCM.

Macquarrie, J. (1972), *Existentialism*, London: Hutchinson.

Maier, B. (2009), *William Robertson Smith: His Life, his Work and his Times*, Tübingen: Mohr Siebeck.

Manchester, R. and B. Manchester (1996), The New Zealand Association of Psychotherapists. Te Roopuu Whakaora Hinengaro. Notes Towards a History. A Chronology of the First Fifty Years. 1947–1997. Unpublished booklet.

Martin, K. (2018), 'Transcultural histories of psychotherapy', *European Journal of Psychotherapy & Counselling*, 20, 1, 104–19.

Mears, I. and L. E. Mears (1931), *Creative Energy: Being an Introduction to the Study of the Yih King, or Book of Changes, with Translations from the Original Text*, London: John Murray.

Midgley, M. (2002), *Evolution as a Religion: Strange Hopes and Stranger Fears*, revised edn, London: Routledge.

Miller, G. (2004), *R. D. Laing*, Edinburgh: Edinburgh University Press.

Miller, G. (2007), 'A wall of ideas: the "taboo on tenderness" in theory and culture', *New Literary History*, 38, 4, 667–81.

Miller, G. (2008), 'Psychiatry as hermeneutics: Laing's argument with natural science', *Journal of Humanistic Psychology*, 48, 1, 42–60.

Miller, G. (2010), 'The apathetic fallacy', *Philosophy and Literature*, 34, 1, 48–64.

Miller, G. (2018), 'Madness decolonized?: madness as transnational identity in Gail Hornstein's *Agnes's Jacket*', *Journal of Medical Humanities*, 39, 3, 303–23.

Monteith, W. G. (2000), 'Iona and healing: a discourse analysis', in M.

Bowman and S. Sutcliffe (eds), *Beyond New Age: Exploring Alternative Spiritualities*, Edinburgh: Edinburgh University Press, 105–17.

Moore, J. R. (1979), *The Post-Darwinian Controversies: A Study of the Protestant Struggle to Come to Terms with Darwin in Great Britain and America, 1870–1900*, Cambridge: Cambridge University Press.

Moore, J. R. (1985), 'Evangelicals and evolution: Henry Drummond, Herbert Spencer, and the naturalisation of the spiritual world', *Scottish Journal of Theology*, 38, 3, 383–417.

Morrison, W. D. (1904), '*Social Origins and Primal Law* by Andrew Lang and J. J. Atkinson [Review]', *International Journal of Ethics*, 14, 2, 246–50.

Morton, T. R. (1977), *The Iona Community: Personal Impressions of the Early Years*, Edinburgh: The Saint Andrew Press.

Muir, W. (1987), *Imagined Corners*, Edinburgh: Canongate.

Mullan, B. (1995), *Mad to Be Normal: Conversations with R. D. Laing*, London: Free Association.

Murray, J. A. C. (1938), *An Introduction to a Christian Psycho-Therapy*, Edinburgh: T. & T. Clark.

Neisser, U. (1967), *Cognitive Psychology*, New York: Appleton-Century-Crofts.

Newlands, G. (1993), 'Theologies at Glasgow in the twentieth century', in W. I. P. Hazlett (ed.), *Traditions of Theology in Glasgow*, Edinburgh: Scottish Academic Press, 99–106.

O'Brien, E. (2013), *Country Girl*, London: Faber and Faber.

Oeming, M. (2006), *Contemporary Biblical Hermeneutics: An Introduction*, trans. J. F. Vette, Aldershot, Hampshire: Ashgate.

Olssen, E. (1981), 'Truby King and the Plunket Society: an analysis of a prescriptive ideology', *New Zealand Journal of History*, 15, 1, 3–23.

P. S. (1965), 'Margaret Rutherford Allan: I', *Davidson Clinic Bulletin*, 77, 2–5.

Partridge, E. J. (1937), *Baby's Point of View: The Psychology of Early Babyhood*, London: Oxford University Press.

Peters, J. (1989), *Frank Lake: The Man and his Work*, London: Darton, Longman and Todd.

Phelan, S. (2017), 'Reconstructing the eclectic psychiatry of Thomas Ferguson Rodger', *History of Psychiatry*, 28, 1, 87–100.

Pols, H. (2018), 'Towards trans-cultural histories of psychotherapies', *European Journal of Psychotherapy & Counselling*, 20, 1, 88–103.

Power, R. (2006), 'A place of community: "Celtic" Iona and institutional religion', *Folklore*, 117, 1, 33–53.

Raitt, S. (2004), 'Early British psychoanalysis and the Medico-Psychological Clinic', *History Workshop Journal*, 58, 63–85.

Rapp, D. (1990), 'The early discovery of Freud by the British general educated public, 1912–1919', *Social History of Medicine*, 3, 2, 217–43.

Raschid, S. (ed.) (2005), *R. D. Laing: Contemporary Perspectives*, London: Free Association.

Renwick, C. (2010), 'Patrick Geddes and the politics of evolution', *Endeavour*, 34, 4, 151–6.

Richards, G. (2011), *Psychology, Religion, and the Nature of the Soul: A Historical Entanglement*, New York: Springer.

Rillie, J. (1988), 'The Abenheimer/Schorstein Group', *Edinburgh Review*, 78–9, 104–7.

Ritvo, L. B. (1990), *Darwin's Influence on Freud*, New Haven: Yale University Press.

Roazen, P. (2001), *The Historiography of Psychoanalysis*, New Brunswick, NJ: Transaction Publishers.

Robertson, D. (1963), 'Freud – or the New Testament', *Life and Work*, 18, 8 (August), 239.

Robertson, S. A. (1932), 'A Scottish tribute', *Sociological Review*, 24, 3, 395–400.

Robertson Smith, W. (1894), *Lectures on the Religion of the Semites: First Series: The Fundamental Institutions*, London: Adam and Charles Black.

Robertson Smith, W. (1907), *Kinship and Marriage in Early Arabia*, new edn, London: Adam and Charles Black.

Rushforth, M. W. (1953), 'Religion: sins and sinners', *Davidson Clinic Bulletin*, 30, 1–10.

Rushforth, W. (1933), *The Outstretched Finger: Notes on Child Psychology for Parents and Nurses*, Edinburgh and London: Oliver and Boyd.

Rushforth, W. (1959), 'Dr Hugh Crichton-Miller', *Davidson Clinic Bulletin*, 52, 9–10.

Rushforth, W. (1962), 'Psychology learned in India and practised in Scotland', *Journal of the Indian Medical Profession*, 9, 2, 4098–100.

Rushforth, W. (1983), *Something is Happening: Spiritual Awareness and Depth Psychology in the New Age*, London: Gateway.

Rushforth, W. (1984), *Ten Decades of Happenings: The Autobiography of Winifred Rushforth*, London: Gateway.

Rushforth, W. (1985a), 'Flag day: the clinic in contact with the man in the street', *Life's Currency: Time, Money & Energy: An Anthology of Shorter Writings of Winifred Rushforth*, Bath: Gateway, 169–70.

Rushforth, W. (1985b), 'The Well', *Life's Currency: Time, Money & Energy: An Anthology of Shorter Writings of Winifred Rushforth*, Bath: Gateway, 150–2.

Sandison, R. (1984), 'Commentary: prophecy, spirit and psyche', *Group Analysis*, 17, 3, 248–50.

Sanford, J. A. (1984), 'The life of Fritz Künkel', in J. A. Sanford (ed.), *Fritz Künkel: Selected Writings*, New York: Paulist Press, 1–5.

Scharff, J. S. and D. E. Scharff (eds) (2005), *The Legacy of Fairbairn and Sutherland: Psychotherapeutic Applications*, New York: Routledge.

Scott, B. (2014), *Testimony of Experience: Docta Ignorantia and the Philadelphia Association Communities*, Ross-on-Wye: PCCS.

Segal, R. A. (2008), 'William Robertson Smith: sociologist or theologian?', *Religion*, 38, 1, 9–24.

Seligman, E. (1983), 'Obituary: William P. Kraemer, M.D.', *Journal of Analytical Psychology*, 28, 3, 269–79.

Sempervivum [Online]. Available at <http://www.sempervivum.org.uk/> [last accessed 25 July 2019].

Sessa, B. (2010), 'Dr Ronald Arthur Sandison', *The Psychiatrist*, 34, 11, 503.

Shamdasani, S. (2003), *Jung and the Making of Modern Psychology: The Dream of a Science*, Cambridge: Cambridge University Press.

Sharpe, C. (2016), 'From the individual, to the relational and communal: the Kirk's influence on three Scottish thinkers: Ronald Fairbairn, John Macmurray and Ian Suttie', *Ethics and Social Welfare*, 10, 3, 224–38.

Showalter, E. (1987), *The Female Malady: Women, Madness and English Culture, 1830–1980*, London: Virago.

Sigal, C. (2005), *Zone of the Interior*, Hebden Bridge, Yorkshire: Pomona.

Smith, R. G. (1966), *Martin Buber*, London: Carey Kingsgate.

Stepansky, P. E. (1983), *In Freud's Shadow: Adler in Context*, Hillsdale, NJ: Analytic.

Stevenson, J. W. (1958), 'The double miracle: misunderstanding about the spiritual healing Report?', *Life and Work*, 13, 151 (July), 157–8.

Stewart, J. W. (2006), 'An "enigma to their parents": the founding and aims of the Notre Dame Child Guidance Clinic, Glasgow', *The Innes Review: The Journal of the Scottish Catholic Historical Association*, 57, 1, 54–76.

Stocking, G. W. (1965), 'On the limits of "presentism" and "historicism" in the historiography of the behavioral sciences', *Journal of the History of the Behavioral Sciences*, 1, 3, 211–18.

Sutcliffe, S. (2003), *Children of the New Age: A History of Spiritual Practices*, London: Routledge.

Sutcliffe, S. (2006), 'Rethinking "new age" as a popular religious *habitus*: a review essay on *The Spiritual Revolution* (Heelas and Woodhead 2005)', *Method and Theory in the Study of Religion*, 18, 3, 294–314.

Sutcliffe, S. (2010), 'After "the religion of my fathers": the quest for composure in the "post-presbyterian" self', in L. Abrams and C. G. Brown (eds), *A History of Everyday Life in Twentieth-Century Scotland*, Edinburgh: Edinburgh University Press, 181–205.

Sutherland, J. D. (1973), 'The Davidson Clinic: an appreciation', in J. Darroch (ed.), *The Davidson Clinic 1939–1973*, Edinburgh: Bishop & Sons, 25–8.

Sutherland, J. D. (1989), *Fairbairn's Journey into the Interior*, London: Free Association.

Suttie, I. D. (1935), *The Origins of Love and Hate*, London: Kegan Paul.

Suttie, I. D. and J. I. Suttie (1932a), 'The mother: agent or object? [part 1]', *British Journal of Medical Psychology*, 12, 2, 91–108.

Suttie, I. D. and J. I. Suttie (1932b), 'The mother: agent or object? [part 2]', *British Journal of Medical Psychology*, 12, 3, 199–233.

Swedberg, R. (2012), 'Theorizing in sociology and social science: turning to the context of discovery', *Theory and Society*, 41, 1, 1–40.

Teilhard de Chardin, P. (1959), *The Phenomenon of Man*, trans. B. Wall, London: Collins.

Underhill, E. (1960), *Mysticism: A Study in the Nature and Development of Man's Spiritual Consciousness*, 12th, revised edn, London: Methuen.

Vaihinger, H. (1924), *The Philosophy of 'As If': A System of the Theoretical, Practical, and Religious Fictions of Mankind*, trans. C. K. Ogden, London: Routledge.

Van Deusen Hunsinger, D. (1995), *Theology and Pastoral Counseling: A New Interdisciplinary Approach*, Grand Rapids, MI: William B. Eerdmans.

Wallis, R. (1976), *The Road to Total Freedom: A Sociological Analysis of Scientology*, London: Heinemann.

Watson, J. B. (1913), 'Psychology as the behaviorist views it', *Psychological Review*, 20, 2, 158–77.

Watson, W. (1946), 'Does Christ still heal?: a mystery science does not solve', *Life and Work*, 1, 6 (June), 129–30.

Watts, F., R. Nye and S. Savage (2002), *Psychology for Christian Ministry*, London: Routledge.

Weatherhead, L. D. (1951), *Psychology, Religion and Healing*, London: Hodder & Stoughton.

Weir, F. (1973), 'The Fellowhip of Healing', *Life and Work*, 29, 7 (July), 18–19.

Wellspring Scotland [Online]. Available at <https://www.wellspring-scotland.co.uk/> [last accessed 25 July 2019].

West, W. (2000), *Psychotherapy and Spirituality: Crossing the Line between Therapy and Religion*, London: Sage.

Wheeler-Barclay, M. (1993), 'Victorian evangelicalism and the sociology of religion: the career of William Robertson Smith', *Journal of the History of Ideas*, 54, 1, 59–78.

Whyte, J. A. (1967), 'The new Church?', *Contact*, 19, 19–23.

Wilson, J. R. (1973), 'The distinction between pastoral care, pastoral counselling and psychotherapy', *International Journal of Social Psychiatry*, 19, 3/4, 192–206.

Winnicott, D. W. (1965), 'Ego distortion in terms of True and False Self', *The Maturational Processes and the Facilitating Environment: Studies in the Theory of Emotional Development*, London: Hogarth Press and the Institute of Psycho-Analysis, 140–52.

Wood, M. and C. Bunn (2009), 'Strategy in a religious network: a Bourdieuian critique of the sociology of spirituality', *Sociology*, 43, 2, 286–303.

Woodhead, L. (2007), 'Why so many women in holistic spirituality? a puzzle revisited', in K. Flanagan and P. C. Jupp (eds), *A Sociology of Spirituality*, Aldershot: Ashgate, 115–25.

Young, A. (2006), 'Remembering the evolutionary Freud', *Science in Context*, 19, 1, 175–89.

Young, R. B. (ed.) (1983), *The Story of St Bride's Parish Church, Edinburgh, 1880 to 1973*, Edinburgh: no publisher.

Zaehner, R. C. (1957), *Mysticism: Sacred and Profane. An Inquiry into Some Varieties of Praeternatural Experience*, Oxford: Clarendon Press.

Index

EU representative:
Easy Access System Europe
Mustamäe tee 50, 10621 Tallinn, Estonia
Gpsr.requests@easproject.com

www.ingramcontent.com/pod-product-compliance
Lightning Source LLC
Chambersburg PA
CBHW071534300326
41935CB00049B/1478